NAZI PSYCHOANALYSIS

VOLUME I

T0337897

NAZI PSYCHOANALYSIS

VOLUME I
Only Psychoanalysis Won the War

VOLUME II
Crypto-Fetishism

VOLUME III
Psy Fi

NAZI PSYCHOANALYSIS

VOLUME I

Only Psychoanalysis Won the War

Laurence A. Rickels

FOREWORD BY BENJAMIN BENNETT

University of Minnesota Press
Minneapolis • London

Nancy Barton grants permission to the University of Minnesota Press for the use of the image "Untitled—Testing" in *Nazi Psychoanalysis*.

Every effort was made to obtain permission to reproduce the illustrations in this book. If any proper acknowledgment has not been included here, we encourage copyright holders to notify the publisher.

Published by the University of Minnesota Press
111 Third Avenue South, Suite 290
Minneapolis, MN 55401-2520
http://www.upress.umn.edu

Library of Congress Cataloging-in-Publication Data

Rickels, Laurence Arthur
    Nazi psychoanalysis / Laurence A. Rickels ; foreword by Benjamin
    Bennett.
        p.   cm.
    Includes bibliographical references and index.
    ISBN 0-8166-3696-6 (alk. paper) — ISBN 0-8166-3697-4 (pbk. : alk. paper)
        1. Psychoanalysis—Germany—History.   2. Psychoanalysis—Political
    aspects—Germany—History.   I. Title.
    BF173 .R49 2002
    150.19'5'0943—dc21   2001005185

Printed in the United States of America on acid-free paper

12 11 10 09 08 07 06 05 04 03 02   10 9 8 7 6 5 4 3 2 1

CONTENTS

Foreword

B E N J A M I N   B E N N E T T

Even without the general title of the three-volume project, we would know immediately what war is referred to in the title of the present volume. World War II is the only war we speak of, with such simple, axiomatic confidence, as having been "won." We Americans, that is. (Ask Tom Brokaw, or Tom Hanks.) But in *Only Psychoanalysis Won the War*, the whole idea of winning, especially for Americans, becomes an issue.

> American propaganda . . . never stopped constructing permanent victims whose makeshift struggle against all odds somehow attains the precision of victory. Even when you're winning, Allied propaganda or group psychology to this day requires that you win—just like a victim. To win outright, right from the start, would turn even you into some kind of Nazi.

Psychoanalysis, however, is here excused from this condition of victorious victimhood and shown to be something like an outright winner after all, in that its intimate involvement (on both sides) in practically everything that was new about this war—in industry, technology, communications, propaganda, even aviation—contributed fundamentally to the development of an augmented entity that our author calls "greater psychoanalysis." Perhaps we can gain perspective on this situation, and on the whole project of *Nazi Psychoanalysis*, by stepping back a quarter millennium or so.

To the extent that a main point exists, the main point of Johann Georg Hamann's *Aesthetics in a Nutshell* (1762) is probably that scripture and history, and indeed nature itself, are all versions of a single text, a single divine writing, and that the purport of that writing depends radically on how the reader approaches it, which in turn never fails to involve the question of who the reader really is. These last two ideas are set forth with perfect clarity, toward the end of Hamann's text, in a pair of quotations, the first in Latin from St. Augustine, the second in German from Luther. But rather than call Augustine by name, Hamann cites him as "the Punic church father," with a footnote mark on the word "Punic." And if one follows that lead, if one descends here into what Laurence A. Rickels likes to call the text's "footnote underworld," one is dragged further and further away from anything like a main point. That "Punic" refers to Augustine's Carthaginian origins, Hamann doesn't bother to tell us; we're supposed to know. Instead, he begins with a reference to Johann David Michaelis's condescending remarks about Augustine's Latin style, and then jumps, via a pun (what else?) on the word "Punic," to the idea of "punning" as developed in an early-eighteenth-century English treatise (necessarily English, since "pun" in German is merely "Wortspiel") that is variously attributed to Swift and Sheridan, and jumps from there. . . . You see what I'm getting at, and if you have looked at the main text of the present book, you probably see something of my reasons for starting with Hamann and punning. Like Hamann, Rickels has important points to make, about the structure and growth of psychoanalysis, and in general about the impossibility of marking off areas in modernity that are somehow sheltered from Nazi contamination. And like Hamann— who must at all costs deny systematic Lutheran theology access to his texts, lest his thought be co-opted into reinforcing exactly the postlapsarian division between scripture and nature against which it is directed—Rickels has excellent reasons for what he terms his "user-unfriendly" procedure. Psychoanalysis, as Rickels means it, is not, strictly speaking, susceptible to being written or known "about." The pretense of possessing an objective or innocent verbal instrument with which to take hold of psychoanalysis violates the discursive implications of the subject matter in exactly the same way that Hamann's Christianity is violated by theological systematics.

Does it follow, then, that the present work is accessible only to strict insiders, only to psychoanalysts? In fact, psychoanalytic literature abounds with formulations of the peculiarly evasive quality of its core discipline; perhaps the best known is Jacques Lacan's remark that what the unconscious "is" cannot be disentangled from the circumstances of its discovery and the person of its discoverer. The theory of psychoanalysis, we are told, is never fully detached from its object, never in command of it, but always itself a self-relativizing instance of analytic procedure; in Rickels's arguments, specifically, it is the analytic mechanism of transference that turns out repeatedly to be operative, on a large public scale, in the history of the discipline. Everything is provisional or heuristic in psychoanalysis; there is no level of abstraction at which the discipline might in principle stand wholly revealed to the gaze of pure intelligence. (We think of the aspirations of Hamann's Wolffian contemporaries.) Understanding is never distinct from practice, and to "understand" a work such as Rickels's is therefore always in some sense to be a practitioner. But in exactly what sense?

The parallel case of Hamann continues to help us here. To be an insider with respect to Hamann means to be the adherent of a special kind of transtheological Christianity, or at least to recognize its presence as an analogue in one's own philosophical practice. Therefore it is not hard to imagine why Hegel and Kierkegaard should be among Hamann's prominent admirers. But to find Goethe in this group, the older, "classical," self-consciously heathen Goethe, is a bit startling. And yet it is true that Goethe, who was in possession of some interesting manuscript material, for a long time considered actually editing Hamann. In book 12 of *Dichtung und Wahrheit*, he characterizes Hamann as follows:

> When a person speaks, he must become for the moment one-sided; there is no communication, no written doctrine, without particularity. Since Hamann, however, was once and for all opposed to this sort of separation, and since he desired to speak in the same all-embracing manner in which he felt, imagined, and thought, and since he demanded the same of others, he stood in opposition to his own style and to everything that others could produce. In order to accomplish the impossible, he therefore lays hands on all conceivable elements of writing.

This does not read like unequivocal praise, and in fact, a few lines later, Goethe speaks of a historical "darkness" into which Hamann's writings descend. But then, toward the end of the same long paragraph, we hear that if we take the trouble to look up some of Hamann's references, we encounter

> an ambiguous double illumination which strikes us as highly agreeable, as long as we resolutely avoid requiring what one would usually call an "understanding" of it. Such pages therefore deserve to be called "sibylline," because one cannot take them in and for themselves, but must wait for the occasion when one is specially moved to seek refuge in their oracular quality.

Surely, when he speaks of "seeking refuge" in Hamann, Goethe is not referring to any specific religious content. What he means can only have to do with Hamann's attempt at an impossible "all-embracing" form of writing. Hamann's texts, I mean, are a place where one seeks refuge *as a writer*, as a practitioner of writing, as a struggler with the "one-sidedness" of writing—not because Hamann in any degree solves the problem of writing but because, by straining its limits, he *situates* that problem, thus profiles it for us and offers us a "scene of writing" in which our particular performance, though still indelibly marked with futility, makes a kind of quasi-dramatic and historical sense after all.

And by alluding to Derrida's essay "Freud and the Scene of Writing," I mean of course to make the connection with psychoanalysis and Rickels. The kind of practitioner implied as the reader of Rickels's trilogy, I contend, is a *writer*, in the sense obliquely suggested by Goethe for Hamann.

> Freud [writes Derrida] *performed for us the scene of writing*. But we
> must think of this scene in other terms than those of individual
> or collective psychology, or even anthropology. It must be thought
> in the horizon of the scene/stage of the world, as the history of
> that scene/stage. Freud's language is *caught up* in it.

The "one-sided" move of the writer—which Goethe vaguely calls "separation," whereas Derrida would relate it to *différance*—not only is imposed
by the world but also in a sense *establishes* the world as a "scene" (and
how else would it become "world" in history?) by performing it. Derrida
suggests that in writers like Freud, this quality of performance lies closer to
the surface than elsewhere. But writers like Hamann—and Rickels—still
constitute a special class, in that their performance is informed by a depth
of resistance (a "user-unfriendly" stance "in opposition") that strains the
boundaries, and thus marks them, and so *sets* the scene of writing. Not permanently, not once and for all: if this were possible, then "one-sidedness"
would not be a necessary attribute of writing after all. Rather, as a moment
of respite or "refuge," a kind of breathing space. This does not mean that
one must "actually" be a writer to read Rickels with profit. But one does
have to be able to adopt a writerly point of view, to read without falling
into the comfortably dependent relation of consumer to a presumed pro-
ducer, to manage one's handling of the text so that there is in the end no
strict "user" for anyone to be unfriendly to. One must approach Rickels not
in terms of "the oppositions sender-receiver, code-message" (these "coarse
instruments," Derrida calls them), but rather so as to engage (Derrida again)
"the *sociality* of writing as *drama*."

To be less cryptic about it, one can in fact formulate as a proposition
the basic implications of Rickels's difficult style. His use of wordplay and
allusion and quotation insists constantly on the point that neither knowledge itself nor the objects of knowledge can reasonably be said to exist in a
manner that is strictly prior to, or at all independent of, the discursive acts
and techniques by which they are shaped, the verbal garments in which
they make their appearance to us. Which means, in turn, that there is no
way of describing a clear division between the referential and logical structure of argument on the one hand, and, on the other, the structure of relations (the arbitrarily grammatical as well as the associative and allusive)
that constitute the general verbal horizon in which we happen to be operating. Rickels's particular talent as a stylist is his ability to keep this proposition in the foreground of his presentation, even while suggesting a large
number of specific and cohesive interpretive arguments on another level.

And just this foregrounding, in turn, is crucial in relation to the subject matter, including the inseparability of theory and practice in psychoanalysis, and the impossibility of establishing a strict division between the two concepts in the work's main title. Foregrounding, however, is the form in which this point appears in Rickels, not formulation; for formulation (including the one I have just suggested) automatically offers its reader the safe, separated position of a consumer (we recall Goethe on "separation"), which contradicts exactly the point being formulated. Formulation requires understanding as a response. But as Goethe says of Hamann, "understanding" is out of place here. How can this be? What do we *miss* in the present text by "understanding" it?

Rickels answers this question when he speaks of his project as the "excavation" of material and the maintenance of its "materiality." The trouble with systematic argument in general, and our understanding of it, is that it (so to speak) dematerializes its material, imposes on the material an order that supplants the structure of the experience of finding it more or less unprepared. This is not to say that either Rickels or we are trying to preserve cultural-historical material in something like an "original" state—a state of the sort that can in fact never reasonably be said to exist. Nor can either we or Rickels reliably reproduce the more or less immediate experience of seeing our not-seeing psychoanalysis. (The ocular metaphor in the pun "Nazi = not-see" produces a contradiction for the understanding here, but not a material impossibility in experience.) Nor, finally, does Rickels ever actually avoid systematic argument. Rather, by the use of balance or tension between argumentative and associative structures, Rickels positions his reader— constantly, from sentence to sentence—so as to enable him or her to go as far as possible (whatever that means in each particular case) toward recovering the materiality of the work's material, without ever losing hold of its (argumentatively established) significance. Materiality, moreover, is also the key to Rickels's use of quotation. A style based heavily on quotation, once a certain density is arrived at—as in Rickels (or Hamann)—begins to body forth the understanding that meaning in language is never really anything *but* quotation, that *langue* and *parole,* in other words, the governing linguistic system and the mass of actual instances, are not really distinct, that language, even in that aspect that is systematized in grammars and lexica, is entirely constituted by the accumulation of material in the form of particular utterances. Indeed, Rickels's fondness for pop-cultural quoting establishes this point at a more immediate level of linguistic practice than, for example, Hamann's quoting mainly from scripture and classics plus commentaries and glosses.

To the extent that a main point exists, the main point of *Nazi Psycho-analysis* is probably that Nazism cannot be isolated in the structure of modernity, that no element of modernity can be thought adequately without thinking its Nazi component. "That's right, it's about facing the continuity that was there: Nazi psychoanalysis, Nazi Marxism, Nazi deconstruction." But this is not a point that can be "understood" in the normal sense of the word, for understanding it would produce a detached critical perspective for the understander, hence an element of modernity (precisely the intellectual juncture at which this understanding takes place) that is thoroughly purged of any Nazi contamination after all. The point, rather, as Rickels suggests, must be "faced" in all its immediate material undigestibility. Or seen from a different angle, it must be *performed*, as Rickels's style performs the identity of meaning and quotation. If you want theory, you go to Derrida, who in fact produces what is in essence a neat theory of "greater psychoanalysis" in his argument on how the opening of Freud's discourse "to the theme of writing results in psychoanalysis being not simply psychology—nor simply psychoanalysis." But in Rickels, what you get is better termed, if not perfectly termed, performance.

For this reason, finally, I will not attempt to do more than Rickels himself does, in the matter of summarizing the present volume, when he indicates that the principal jumping-off point for his arguments here is the importance of the treatment of war neurosis in World War I, its importance both for the development of Freud's theorizing and for the establishment of a reputation of therapeutic efficacy for psychoanalysis. Instead, I will simply point the reader toward one or two of what happen to strike me as the most interesting pieces of material. For example, the chapter "Faust, Freud, and the Missing Entries—into War" covers an enormous intellectual and historical span, from an editorially suppressed reference to the "two souls" in Faust's breast, to war neurosis and the doubling of narcissism, to the relation of earlier and later Freudian systematics (down to *Civilization and Its Discontents*), to technology and the sketching of an argument for the equation "group psychology = total war = psychological warfare," which is a main part of the whole work's focus on "continuity." And then here is a series of sections presenting an argument on the history of insurance that is linked associatively, by the word "Sicherung," with war neurosis, thence with homosexuality and gender questions, and in passing finds most of its material (like a rabbit out of a hat) reassembled in the figure of Franz Kafka.

It is true that some readers will still be bothered by the associative aspect of this writing, by the virtual structural equivalence in it of "real" historical or factual relations and those verbally mediated relations, as it were material puns *(Sicherung/Versicherung)*, that one is tempted to call "coincidence." But the thing about coincidence in this sense is that it refuses to go away; there is no home for it, no grave, in our filing systems. A strictly real relation gets used up in its reality and so always gets left behind, disposed of, by any reasonably adequate representation in language. But a coincidence, whose substance is both verbal *and* factual, or at least the sort of pregnant coincidence that is repeatedly brewed up by Rickels's broad knowledge and analytic skill, sticks in the craw of language, so to speak, and confuses the comfortable triangle of producer-consumer-object, as if reality had wrenched the instrument from our hand and were writing itself. The separation between reality and writing, the space of a presumed visibility that hides not-seeing from view—or as Hamann (who else?) would say, the separation between nature and scripture, which makes space for us to accept, for instance (as not-seeingly in the eighteenth century as in the twentieth), the notion of an enlightened politics—this separation is not transcended so much as it becomes, for the time being, in a manner of speaking, hard to swallow.

In other words, as long as you expect Rickels to do something for you— to teach you, to improve you, to take you somewhere—as long as you insist on something "positive," you will be disappointed. Reading, in the age of the novel, is generally understood as the mental equivalent of traveling. When you read—as when you place yourself physically in unfamiliar surroundings—you take a kind of vacation from your identity. This applies not only to the reading of novels, where it is obvious, but also to the reading of expository texts, where you try to be objective or open-minded (which means, not yourself), in order to understand the writing "in and for *it*self." But this attitude is as misplaced with Rickels as Goethe says it is with Hamann. You are never going to have all of this book anyway. The way you in fact are, as yourself, named, scarred, broken, accidental, radically compromised, like modernity *it*self, is how this book wants its reader, and how you, the reader, want the book.

Achtung

A PREFACE TO *NAZI PSYCHOANALYSIS*

> Ruth Eissler reports the successful analytic treatment in a case
> of acute paranoid delusion. A young woman whose mother is
> of German ancestry accuses herself of being an "innocent Nazi
> spy" when her husband, a member of a depreciated minority
> group, is about to be drafted. In one of his last papers, Freud
> has asserted that each delusion contains a kernel of historic
> truth from infantile sources. In Eissler's case, the "truth" is a
> miscarriage of the mother at the height of the patient's Oedipus
> complex. The traumatic position was later fortified when a girl
> cousin died of tuberculosis. She had been closely attached to
> this girl and employed a secret code in communication with
> her. This code she unconsciously used in her psychotic episode
> again, thus getting magically in touch with the dead. In her
> paraphrenic language, "Nazi" was really "not see"—referring
> to the magic destruction of the unseen rival.
>
> **—FRANZ ALEXANDER AND GERHART PIERS, "PSYCHOANALYSIS"**

If we were to list all institutions that supported this project and, on the other side, the many distinguished addresses that could not follow at all, rejected it out of their hands, we would be reminded, more by metonymy I suppose than by any direct reference, that there was, after all, the one side that won the war. I hope this reassurance will in some measure uncanny-proof my thousand-page *Reich*. All you consumer fascist types, you know who you are, cannot be stopped from policing the middlebrow beat to which intellectual discourse was condemned long time ago. But it is still important to keep up with the symptomatic character of these conspiracies of mediocrity and tag the show of not understanding at all as no more, no less, than resistance.

What may strike some as obstructive in this manner of genealogy or total history is less the style of writing or argument than the insistence on staying with the materials in the juxtapositions in which they can be and have been thought. The book is nonphobic about what comes its way. But most important of all, the space of this tension between low and high, literary and historical, material and interpretation comes right out of the force field of Freud's legacy. It's an allegorical tension that comes down to the unrepresentable gap lying between the in-session experience of the transference and the shorthand of analytic theory. Here we find the materiality of psychoanalysis, through which all concepts continue to pass. The silent but pressing inclusion of this tension in psychoanalytic theorizing was what Freud was listening to when he allowed for a distinction between his science and philosophy. It's what I want you to hear whenever you, dear reader, already a survivor of the collision between "Nazi" and "Psychoanalysis," come across, in the reading that lies just ahead, juxtapositions or even contaminations of seemingly undigested blocks of time or language. Mourning is the model of this work. It's work, all work, that takes the time—the times—it takes to mourn. It's time to be user-unfriendly.

In the course of the dig, as they all rose to consciousness, the materials kept on putting in uncanny connections between so many of the split-off, discontinuous segments of our standard tradition or reception of good modernism, good psychoanalysis. The influence we now see come out in the watch of the materials relies on a sense of audience that puts on Freudian ears to listen behind the lines: out of the noisy wear and tear of resistance there emerges one genuine line of influence, the kind that represents real change. A clean transferential cutting in of "the father," say, into the place of the analyst or therapist can promote the immediate cause of healing; but in matters of influence—a matter psychoanalysis alone made an issue of its science, also in the sense that there was no influence until we learned how to interpret for the transference, the resistance, the defense—the intactness of a foreign corpus inside another's identity or identification indeed symptomatizes a host or ghost of issues but does not, finally, give the measure of any influence.

The least likely place to look, therefore, which was where previous studies of the Nazi history of psychoanalysis and the psychodynamic therapies tended to start and stop, is the small band of certified analysts who stayed on in Germany after 1933 (only one "Aryan" analyst felt it was the time to leave with his Jewish colleagues) and formed compromises that, out of context of the big influence, and slipping into and around see-through rationalizations, seem but an abject of study. Even the wider bandwidths measuring the entire eclectic setting of the old analysts back together again with their former competitors, the Adlerians and Jungians, who thought they had split psychoanalysis once and for all, only come in shortwave. There was the obvious prestige and scope of application of psychotherapy with full state support. The backing the German Institute of Psychological Research and Psychotherapy received was given directly, no problem, or it came, in triumph, at the end of another corridor skirmish with bio-neuropsychiatry. Psychotherapy openly maintained its outright lead in the contest with psychiatry until after Stalingrad, the analytic-therapeutic influence became less public in its broadcasting out to the war effort. But there is evidence that frontline work with schizo soldiers was still being conducted in ways and means compatible with greater psychoanalysis. The corridor wars between analytic psychotherapy and neuropsychiatry, which had already commenced upon Freud's first full entry into the field of psychological interventionism by way of the extremely good rep psychoanalysis received during World War I as treatment of choice for war neurosis, frame the ambiguous status and conflicting verdicts or second opinions that affected the nonreproductive members of Nazi German society. At the therapeutic end of the corridor, homosexuals were under treatment to be healed (with all the other neurotics, including the symptomatizing soldiers); but if the neuropsychiatrists got hold of them, they went the one way of all the other untreatables. This split-leveling of homosexuality occupies the bottom line of projections ultimately held in common and in conflict at all ends of the corridor.

But even the Institute-sized networking of the materials sets a limitation on the ranging of Freud's effects, which were rolled over beyond the jurisdiction of the reunified analytic psychotherapies. Psychotherapeutic standards of correctness and correction, according to which every German was to be given one more chance, were too popular to be contained within the history of one institute. From the close of World War I through the end of World War II, Germany was a pop-psychological culture of all-out healing. Before the baton could be passed to California, the current finish line of eclectic psychotherapy for all, the big splits between the Germanys and between a good German psychoanalysis and a disowned German neoanalytic therapy were all that the Germans, their victims, and their conquerors could do to defend themselves.

Nazi Psychoanalysis reconnects all the outposts of frontline intrapsychic theorization and treatment inside the orbit of the central psychotherapy institute in Berlin. One more jump cut through the material, one that once again doesn't follow Institute guidelines, tunes in the otherwise least likely candidates for analytic influence, military psychologists trained in psychotechnical methods. In particular, their specialized understanding and management of the relations obtaining between pilots and their flying machines reflect a Freudian influence strong enough to receive and transmit between the lines. These psychotechnical relations, which were seen to be always shock-absorbed with what was fundamentally traumatic about artificial flight, follow the intrapsychic model where few analytic thinkers had gone before, right up to the head of the receiving line of Freud's reading of technology. It was this double reading of a Freudian techno-criticism that my first two books, *Aberrations of Mourning* and *The Case of California*, already sought to raise to consciousness from between the lines of Freud's studies of psychosis, melancholia, perversion, and group psychology. In *Nazi Psychoanalysis*, which marks the final installment of my trilogy on "Unmourning," the long haul through tracts on war neurosis, military adjustment, and psychological warfare, all of which had been abandoned, now in the ditches of one world war, now inside the air-raid shelters of the other one, leads to a reconstruction of what can be called to this day "greater psychoanalysis." By World War II, between the air-raid sheltering of the populace in a group-therapeutic mode and the intrapsychic wiring of the pilot to his machine, an axis of technologization was being followed, up through cybernetics (both in Gregory Bateson's sense of feedback and in Jacques Lacan's staging of the rearview mirror) all the way out to the fantasy horizon of science fiction, which is where this book begins again.

What the particular science fiction that was Nazi Germany tried to outfly belonged to the gravity, the grave, of earthbound or limited supplies, which each time marked the spot the German war machine was in when the world came to war. To open up the underworld commentary that runs with the flights of techno-fantasy, focus can be fixed on an ambiguously held term or introject, the German word *Bestand,* in which the notions of reserve supplies and staying power are combined, and which goes by "standing reserve" in translations of Heidegger's use of the word (in his essays on technology). Here we find the melancholic scarcity or lack that through total mobilization was to be transformed, like a wound, as in takeoff, into the miracle of flight all the way to fetish victories of rocket or robot bombing. But the itinerary of flight was all along skipping another beat around the rush for prospects for technologization and group psychologization. It was the master beat of reproductive coupling. By the time of his essay on fetishism, Freud was staying tuned to the impulses of gadget love that we've been jamming with ever since the onset of technologization. Techno-fantasies or science fictions have, at least since the eighteenth century, special-featured the overcoming of a crisis in reproduction through the self-replicating prospects of immortality now (in other words, without the loss of generation). This is the place of tension to which Freud assigned the fetishist, after first discovering it over the symptomatizing body of the war neurotic: between, on one side, the attractions of splitting or doubling within a borderline zone lying across neurosis and psychosis and, on the other side, the requirements that are still and for the time being with us, the same old ones that only reproduction can keep on fulfilling for the survival of the species. Thus through the fetish future that science fiction holds open and shut, the continuity back then that we're addressing here for the first time can be brought back into real-time proximity with the live or dead issues that currently occupy the media grounds for our existence.

Achtung contains the word of caution but also the word for respect. In the course of gathering all the materials that fit my monster topic, I benefited from many leads given me by the following individuals I think/I thank: Nancy Chodorow, Mark Grotjahn, Werner Hamacher, Elliot Jurist, Peggy Kamuf, Friedrich Kittler, Wolf Kittler, Peter Loewenberg, Karl Rickels, Avital Ronell, Lorraine Ryavec, Renate Schlesier, Ursula Schreiter, Lawton Smith. My project was supported by fellowships from the Alexander von Humboldt Foundation, the Center for German and European Studies (University of California–Berkeley), the Interdisciplinary Humanities Center (University of California–Santa Barbara), and the Academic Senate (University of California–Santa Barbara). It took me more than two years to place this book. My *Achtung* has therefore been won in the first place by the University of Minnesota Press. Thanks to William Murphy and Doug Armato for their support of my project.

When I first opened up shop with the materials of Nazi psychoanalysis in 1991, I right away enrolled in a local clinical psychology graduate program and commenced my training as a therapist in the setting of licensure in California. My training in California as just another psychotherapist whose eclecticism remains, by training, stuck on the parts of psychoanalysis that "work" afforded me the next-best thing to being there, at the Nazi German institute of psychotherapy in Berlin. Alongside the archival labors—along for my metabolization of those materials—this field-tripping hands-on portion of my analytic research must be admitted as equally formative in the development of the study of Nazi psychoanalysis.

This study was completed in 1995. Beginning in 1991, I presented papers and published articles advertising my discoveries and their final destination as part of work I was pursuing at book length. Discoveries I had made, for example, in the prehistory of Nazi German investments in psychotherapy that had their primal scene in Freud's World War I reading of war neurosis, among other headlines from the trenches of my dig, were thus fixed in the same space as my name. Nineteen ninety-five remains the cutoff point for my published interest in contemporary accounts of these "same" histories. If a certain first-generation historian of Nazi German psychotherapy, who is given credit for his study in the first volume of *Nazi Psychoanalysis* in the exact amount due, has since 1995 published an "expanded" new edition of his work that suddenly takes another look at the materials by the stolen fire of my work (admittedly reduced to a night-light by the shame of it), then I can only make the referral to Karl Kraus, who had all there is to say about the double failure in journalism and prostitution that leaves the loser only one option by default—the small-change careerism of the academic historian. Perhaps there is an affirmation here, after all, in the way my work goes into others' works and words without saying or commemoration. I am reminded of a most exciting moment in the late 1980s when (I was attending the annual meeting of the International Association of Philosophy and Literature) I watched someone steal the display copy of *Aberrations of Mourning* from the conference book exhibit. There is honor from thieves.

On a clear day you can see psychoanalysis both in the recent primal past and in the future now. The overdetermination of a Freudian influence is not about a responsibility or codependency diagnosis (the deep sitting-stuck fear of the overprotectors). Only the analytic discursivity is in positions to contain the Nazi symptom, for even historically, the symptom we're all still struggling to bust was already highly saturated with psychoanalysis. Another healing, more long term in its scheduling, more long span in the attention that can be given in-session materiality, is still in order, on order, in the works. Let the closure begin.

INTRODUCTION

1994

Being suddenly face to face with photographs of analysts as members of an institutional staff that included men in Nazi uniforms, seeing on the page of a Nazi newspaper, capped by a swastika, an article by a prominent psychoanalyst entitled "Psychoanalysis and *Weltanschauung*"—the obvious reference being to National Socialist *Weltanschauung*—these things gave us a sick feeling. What were analysts, people we think of as our professional and spiritual kin, doing with them?—the "them" being the one unambiguous symbol of evil in our historical time and for many of us the murderers of our people.

—ANNA ANTONOVSKY, "ARYAN ANALYSTS IN NAZI GERMANY:
QUESTIONS OF ADAPTATION, DESYMBOLIZATION, AND BETRAYAL"

That psychoanalysis in particular should have been made to conform as the tool of the ruling power appears to me an untenable, tendentious claim. If the charge is made that "psychoanalysis" was deformed during this period and that this deformation has been transmitted consciously or unconsciously into the present, then what first must be clarified is what the proper embodiment of psychoanalytic tradition was then and is now and how then and now it must continue to develop and assert itself with regard to the challenges of the time and social change. I can only say that at that time psychoanalytic dialogue gave me a first experience in my own case of the liberating dynamic of the treatment process. And the possibility of such a positive practice seems to me still the most important direction for the true tradition and fruitful further development of psychoanalysis.

—WALTER BRÄUTIGAM, "REVIEW OF THE YEAR 1942:
OBSERVATIONS OF A PSYCHOANALYTIC TRAINING CANDIDATE
AT THE WARTIME BERLIN INSTITUTE"

In 1994 a conference entitled "Psychoanalysis and Power" held at the New School for Social Research brought together analysts from Germany and New York only one doorway away from what appeared, at first sight, to be the centerpiece of the meeting, the reconstruction of a 1985 exhibit documenting the German history of psychoanalysis before and after 1933. What history was already slow to show in 1985 was first assembled for the International Association's Hamburg Congress to mark the spot everyone was in during this first return of International Psychoanalysis to postwar Germany. At the Hamburg Congress, it had to be admitted that psychoanalysis, even if by many other names, had in fact never left but had remained behind, a functional part of mobilized life in Nazi Germany. French analyst Janine Chasseguet-Smirgel, the queen of radically conservative diagnoses of perversion or adolescence in mass culture, was the chairman of the program committee presiding over the 1985 congress between Allied and German analysts that was to repair the split ends of the International while keeping the pair, the us is not them, intact. A couple of years later, in the *International Review of Psychoanalysis*, she let the record show the removal of loud and clear boundaries from the history of psychoanalysis during World War II. It was the unexpected side effect brought on by the return to Germany. Although anticipated as traumatic within a force field of persecution and denial, the encounter that all were prepared to take interpersonally and ideologically threw up instead an intrapsychic continuum of transferential objects that took the congress-goers by surprise: "At the same time we began to pick up stronger and stronger echoes of the conflict that had been raging among the German analysts for some years—a conflict which, as it happened, was now coming to a head—about the history of German psychoanalysis under the Nazi regime. The members of the Program Committee and the President of the IPA himself learned on this occasion that a stubborn legend (stubborn because of its credibility) now had to be given up—namely, that of the 'liquidation' of German psychoanalysis under the Third Reich" (435).

Between 1985 and 1994, the transmission didn't copy. We were as close to, yet as far away from, analysis of the Nazi phase of psychoanalysis (whether or not we had all already, by rights, completely passed through it). Even or especially the very juxtaposition of names—"Nazi psychoanalysis"—had yet to make the preliminaries of metabolization or the standard reception. What neither sinks in nor swims along the surface of received history is a loss in clarity of boundaries, a loss that counts as traumatic (although the point of impact is not trauma as such but the onset of panic attack). In other words, we're not talking the happening kind of trauma that keeps on repeating itself in building up an anxiety defense (as in our ongoing relations with the Holocaust) but the kind that goes the roundabout route of repression and displacement or, in other words, doubles as origin of identification (which is always a way of being what one at the same time not sees). But the two kinds of trauma and trauma transmission seem coimplicated on the projection screens of resistance. It's as though the unambivalence and unmournability of our relations with the Holocaust required only one kind of boundary. Admission of "Nazi psychoanalysis," as something new and something historical, demands interrogation or patrolling not only of differences between good and evil but also of the border tensions between therapeutic and political modes of correctness or between the intrapsychic and interpersonal takes on conflict.

But if psychoanalysis is to maintain the primal-scene hierarchy of aberrations of identification (along the lines of Freud's own insistence that a specific, even linear, trauma transmission schedule be upheld for the history of the Wolf Man's symptom formation or, later on and on a larger scale, for the delegation of monotheism), then certain continuities on the side of civilization require the training of a steady focus. John Kafka, another conference-going participant in, and witness to, the wipeout of the return of psychoanalysis to Germany in the wake of its repressed history, observed that a diversification-of-holocausts rationalization props up the discontinuity defense of German resistance:

> Elements of denial of the special obscenity of the Nazi Holocaust have sometimes become apparent to me, a denial not so much of its magnitude but of its special institutionalization, its "industrialization," the juxtaposition of ultimate degradation with a setting in which Kultur and civilization were proudly proclaimed. The syndrome of "dedifferentiation of holocausts" can manifest itself by a shift of focus to other historical or current events, injustices, tragedies, and slaughters. This dedifferentiation of holocausts is often an ego-syntonic and almost unassailable defensive reaction. . . . Similar defensive operations were much in evidence at the Hamburg Congress. . . . Think of a comment about the living reality of anti-Arab discrimination and cruelty compared with the merely historical concern with the Holocaust. (302–3)

That's also why one Allies-only brand of study of the Nazi period, right down to the punctuation at the end of a sentence that Good hands down to Evil, cannot press for representation here, precisely because its branding operations require that psychoanalysis be awarded a blank within the history of Nazi Germany. What will henceforth go, once we're out with this brief spot, without coverage in *Nazi Psychoanalysis* is the resistance through oblivion that continues to keep standard historical reception from checking up on itself. As recently as Robert Jay Lifton's *The Nazi Doctors*, blanket coverage gets extended to psychoanalysis that, as Jewish science, can only have been cleanly excised from the German socius with the Nazi ruler. If you take the shortcut of the index, the single "psychoanalysis" entry gets you right in the paraphrase of some Nazi diatribe against the Jewish degeneracy Freud turned into a science. But forty pages later, down in the footnote underworld, it is admitted that the Nazi split-leveling of distinctions also dropped analysis inside the blender. But that indigestible bit just drops to the side, the inside of what's been repressed. Lifton gets out of the air pocket he hit below by diverting attention to a current notion of the benign Nazi. As a result of this scramble, any followers of the bouncing designation or affiliation of psychoanalysis have been left only untenable positions to hold for a longer look at the meaning of this medical conjunction between healing and murdering.

On an international scale, Lifton was a close associate of Alexander and Margarete Mitscherlich, whose interpretation in *The Inability to Mourn* of postwar German nonrelations with the past he helped introduce and popularize in the United States. Lifton, then, awards the history of psychoanalysis a kind of blank checking account in which the so-called Jewish science cannot be received as anything but another victorious victim of the Allied struggle against Nazi hegemony. American propaganda—here's looking at it, kid—never stopped, at least down the corridors of screen memory, constructing permanent victims whose makeshift struggle against all odds somehow attains the precision of victory. Even when you're winning, Allied propaganda or group psychology to this day requires that you win— just like a victim. To win outright, right from the start, would turn even you into some kind of Nazi.

West German analyst F.-W. Eickhoff, who attended the 1985 meeting, set up for that occasion stations of a crossing whereby trauma skips the generation it takes to transmit a legacy and slides down its secret swift passage (the so-called "telescoping" of generations). Eickhoff follows French analyst J. Cournut's reading of Freud's notion of a "borrowed unconscious sense of guilt," which he rushes to connect with the Mitscherlichs' *The Inability to Mourn*. What Eickhoff borrows from the Mitscherlich couple is their inside view of a German state of melancholia or zombieism that results not so much from not mourning the victims of Nazi Germany as from the irreparable, unmournable break with the leader; in this missing place of the father (who in his postwar German incarnation stands in only as placeholder for the greater reality of the recent past), desymbolization and derealization of the present, of the father's symbolic presence, set a spell. Thus in transposing from Cournut's reading of the Freud case study to his own case work, Eickhoff leaves no body, no object around to be lost or found. The deposit made inside the young woman in the first case comes from the father and consists of his unconscious work of mourning over her mother, whose early departure left him unfinished even with the beginning of acceptance.

For Eickhoff's purposes, however, "the father's miscarried mourning... clearly has less to do with the patient's mother than with the 'Third Reich,' with which the father was profoundly and culpably involved in a manner that has remained concealed to this day" (327). The catchiness of the Mitscherlichs' thesis—that the loss of the ego ideal, Hitler was its name, was the loss the Germans unacknowledged and symptomatized—overrelies on two guilty assumptions: one, Hitler was an object that could be lost (rather than, say, already the phantomization, now friendly, now vengeful, emanating in turn from another reception of unacknowledged losses) and, two, that the Germans had no internal-world connection with the public enemies of National Socialism. An open combination of "German" and "Jewish" "identities," unacceptable, understandably so, to many whose work through ambivalence cuts off the cutting in of identifications that could blur or jam together the legacies of victim and persecutor (and silent partner), represents just the same a lasting understanding that the Nazis' goal of total segregation of (blood)lines of identification cannot be realized, not then and not after the fact, after all, in the names (taken in veins) of their victims.

The topic garnishing the Hamburg meeting was "Identification and Its Vicissitudes." There were a couple of ways to frame the trauma work coming out of or going to a Congress topped off with this agenda of identification. On her own psyche, Israeli analyst Rivka Eifermann discovered that she was well on her way to one method of getting the work done. It was another transmission of trauma, one that will admit objects to be lost or retained. If it was the other's transmission, which can never name itself as other, then as long as the Mitscherlich model continued to block the 1985 intersection, it was missing-in-recognition. By the time Eifermann was recalling, as her most vivid souvenir of the Hamburg Congress, the lord mayor's applause-winning declaration that if Germans count Goethe on the roster of their identifications, then they must count in Hitler too, she had started seeing through the screening device that had protected and projected a secret ambivalence. It was these living bookends of the good and the bad German that had for some time been framing her own mixed feelings as though unmixed. Upon returning to Germany in the year of the Hamburg Congress, she found herself in Munich delivering her lecture in German, which was considerate to be sure, but, nice try, a mess of slow, stumbling reencounters with her original mother tongue. On second thought, she recognized that she had inflicted on the locals a reduction of the range of her own expression to that of the three year old she had been when forced to leave Germany, and had thus at the same time extended her childhood rage to include the share that the suffering audience was going to pay her back. After the fact, then, she was able to reconstruct "Germany" and "the Germans" as her "transference objects": "I had been relating to Germany and the Germans in ways that largely correspond to transference relationships as they occur in the analytic situation, and that my ways of relating were unconsciously driven by deep ambivalences" (246). The unconscious fantasies that were thus reanimated "related to 'good' and 'bad' aspects of my internalized love objects and their derivatives" (247). The idealizing trend she discovers in the network of these aspects and objects is caught by the phrase "If it were not for." That's another way of focusing on what would ideally have been, if it could have been. The pain that found the little voice of the girl persona who acted out on her audience ("the Germans") became disconnected at least (at last!) from the vaster network of demons and ideals. Ambivalences may be unresolvable, but once you are able to take them on one at a time, the load or overload has been made lighter, easier, "as each stands less in the service of the other internally" (256). Left untouched in Eifermann's case, "Germany" had become the kind of discrete secret that patients determine on occasion to keep from the analyst and that immediately expands on first contact to act as a screening or scrambling device covering a whole field of associations. "Only painful recognition, like the one that I could still, today, unconsciously associate my brother with 'Nazi,' can aid further resolution and lead to acceptance of ambivalent feelings. Such recognition also can, as in my case, help pave the way to new realizations: it was through my feelings of love and deep loss with regard to my brother Ya`acov that I came to recognize and to face my deep longing, love and feelings of loss with regard to Germany" (255).

At the 1994 meeting on the powers that continue to be with or within psychoanalysis, Karen Brecht, one of the cocurators of the 1985 exhibition that nearly a decade later was coming down the New York reassembly line, was also back, like the wandering witness, decade upon decade, to always the same forget-together. She delivered a reassessment of Alexander Mitscherlich's career that turned a high beam on Mitscherlich's make-believe (or, at least, premature) identification of himself as analyst and on his underlying idealization of this fantastic relationship to Freud. Mitscherlich in fact graduated from a German tradition of psychosomatic medicine, the routes to which during the Nazi period he neither traveled nor, then as later, seemed to know about. But the foreclosure Brecht announces cuts out a wider birth—of therapeutic eclecticism—that cannot but prove Mitscherlich rightfully heir-conditioned, after all. The psychosomatic trajectory overlaps in its origins with the eclecticization and reunification of all psychoanalysis-based therapies (a basis that underlies both the more compatible and more resistant offshoots). We tend to read the history of psychotherapy in terms of its growing distance from Freud, but if we were to read the same span of intention the other way, we'd have the very measure of Freud's unstoppable influence. A citizen of "greater psychoanalysis" without knowing it, Mitscherlich took advantage of the postwar need for a split between the Before and After, between the two Germanys, to introduce and maintain a split of his own making, the splitting image of two societies claiming to represent psychoanalysis in Germany (the DPG and the DPV), one receiving international recognition, and the other getting the former's scapegoat role. And yet both societies counted among their founding members analysts and therapists who had worked in Nazi Berlin at the German Institute for Psychological Research and Psychotherapy (which, following the leader, Matthias Göring, the more famous Göring's cousin, was popularly known as the "Göring Institute").

Mitscherlich got away with claiming to be the sole custodian of a purely victimized Freudian tradition that the Allies brought back. Unwittingly, he was telling a part truth; the lie involved the discontinuous break in the programming, the break he gave himself as pioneer. Just the same, when it came time to set up his own center for psychosomatic and psychotherapeutic treatment (later to become the Sigmund Freud Institute), he was able to cite the Nazi Berlin therapy center as model. His main mentors had both been associated with the Berlin operation. The most famous of the two, Viktor von Weizsäcker, who studied the play era of childhood and the gray area of psychosomatics during the Third Reich, was another curious agent of an expansionism of psychotherapy that keeps coming down to the influence of Freud. Thus Mitscherlich was quoting von Weizsäcker whenever he assumed or pronounced that the destiny of psychosomatic medicine was tied to its compatibility with psychoanalysis.

If Mitscherlich founded anything, it was the postwar German tradition of sociocultural criticism that capitalized on the benefits and interest accruing from the merger that's been going through for the duration of the twentieth century and beyond between a more or less Marxist sociology and a psychology equally mixed and matched or mismatched with psychoanalytic associations. Mitscherlich thus formulated in his book on unmourning a kind of cultural criticism or cultural studies that lubes with loosely used psychoanalytic concepts the same old social contexts and standards of interpretation for a better fit with their objects and objectives. Already in 1988 Brecht was able to forecast the conclusion she would be coming to at greater length at the New York Congress: "His critical argument with National Socialism provided a suitable front behind which the true history of psychoanalysis in Germany conveniently disappeared" (246).

The Californians

In California in the 1970s, the crypt of the missing era was first opened up by Geoffrey Cocks, at the time a history grad student whose open-headedness all over the different sides of the topic's untenable identification produced a dissertation that was unique in being able to organize the polymorphousness of the contradictory material: he produced a kind of neutrally upbeat history of psychotherapy today, whether in Germany or in California, based on the standards of professional upward mobilization, insurance coverage, and recognition by the military and the medical establishments. The dissertation went out in book form in 1985: *Psychotherapy in the Third Reich: The Göring Institute*. (The material that can be assumed, by movie rights, to be his own was reported in *Lingua Franca* to be under way as screenplay. May he score another first, a non-identification-stuck projection of Nazi compromise formations.)

> What has heretofore escaped notice, however, was the surprising opportunity for those who remained in Germany. A number of lesser-known physicians and laypersons involved in the practice and propagation of all types of psychotherapy, including psychoanalysis, were now, through a confluence of conditions, in a position to foster its professional exercise and promulgation. Even at the zenith of Nazi persecution, an important degree of professional continuity was maintained. And furthermore, the particular conditions that prevailed beginning in 1933 allowed these psychotherapists to achieve an institutional status and capacity for practice that has been unrivaled in Germany before or since. (3)

What's missing from histories of psychoanalysis, modernism, and National Socialism is the continued existence of psychoanalysis in Nazi Germany. In the search for all the other contexts of this missing era, Cocks's surefire history holds the romantic lead in pulling up longer-term German traditions or legacies (notably the German psychologies and philosophies of romanticism) in which the congruence between Nazi commitments to total fitness and psychotherapeutic holism would count down as late arrival. But this is where Cocks falls for the busywork of Nazi psychotherapists who sought to establish an alibi in the prehistory of psychoanalysis that would wipe out the peaking of Freud's original influence through their own institutional efforts on behalf of therapeutic eclecticism or reunification. First there was the problem of a bio-influence expressed in the yodeling of neologisms around "Jew," recast as the adjectivalized verbs *verjudet* or *angejüdelt*. And then for the same reason, only more biographically than biologically determined, there was the all-points lookout for another historical dating of priority in the discovery of the unconscious, repression, drive, identification, and projection, among other terms, that could be awarded to, say, Paracelsus, Leibniz, Carus, Goethe, Hartmann, or Nietzsche. But who Carus? How can there still be a return to romantic sources that travels (fast!) outside the frame of reference and resistance to Freud? At the more current end of reception and misrepresentation, the alterations Cocks sees psychoanalysis get fitted for in order to attend the neopsychoanalytic movement are in fact changes down the receiving line of treatment that really give a measure of the extent of the Freudian system's expansion through alteration of the middlebrow range of health professionalism.

As Richard Grunberger observes down the Third Reich's halls of justice (where "retrospective legislation became an integral feature of Nazi legal practice," the law one of retroactivity, and the precedent for what was already reset to have gone), the retrofitting of contexts to fit Nazi ideology's investment and emplacement in so many institutions and discourses was one of the more happening trends (122). The Nazis indeed launched virtual time travel missions into the past (as in the film *Jud Süss*, in which the Frankfurt school's dialectical hold on the Enlightenment is pulled out by these routes) to alter it in such a way that passage to the present would have to change its booking too, and thus the immediate past or present of an established precursor or alternative tradition would stand or fall corrected, circumvented, even vaporized. But time traveling is only as effective as the next guy's denial of the Oedi-pedagogical imperative of one-way transmissions. Cocks assumes that the fantastic tampering by Nazi German psychotherapists with the historical contexts of their discipline was the determining force in the way they went about or got around the legacy. Just the same, if we let Cocks's record speak for itself, the revisionist commentary that tried outrunning Freud in history and in theory could not touch the up-to-date practice of psychotherapy that had never before been more dependent on a thorough knowledge of analytic techniques.

> Freudian theory and practice, though loudly condemned in Nazi Germany, thus actually survived by two means. The first was the sheer fact that psychoanalytic thought had already penetrated into almost all systems of psychotherapeutic theory and praxis; the second was the persistence of the practice of psychoanalysis itself in both its orthodox and neo-Freudian forms. The growing neo-Freudian orientation was of particular importance,

for by 1933 psychoanalysis had not only been attacked, accepted, and adapted from without, but altered from within in such a way as to provide some lines of congruence with the approved psychotherapy of the Nazi era. (16)

Rather than consider psychoanalysis as so altered from within that in 1933 there was enough compatibility between its new self and the new other therapy to explain its survival in the stampede of approval of psychotherapy in Nazi Germany, I would underscore instead that Freud's influence was so unstoppable that even in Nazi Germany, Jung's outright objections to including psychoanalysis within the new order of therapeutic eclecticism were, in practice, ignored (while as words from a sponsor, they were broadcast to lay claim to something new and Aryan rather than the old guy's thing the Germans were sticking to because it worked).

1985

1985, the year Cocks's study went out in book form, the year of the Hamburg Congress, also saw publication of the main German-language history of psychoanalysis in the Third Reich, Regine Lockot's *Remembering and Working-Through: On the History of Psychoanalysis and Psychotherapy in National Socialism*, and, same year, same language, Peter Riedesser and Axel Verderber's *Mobilization of Souls: Military Psychiatry and Military Psychology in Germany and America*. Lockot supplements Cocks's documentation with greater analytic attention to the in-session dynamics that tend to be overlooked by mainstream spans of historicization. She sees a series of vacuum packings promoting therapy at large throughout Nazi Germany and psychoanalysis in particular within Nazi German psychotherapy.

> During the Nazi period psychotherapy was supported financially in a form even now not yet matched. The reasons for this are not to be found in an altered psychic sensibility that caused people to look for help more emphatically and more intensively—and it is furthermore doubtful that psychotherapy per se was a conformist instrument that made citizens who were still resisting the new order psychically more available for the change—rather it seems that the development of psychotherapy benefited enormously from the vacuum National Socialism created. The annihilation of cultural traditions left behind vacancies that National Socialist ideology was not equipped to fill. (314–15)

> Although psychoanalysis could be referred to, if at all, only critically, the representatives of German psychic healing [*Seelenheilkunde*] could not forgo the technical knowledge and experience of the psychoanalysts. (313)

But this opportunity provided only a half-life to both staying powers, much as, in the case of patients whose psychotherapy fills or compensates for vacancies in their lives, any therapeutic intervention has little to say or long to stay.

> The politics of the German Institute mirrors in essence the "greater" politics and Germany's usurpationist claims. International contacts were severed, the German psychotherapists attempted to build a new National-Socialist society under German rule. This attempt miscarried, the war brought Germany's defeat. (315)

Lockot's study wins the prize for staying inside psychoanalytic thinking while getting the historical work done. She also has her Freudian ears on when going over the same material that others have overlooked or passed on. A speech by Dr. von Kogerer in which the military psychiatrist extensively criticizes psychoanalysis is taken by Lockot as proof that, beyond the evidence of resistance to Freud, it is the body of knowledge that von Kogerer tampers with, knows, and gnaws on—down to the details—that has him under the influence (228). In Lockot's study, repetition, the silent partner in the title, the third term and it's out, is to be replaced by the remembering and working through her title loudly proclaims. Replacement is her duty, given her understanding of repetition as the sort of second chance or comeback that allows a repetition of the first time full of mistakes, but this time with everything right and what's too bad made good. Indeed, as Freud pointed out with regard to the children playing doctor, such repeats are usually only gratifying if active and passive positions or operations can be exchanged the second time around. Thus there's the history Lockot is attempting to remember and reconstruct, and then there's the other history, already there, repeating on automatic. "That is to say that the history of psychoanalysis/psychotherapy in National Socialism can be completely recorded once the postwar history has been interpreted under the aspect of repetition. Sometimes the work of interpretation is taken over from us and performed for us by the very agents of the history" (10).

To this day whenever "remembering, repetition, and working-through" comes on in a German setting, it's not the Freudian brand or band that's playing but rather the Mitscherlichs doing a cover. The monumental simplicity of Lockot's model, in particular as it extends at once into repetition and into the sociohistorical relation, owes more to the Mitscherlichs, more than she perhaps bargained for, than to Freud. In the following, Lockot compacts the repetition model prescribed in the foregoing paragraph to follow out the displacement of affect across a family gap of generations.

> The Nazi period in particular, at which time even mass murder was accomplished as bureaucratic business as usual, seems inclined to awaken in the observer precisely those emotions that were lacking at the time. The readiness for this, in this case to react affectively, lies in one's own drive impulses, which are re-experienced in their projection onto history. Just as the depth of a psychoanalytic treatment depends on the analyst's anxiety-free confrontation with his own drive impulses, as he can only then admit the rejected stirrings of the analysand, so the excavation of the historical reality that's reflected in the analyst can succeed

only to the extent that he, by becoming aware of and working with his countertransference, keeps on pushing his inquiry onward. (22)

Between the lines there is a lockout of the Jewish victim's perspective or reality (or running continuity) that aims its second barrel at the one transferential object always sure to be there, given the ethnicity of the father of psychoanalysis, along for the setting. Chasseguet-Smirgel makes this transference interpretation, one that comprehends all psychoanalysts, who are "in effect of Jewish stock, through their identifications with Freud and the pioneers of psychoanalysis, and should therefore perhaps think about the links between Judaism and psychoanalysis—and hence themselves" (433). Brought to consciousness through transference work, the objective or objectional part of the session that's Jewish bears good news and spares the messenger of the transference. It's where the slip, once it has set out across the transference, can be re-paired inside the couple relations we hold in analytic reserve with this father. The saving fiction of the couple goes cannibalistic when it produces, projects, requires that "perversion" stay in the other place. The line of reproduction that the couple formation even of individual therapy automatically gives us falls back behind the front lines of a newly narcissistically aggrandized psychic field or no-man's-land that psychoanalysis discovered inside the shell-shocked soldier. It's an investment that gets diversified, as we'll see, on all sides of World War II (at the latest). But in the meantime, the retrograde position is a giveaway address for arguments to fall back on. The problem with *The Inability to Mourn* is contained in the coupling of its authorship. Alexander Mitscherlich and Margaret Nielsen-Mitscherlich give their highest rating to true mourning, which, by definition, presupposes that the other loved and lost was related to the survivor through a difference modeled on the way "a man and woman can enrich one another through the experience of their differences" (39). Riedesser and Verderber owe their work of automatic violence control to having seen Roth—Karl Heinz Roth, whose essay on the sheer torture of the treatments shell-shocked soldiers received has only one model in the duo's view: Alexander Mitscherlich's 1949 documentation of medical war crimes (in which, since any treatment of psychology was left out, it's easy to take sides). Their own team spirit comes down to the same used model of difference that was parked between the Mitscherlichs. The two men dedicate their study together to one future: "For our children Dirk, Hannes, Marian."

A Couple More Mistakes

A traveller along the main southern-highway route from
California to the Gulf of Mexico will come across a huge sign
marked, "The Great Divide." One arrow points to the east, the
other to the west. There is nothing else the eye can fix upon to
mark the boundary-line.... A problem similar to that of the
traveller at the continental divide is presented to every observer
who surveys the Nazi culture programme. Except here at
critical points there are no boldly worded sign-posts to tell the
direction of flow. Yet without knowledge of the dividing-line,
and the direction, the leading purposes, being pursued, no
evaluation—scientific or otherwise—of any Nazi programme
has any meaning.

—ROBERT BRADY, *THE SPIRIT AND STRUCTURE OF GERMAN FASCISM*

In the "Personal Afterword of the Authors" Riedesser and Verderber share
with the reader their struggle for self-control over their raging selves in
order to keep the commentary from running off at the mouth. In the Person-
als section, then, they recall how each time they took a break and returned
to the project, they couldn't help themselves: they had in the meantime "repressed" the open horror that the documents they excavated cynically spelled
out. (It's hard to imagine that they didn't know that the Nazi Germans
were thick as war criminals with the party's public, published agenda.) This
afterthought or afterimage of a "repression" is as close as those two come
to intervening in their material, which preselects itself in headline fashion.
The repress release plays back the tapes of the official record of how the
psychologists and psychiatrists who applied themselves to military concerns
understood or advertised their contribution. If not careerism, then the self-
deception that's a big part of self-love, will certainly promote a deliberate
segregation of one's own work from the other's work. Thus we are left with
the self-promotion of characterological or holistic psychologists claiming
their distance from any contact whatsoever with psychoanalytic and Gestalt
models. It doesn't matter that academic psychologists lend themselves to
polemical citations for their own originality; the corridor race for government approval in the undecided space of ideological protest, which they
had to run against the more powerful agencies of psychic treatment (psychiatry and psychotherapy), automatically resituates the rise to monopoly
position of the Leipzig School of Personality Theory. The authors refer to

Cocks's dissertation work on Nazi psychotherapy and for that moment are aware that a certain adherence to psychoanalysis stuck to the Third Reich. But when they get around to covering and quoting the psychologists, they forget what they had by Cocks's proximity and proxy only several pages ago also already known. Now we're expected to believe with them the psychologist Oswald Kroh, who crows in 1941 all about the Nazi revolution's permanent removal of the "hocus pocus" or "ghost" *(Spuk)* of Freudian and Adlerian analysis (Riedesser and Verderber, 68).

One year before the run on studies of the Nazi military-psychoanalytic complex, Ulfried Geuter published a study clearly inspired by Cocks's emphasis on professionalism as a focus for reconstruction of the missing era within institutional history: *The Professionalization of German Psychology in National Socialism.*

> It became clear during study of the source material ... that a series of mysteries could be explained, developments interpreted, texts and materials set in order and understood, if the history of psychology in National Socialism was approached from the side of the professionalization of psychology—its development from an academic discipline to a profession with areas of application, in possession of specialized job opportunities and of its own system of training. The striving of the discipline for professional status proved to be the driving force of its development during this period. The choice of this methodological approach to the history of psychology thus followed out of the material, even if now the written version proceeds from method to material. (14)

Geuter brackets out the area Cocks covered not only because their studies are too proximate but also because psychoanalysis and psychology had gone their own ways. Even though psychologists borrowed from psychoanalysis in open or tentative fashion, the lack of critical assessment of, and interaction with, Freud's science at the same time does not register the kind of reception that would indicate influence (Geuter, 27). The psychoanalysts kept to themselves in their own institutes, which were then dissolved but reabsorbed within the German Institute for Psychological Research and Psychotherapy, the address for the reunification of the main depth-psychological or analytical approaches. Psychologists enrolled at the institute to attend seminars and lectures and to receive psychotherapeutic training. The new careers in child and teen counseling that were opening up for psychologists at that time had in fact originally been trail-blazed by analysts of diverse schools. Matthias Göring, Hermann's cousin, who was named the head of the Nazi Berlin institute and had trained as an Adlerian, was prior to his career move to Berlin in charge of a children's counseling center in Wuppertal. Geuter's criteria for locating an influence are overly strict. His material suggests many points or overlaps of contamination with the psychoanalytic structures internal to so many receptions at the time. Military psychology's criteria for selecting soldiers right down to their psychotechnical fit with certain specialized duties were ultimately based on characterology, the psychology of the whole personality that allegedly displaced psychoanalysis and Gestalt psychology with something totally new.

> It is interesting in this connection to consider Freud's reception within characterology. Freud is recognized in the thirties as a "character-morphologist." The strata-theorists [Schichttheoretiker] borrow his structural theory as their strata theory, but kill off the vitality of the Freudian model by pulling out the thorn of drive theory and taking away from the model its internal dynamic. Also they do not acknowledge a superego; for at the latest by that point they would have had to admit the social-critical potential of the model. (189)

Once again Geuter's criteria exceed most expectations, which, for many of us, are in fact greatly confirmed: superego says that these psychologists admitted into their work for the German military extensive compatibility with Freudian models.

For Riedesser and Verderber, Freud functions as the kind of split-off object to which one can remain partial, hating it and loving it too. Outside their brief consultation with Cocks, to which Freud was after all invited, the two authors leave the father of psychoanalysis standing alone in the archive of materials they unpack with both eyes open. Psychoanalysis is at the same time kept from entering, in the span of their genealogy, the compromised or eclecticized field of therapy across which German and American experts continued to draw once and future battle lines. Riedesser and Verderber make mistakes in how the material gets distributed between foreground and background; often the better half is completely omitted. Thus they are relentless in tracking the testing drive of U.S. military psychology and psychiatry to the point of totally missing the shift also taking place over there toward greater connection with psychoanalytic, Gestalt, and characterological approaches, a new modality swing that, beginning in 1941, sent several psychoanalysts to top positions in the military medical establishment. Riedesser and Verderber are equally tenacious in registering the claims of the German military to have consistently targeted so-called psychopaths as a military exclusion (a pattern that fits the authors' political take on "psychopathy" as always left-wing protest). In the United States there was indeed, as they emphasized, a trend toward considering ways in which those unfit in peacetime might just the same have the right psychic fit for wartime purposes. But the direction the trend took postwar in Britain and the United States was toward increased disambiguation of the psychopath's diagnostic reception, one extended to delinquents and deviants alike, who thus came under the hearsay of criminalization and pathologization. With all the painful amount of reading to which they lay claim, you would think that Riedesser and Verderber would have caught Otto Wuth and Max Simoneit (two figures whose pronouncements they otherwise cover extensively) proposing the compatibility of some psychic disturbance such as psychopathy with the new techno-specializations required by modern warfare. Cocks and Lockot don't overlook the surprising aside recollected by Nazi psychiatrist Oswald Bumke (whose boom-boom diagnoses of "psychopaths" are readily available for citation): the observation Ernst Kretschmer shared with Bumke was about a funny thing that happened on the way to 1933: "It's a funny thing about psychopaths. In normal periods we are asked to give our expert opinions on their cases; in times of political unrest they govern us" (Lockot, 74–75).

Steady State

Elisabeth Brainin and Isidor Kaminer see all postwar Germans slipping ahead of themselves at the impasse that idealization and oblivion held up in their relations with psychoanalysis and psychodynamic therapy. The consequences of National Socialism for the psychoanalytic movement were outright traumatic. "The 'German Institute for Psychological Research and Psychotherapy' was the dominant psychotherapeutic institution in Germany. Thus the Nazis were the first to permit the practice of 'psychoanalysis' in a state institution" (994). Brainin and Kaminer read the upsurge of interest and investment in psychoanalysis in postwar Germany (aided also by the attainment of total insurance coverage in 1967, thereby marking the late victory of a campaign waged already in the twenties but, in Nazi Germany, mounted with a unified force that left the more lasting impression) as a run on empty, as idealization, even as the kind of rapport with "miraculation" that Freud's most interesting psychotic case, Daniel Paul Schreber, can't stop projecting. When it is a "Jewish science," double idealization through psychoanalysis is abetted, but when the equally available appeal is made to Freud's modernist secularism, then a "Jewish" part gets wiped out in the name of identification.

According to Brainin and Kaminer, Anna Freud's notion of "identification with the aggressor" had last been seen in the treatment of former concentration camp inmates. This move against the victim has "more to do with the feelings of the therapist in the face of the extent of annihilation than with those of the patient." Countertransferences thus "stand together with the defense against narcissistic anxieties about identifying with the victim, and lead at the same time to a refusal to empathize. But isn't it a question of the guilt feelings of the analyst which come out of his own historical position and are defended against by means of this withdrawal of empathy? Don't guilt and shame make it impossible for the patient's story to be seen for the first time as historical reality, so that finally one can begin to work out just how much this reality is perhaps used as a form of resistance in the psychoanalytic process?" (1005).

In Nazi Germany in 1937, the proceedings of the 1936 Marienbad Congress could be discussed and referred to, and even Anna Freud's *The Ego and the Defense Mechanisms* could be reviewed in print. The British Society's prize for the year's best clinical work was awarded in 1937 to two analysts who, tied for first place, were still members in equal standing: Fritz Riemann from Berlin and a Chicago colleague (Dräger, 261–62).

Beginning in 1938, the official psychoanalysts were concentrated under the institutional rubric of "Working Group A." This was a punitive setback following analyst Carl Müller-Braunschweig's transference intrigue with Anna Freud. Upon Austria's absorption within an even greater Germany, Müller-Braunschweig gave himself assurance coverage in Freud's eyes that the Vienna institute would continue, virtually, as always. Set in writing that the Nazis soon hand-held, it made Müller-Braunschweig look like someone who served the family first, according to the letter, and Nazi team spirit only on the side.

The top billing that was still being given through transposition to A-status was dropped from all records of recognition after one of the group members, John Rittmeister, lost his head over "espionage" convictions. This political crisis, which Nazi psychoanalysis was by some "miracle" nonetheless in a position to survive (Baumeyer, 210), is a radical demonstration of the continuity between Nazi Germany and the other modernist nations, one that holds the tension between political and therapeutic standards. Rittmeister left Switzerland in 1937 to join the Berlin institute, where he was soon put in charge of the outpatient clinic, and where he completed his interest in psychoanalysis through training analysis with Werner Kemper. One of the reasons Rittmeister left Switzerland was that his left-wing sympathies had placed him at odds with the authorities; he also felt that the Berlin center was where psychoanalytic work was happening in Europe. He saw no problem, no more than pursuing his analytic interests in Nazi Germany, in his regular involvement with the resistance movement. The other reason he gave for leaving Switzerland to return to Germany, even Nazi Germany, was to take a wife. But going to the chapel, the wife took him to the Rote Kapelle (as the underground organization with which he was busted was called). Following Rittmeister's execution in 1943, a "catacomb" mode of existence was dropped on the remaining analysts, who, remarkably indeed, nevertheless remained, as regards all basic signs of life and more, protected by the Berlin psychotherapy institute. But now they could meet only as an unofficial discussion group restricted to examining issues of "casuistry and therapy," most notably the treatment of stuttering.

Not right away, but increasingly, Freud could be referred to only by work, not by name or specific recognizable terms, and more as work of therapy than as that of theory. But while Freud's books were the toast of the 1933 book warmings, at the institute the same works were available to members right to the finish line. Freud's portrait, however, was removed in 1938 from the spot it was in across the hall from the Hitler portrait, which then stared on out into space without other until 1945. In 1936 Felix Boehm got it from highest authority that psychoanalysis, clearly a useful therapy, should negotiate a merger with the other psychotherapeutic groups. Boehm approached the Jungians first. But although the president of the Jung fan club, Eva Moritz, informed Boehm that financial concerns were making her hedge, behind that scene all bets were off, Jung assured her, regarding any close contact with the ambivalently targeted science. He was having the time of his life hating Freud.

A directive from on high planned that the new center of reunified German psychotherapy would build and draw on the facilities, resources, and experience of the Berlin Psychoanalytic Institute. Up there psychoanalysts met with way less phobicity than what was coming at them from the former colleagues who worked for the competition psychodynamic therapies. No doubt it was the sense of the history of psychoanalysis that the authorities were backing that informs the memorandum or manifesto Boehm and Müller-Braunschweig collaborated on for the new era of compromise formations. They started out advertising psychoanalysis's excellent war record and, for the meantime, emphasized the ongoing efforts of psychoanalysis, as witnessed by the opening of the outpatient clinic with its sliding scale, to make the cure of whatever symptomatology got in the way of socialization (in the way, that is, of going to war) accessible not only down the ranks but, even in peacetime or right on time for a more total war, across class lines (Lockot, 141). By 1944, with the end in military sights, the German Institute was receiving mega-funding: the amount set aside for the therapy center, which had been doubled for 1943–1944, was doubled again for 1944–1945. Was it the end coming soon that was to be therapeutically assuaged and, rather than teaching a lesson, lessened through radical subventions? The patience (and patients) of Germany had already passed the test once, the test of long awaiting the next turn, turn, of a time for war.

The therapy institute was considered basic to the prep work for warfare. Once war started, the institute was awarded the status of "important to the war effort." The Nazi peacetime effort had divided the therapeutic labor of the institute among three deep approaches in support of the war steadfastness of the Germans, soldiers and civilians alike: psychological warfare, frigidity or sterility in women, and male homosexuality that in its final tally counted one promotion and two cure-all efforts. The three-part program was reshuffled for hitting the deck with war on. Psychological warfare was still the number one promotional. Preparedness for war would now be addressed up close, in more direct terms, given the prospect of war neurosis, which the institute would counter and contain with research on the best treatment methods and with a steady supply of specially trained military psychologists.

Kurt Gauger went so far on the resistance curve to proclaim (psychodynamic) psychotherapy as the ideology of the Nazi revolution—"the most political discipline of all the disciplines however is psychotherapy" (Zapp, 131)—all the while taking from Freud all the originality of thought or discovery. It was a dealing he sealed by awarding Freud a star for great "application." By and large, the achievement of psychoanalysis was detached from Freud's name and corpus, which was personalized and credited only in terms of a certain opportunistic or uncanny sense of timing that still returned to Freud. But even if all the pieces of psychoanalysis could be seen to preexist Freud, their reconfiguration around a new sense of timing is what also set off Gauger's counter of recognition. There are indeed whole histories of Freud's redealing the words of another at a better timing. In 1912 Sabina Spielrein had worked the words of the death drive thesis first— and too soon. Freud took the time to bring his first system to completion as the techno-mediatic sensurround of projective haunting in which the death wish is your telecommand. What would death drive or group psychology mean without this preparatory wiring of its reception? Spielrein's death and destruction drive, which flared up preemptively, hot and fast, over and out, performed or symptomatized the drive that's all over you in no time.

If Gauger (even as he tries to declare him history, all the way into prehistory, and make him over as his own epigoner) cannot get around paying Freud, the opportunity and time taker, his overdues, Göring manages to contract a double contamination when he tries putting psychoanalysis in its other place, since it doubles on contact also as the other's place, and then, unstoppably on a roll, as the unconscious. What Göring has been finding lately even and especially in "patients who are pure Aryan [is that] there is often something in the subconscious that appears to us as belonging to another race [andersrassisch]" (Zapp, 106). To jump the gun down this double barrel: do we not have here the beginning of an admission— beyond the bad effects of industrialization, Jewish assimilation, and so on, which the Aryans have been left carrying to longer term—that psychoanalysis, to lip-synch Karl Kraus's stiff upper quip, always also is the disease that it sets out to cure. Because psychoanalysis, owing to Freud's sense of timing, had established itself as the overriding modernist discursivity, whatever overturning might lie in store for psychoanalysis must be administered first by a technique compatible with what's to be found among the psychoanalytic stores. It's like what Freud theorized as the transference neurosis, the inoculative miniaturization and organization in session of the mess of disorders the patient brings to the beginning of treatment. Only it's like the transference neurosis in reverse, going into reverse to implode together with the analytic prospects for a cure the whole system of psychoanalysis, the one that's thus contained by its bad influence, which is under treatment.

Eat Your Words

Another idealization of analysis that has been caught harboring resisters begins by taking the Nazis at their word. The Nazi principle of *Gleichschaltung* (a neologism borrowed from engineering and signifying coordination, harmonizing, or unification with the Nazi agenda) "required a leveling, an adaptation, to Nazi ideals. It required that every institution regardless of its specific nature follow the prescribed regulations. In the case of Freudian psychoanalysis, any abstract formation beggars the reality of how this was achieved with integrity" (R. Spiegel et al., 486). *Gleichschaltung*, which applied itself to both social and lexical units or unities, claimed that different words made the difference. "Psychoanalysis" assumed many code names: even when "psychoanalysis" could still be used (until 1938), when it wasn't answering to "depth psychological treatment of long duration," it was taking calls for "developmental psychological orientation."

In discussion or whenever going audio, it was possible to agree on terms or meanings and exchange them freely at the institute. But publications came under ever heavier handedness of censorship out to purify what others go to the trouble to read. August Aichhorn, one of the first and few analytic experts on adolescence, was up-front about it: he sent a list of diverse analytic terms to Kemper with the request that, for his information, they be corrected to bring them up to date with current usage. In 1944 Kemper committed to writing that it was never a question of replacing certain objectionable terms but that the whole libido theory, for example, had to be rethought, brought into alignment with the new direction. Instead of issuing a decoder, Kemper suggested that Aichhorn create a brand-new language of terms and thoughts. In other words, Kemper was telling Aichhorn that he had to figure it out and do it himself, as though creating something new out of nothing (Lockot, 196). Kemper's own covertly analytic work during this period, *Disturbances in Women of the Capacity for Love,* was finally undecodable as analytic by his colleague Käthe Dräger: "When you read Kemper's book you get the impression that in it psychoanalysis has fallen out through the grid" (Zapp, 40 n. 1).

But if the "Oedipus complex" had to go by "family complex," then Allied developments within the eclecticism mixer were not far behind those of the Nazis: doesn't that "translation" cover the emergence of family systems therapy or theory as something "new"? Psychiatrist Walter Cimbal crashes this admission of the status quo from the Nazi bookend of this celebration of a psychotherapy that would be true to the people, at their service, and "supplement the biological improvement of the race through cleansing and improvement of the atmosphere of family life, in which the German child grows up" (Zapp, 65).

Harald Schultz-Hencke, who had to pay postwar as though the one and only Nazifier or therapeutic eclecticizer among analysts in Nazi Germany, had in fact preempted the struggle for words going down during the Nazi period by his neoanalytic activities (already in the later twenties) in synchrony with the efforts of other international revisionists, such as Karen Horney and Harry Stack Sullivan. In his 1927 *Introduction to Psychoanalysis*, Schultz-Hencke already was taking issue with the added difficulties that psychoanalytic terminology put in the way of a greater following. He preferred using the term "unconscious" only infrequently. His recodings were unstoppable: "captative" for "oral," "retentive" for "anal," *"Desmolyse"* or *"Desmologie"* for *"Psychoanalyse."* Kemper applauded his colleague as the German pioneer in the move to make ever more accessible whatever worked in psychoanalysis. During the pre-Nazi period, Schultz-Hencke also had a friend in Otto Fenichel, who, in his review of the 1927 intro, agreed that the terminology, for better or worse, was not the object of one's commitment. But the editorial note drops its disagreement with the review as though asking a question: "If words (terminology) are really so extraneous and insignificant, then why does one even bother to modify the words, just the words?" (Zapp, 137).

If Nazi psychoanalysis was a science that could not speak its names, then, down to the letter of its laws, psychoanalysis proper was never retained or rescued by its callback to a Nazi space of secondary audition and elaboration. Staying power belonged, instead, to psychotherapy, which enjoyed unprecedented professionalization and spread during the Nazi period of its history. In his review of Cocks's 1975 dissertation, the basis for the 1985 book on the so-called Göring Institute, Lacanian therapist and theorist Hans-Joachim Metzger insists that other words *are* other worlds:

> There were no doubt those among the individuals Cocks refers to as "Freudians" who were and wanted to be what they were: psychotherapists.
>
> If one doesn't view the symbolic constitution of the analytic discourse as extraneous, then one cannot get around accepting the label under which they positioned themselves or allowed themselves to be positioned. One has to believe them.
>
> And that's a lot. And in a certain perspective it offers plenty to think about. Because it turns a light on the period of the emergence of what one today encounters everywhere under the name

"psychotherapy." ... It is the Göring institute and the literature
its members produced in which, as though crystallized, all preconditions, procedures, and aims of nearly all currently practiced forms of psychotherapy can be found, including the pro-
grammatic eclectic attempt of the integration of all in one. (37–38)

But from where he sits within the institution of psychoanalysis, Robert
Wallerstein admits with best regards to its Nazi period another—greater—
view of psychoanalysis that includes the face-off that's really an interface
between "analysis" and "therapy": "Unhappily it is just the point that psychoanalysis is not that different from psychotherapy and enjoys no such
immunity from the human condition, anymore than does any other psychotherapy or any other species of professionalized activity" (369). The make-
believe oppositions set up to protect Freud's legacy, whether between or-
thodox psychoanalysis and, say, the object-relations school or between
psychoanalysis proper, however its precise location is to be identified, and
a mixed-up medley of psychotherapies, only serve to obscure the context
of the difference Freud makes, and that continues to complete itself in the
widest possible circulation of his intrapsychic model through all departments
of psychological interventionism. This widest ranging of the Freudian model
is what is being designated here as "greater psychoanalysis." It is the miss-
ingness of the era of Nazi psychotherapeutic eclecticism or correctness
from our histories of modernism, National Socialism, and psychoanalysis
that requires that we not see (Nazi!) our complete investment in Freud.

Another way to assess or dismiss the continuity overrelies on the short-
cuts of perversion. Analyst Anna Antonovsky is pulled up short by the
weird hybrid of ideology and ideas in the generic articles: "The ideas do
not really mix, but in perverted form a psychoanalytic concept is made to
be the carrier of an ideology inimical to it" (227). The location of "perversion" in this uncanny complex represents one of the frontiers of work to be
done. For now, at the level of wording, in the context of a more value-free
determination both of perversion and of word, this place is marked and
held over for future reading by a word from Derrida: "There's no racism
without a language. The point is not that acts of racial violence are merely
words but rather that they have to have a word. Even though it offers the
excuse of blood, color, birth—or, rather, *because* it uses this naturalist and
sometimes creationist discourse—racism always betrays the perversion of
a man, the 'talking animal'" (292). The resonance is there, between the evolution or perversion and what was first known as "the talking cure."

Before there can be any name-calling there has to be identification, the big I.D. that runs interference, I mean inter-reference, for what Philippe Lacoue-Labarthe and Jean-Luc Nancy call "The Nazi Myth." "It is because the German problem is fundamentally a problem of *identity* that the German figure of totalitarianism is racism" (296). The specifically German rapport with identification has a history that goes back, over and again, to an original trauma.

> The drama of Germany was also that it suffered an imitation *twice removed*, and saw itself obliged to imitate the imitation of antiquity that France did not cease to export for at least two centuries. Germany, in other words, was not only missing an identity but also lacked ownership of its means of identification. (299)
>
> But there is more: it can be said, no doubt, that what dominates German history, from this point of view, is a pitiless logic of the *double bind* (of the double, contradictory injunction with which Gregory Bateson, following Freud, explains psychosis). The malady, in the precise sense of the term, that seems always to have menaced Germany is schizophrenia, to which so many German artists would appear to have succumbed. (299–300)

Double bind will trigger a more direct hit of associations down the pages of *Nazi Psychoanalysis:* Bateson's formulation of the bind (we were in) was syntonic with the worldwidest range of greater psychoanalysis, doubly taking in the connections that were there between technology and the unconscious. Bateson's insight into negative feedback, for example, which he attained on the Allied side, also shot up on the German side with the rockets that owed as much to psychodynamic theories and constructions of the pilot's merger with the automatic functioning of artificial flight as to science fantasy or even to engineering science. The history of Bateson's reception or conception of cybernetics goes back, before that finish line, to the stint he was doing as propagandist earlier in the war, now analyzing Nazi films along the psychoanalytic lines he detected already dotted across the German productions, now projecting National Character treatises or traits that were modeled on an applied mode of psychodynamics that the Germans were the first to mobilize already between the wars. This between time, to continue sliding for a moment down this feedback aside, was really only the lead time it took for the Nazis to follow, understand, and improve on all the public relations and propaganda aspects of the victory that carried the Germans out in the first round of world war, defeat first.

The external frame of reception for a French diagnosis of German schizo-secondariness comes, then, from one original discourse that's not French, nor is it purified by exile. The drama or trauma of imitation and identification that gets set on the Germans was inspired by the work of a West German filmmaker (who was first brought to international attention down tracks already lubed by the Mitscherlich reception).

> The Nazi myth, as H. J. Syberberg (without whose *Hitler, a Film from Germany* the analysis that we attempt here would not have been possible) has so admirably shown, is also the construction, the formation, and the production of the German people in, through, and as a work of art. (Lacoue-Labarthe and Nancy, 303)

But (surprise!) in the time between, Syberberg took his supporters out with sudden attacks of hyper-nationalist, even fascist, and especially anti-Semitic points of view. The greater German (including Belgian) objects of French theoretical commemoration tend to have the phantom's last word. The French couple was responding to Syberberg's good mourning. But in the mourning after, the spook of Nazi adolescence acted out repossession of the reception of loss. This is the double bind of promoting acceptance of the end of all self love affairs with Hitler's lost object. But can the privileging of grief in screen memory ever really come down to and rest with an inability to face loss in the interpersonal register or column? According to available therapeutic models (in and outside psychoanalysis), the true mourner is the one who has lost and acknowledged as lost not the narcissistic prop or replicant (which can only be retained without issue, as in Syberberg's approved style of endless grieving) but the other, the other recognized as distinct, as separate. In the 1990s a cutting-edge industry of grief studies crowded the corridors of academe with the injunction to mourn or be forever fascist. The crude defensiveness of this opposition could not but lead to a word series of misrepresentations (whether given in complicity with or in resistance to the good mourning). To evaluate Syberberg's siren whine for all that was lost to, through, and with Hitler (as one must according to the opposition's progress of elimination) either as the living end of melancholia or as, just the same, a forum for endopsychic insights is tantamount to attributing mourning (or unmourning) to the kind of pathogenic transference, for good or bad, that blocks capacity for insight or exchange in session.

Memoirs

Around 1931 Martin Grotjahn, at the time a young psychiatrist and son of the late Alfred Grotjahn, former dean of the medical faculty at the University of Berlin and professor of social hygiene, applied for psychoanalytic training with the Berlin Psychoanalytic Institute. According to his father's testimony, father knew best when he "torpedoed" the proposal for establishment of a Chair for Psychoanalysis under consideration by the medical faculty in 1918, allegedly on account of that unsavory bit of speculation about the homosexual subtext to early man's control of fire, in particular of his urge to put the flame out with his own burning stream of urine. Since that speculation first appeared in a footnote in *Civilization and Its Discontents*, son Martin had good reason to consider his father's rationalization of his decision a legend in his own time (*My Favorite Patient*, 30). Around 1931 (the year of his father's death) Martin Grotjahn was interviewed, evaluated, and admitted by Max Eitington, Karen Horney, and Wilhelm Reich. His training analysis was with Ernst Simmel: "Simmel put me on the couch without any introduction, preliminaries or explanation. He simply said: 'You know the rules—so why don't you follow them?' These were the last words that I heard from him for a long time to come" (33).

And then it was 1933. "After some months and during an hour with me he got a telephone call from a friend in the police department at the Alexanderplatz, who warned him that the secret police were on the way to arrest him.... Simmel's telephone had never before interrupted an hour so he explained the situation to me. I sat up and reached for one of his cigarettes, an unheard of liberty. Since he assumed that his house was under surveillance, we escaped through the back window from the staircase and climbed down into the backyard, over a fence and into an alley. This was not an easy accomplishment since we both were small in stature" (34). The Promethean liberty obtained by son through "father" was short-lived. "Simmel disappeared for some months or only weeks but then came back, to everyone's surprise. He did not yet believe that anybody could seriously threaten him, an old soldier of the First World War, decorated with the Iron Cross.... He saw me a few more times and made the disarming remark: 'We have broken every rule and regulation of analytic training. I should be put into an analytic concentration camp.'... Another time I felt uncomfortable with my belt. Simmel asked innocently why I did not loosen it? I felt horrified at the idea, uncovering the hidden meaning of the homosexual surrender and its defenses against it. To surrender to my father or

31

his representative Simmel, meant certain death in my unconscious. . . . I am not sure whether I understood the incident at that time or later after my analysis, or now when I write about it" (36–37). But then Simmel really did have to go. He referred Grotjahn to Theresa Benedek. But, go away! Grotjahn just couldn't believe that Simmel hadn't noticed that he would never be able to trust a woman analyst. Instead Grotjahn sent his wife to Benedek while he signed up with Felix Boehm, if only by process of the elimination of all Jewish colleagues.

Grotjahn spent countless hours in analysis with Boehm until his immigration to America in September 1936.

> One dream stands out in my memory. It could well serve as a symbol of my whole analysis: I dreamt I was sitting on a small pile of earth—perhaps a grave?—and eating a red dessert, a kind of jello. For once Felix Boehm came to life and did not wait for my associations but shot an interpretation at me: "You are quietly eating the pickled penis of your father!" I remember feeling at that moment like looking into the deep canyon of my unconscious. I also remember this as the only interpretation I received which simply cannot be correct. (49)

Outside the Promethean complex in which Grotjahn celebrated reunions with Father, the Nazi German setting figured as shorter fuse to the form of resistance known as "acting-out":

> Once I telephoned him and told him that all books of the psychoanalytic publishing house were confiscated by the police in order to be burned. I added naively—and I am embarrassed now to tell this story—that we ought to buy these books for our use. Boehm was loudly indignant that I talked this way over the telephone. He considered that call as inexcusable, a dangerous aggression, a hostile acting-out, endangering his position and perhaps even his life. I was shocked by my carelessness but I must have thought at that time that we, the Gentiles, were above danger of persecution and terror. I felt like a total fool when I only wanted to be "helpful." These were times when any acting-out could mean instant disaster. I learned not to call my analyst. (51–52)

Grotjahn's wife, Etelka, was half Jewish, and their son had some Jewish blood that would come out in the watch for German purity, and so the Grotjahn family's days in Nazi Germany were outnumbered by the longevity of a regime Grotjahn was sure would be overthrown any day now. Before it

came time to leave, Boehm offered Grotjahn the position of assistant director of the outpatient clinic of the Berlin Institute for Psychoanalysis. "I
made up my mind during a summer vacation from analysis to immigrate
to America. I made my decision about leaving Germany without my analyst. When I told him this after his vacation, he was taken aback in disap-
pointment, then silently opposed it, and finally he agreed reluctantly that it
was perhaps the only way out for me, who was married to a woman with a
father born Jewish" (53).

Eighteen years after his Berlin analysis, Grotjahn met Boehm again in
the destroyed city. "Felix Boehm had heard that I was coming to visit Berlin,
wanted to contact me and wrote to a colleague in Beverly Hills for my address. This colleague in Beverly Hills was not on speaking terms with me
and so he did not give me the letter but forwarded my address to Boehm.
When Boehm wrote me he wanted to make sure to meet me—but alone
and not in the presence of Müller-Braunschweig, the only other surviving
analyst in Berlin, with whom he was not on speaking terms!" (55).

For Grotjahn, the arena of individual analysis set him against his father in unresolvable conflict. While in America he became intrigued with
the children's story "Ferdinand the Bull," which celebrated the perverse or
pre-Oedipal but also utopian circumvention of the bullfight between father
and son. In his memoirs he comes back to this fight, and its suicidal resolution, and while dissatisfied with the formulation, even after submitting it
to more revisions than he did any other part of the book, he still includes it,
because it marks "the culmination point of my entire analysis":

> The bullfighter represents and acts out the high drama of seduc-
> ing the aggressor to attack. The perfect, skillful seduction elimi-
> nates the difference between the seducing fighter and the attack-
> ing bull. The unity between attacker and victim, between parent
> and child, is re-established.... Bull and fighter become one and it
> seems not to matter any more who lives and who dies. For a
> split second of perfection in the moment of truth, life stands still
> and becomes death and eternity. (60)

This splitting of the second position treats the split heir to a oneness that
gels because it's still to die for. This marks one culmination point. By refor-
matting analysis to admit first families, then groups, Grotjahn achieved a
more satisfying alternative to the bullring through whatever father knows,
he knows best, the ring of internal recurrence inside his Prometheus complex.

By 1938 Grotjahn was working with Franz Alexander. He contributed
data supporting the success of short-term therapy (based on his own 250

case studies) to Alexander's *Psychoanalytic Therapy,* which appeared in 1946 and in which reference to Grotjahn was given short shrift (Grotjahn, 84). But whatever provocation short-term therapy posed (once again) in the civilian setting, Grotjahn soon joined the war effort in the field of military psychiatry where what's short-term cannot be associated with loss, even or especially given analytic gains. Grotjahn's postwar pursuit of analytic family and group therapy had to wait several years, during which time, while trying to uphold standards at the psychoanalytic training institute in Los Angeles, he developed "analytic battle fatigue" (in the new peacetime world of mixed metaphors) until, finding his "therapeutic efficiency" threatened, he turned to "group work," which then gave him "satisfaction and joy" (127). But the move away from individual analysis was first inspired by Grotjahn's wartime experience treating war-neurotic soldiers.

> I made my rounds on my wards during these visiting hours, going from family to family, and offering my help to activate the natural trend to growth and health in any family which accepted the returning veteran. It was the beginning of what I later in my peacetime practice tried to do with family therapy. I also tried group psychotherapy, in the army first, and many years later in private practice. (105)

Grotjahn's position as resident alien, German no less, in the American psychological war effort brought him to a point of overcoming or accepting his long-standing sense of isolation—as Gentile to his Jewish colleagues, as analyst to his psychiatric colleagues, as German to Americans. Pressed into service as interpreter for German prisoners of war, Grotjahn lost his place in the translation process, speaking English to the Germans, and German to the Americans.

> I worked better as a therapist to the Germans. I was once called to treat one of the prisoners because of his annoying bed-wetting. I put on my best parade uniform and told the man—in German— to his shocked surprise—that he was now in AMERICA—and here NOBODY wets the bed. Absolutely nobody! It worked, not to *my* surprise. During this short but painful identity confusion I had a peculiar dream which I am embarrassed to tell and which was difficult to analyse:
>
> I dreamt I was two man-sized spiders in the Berlin Zoo. My association went to gigantic deep sea crabs off the coast of Alaska. The dream-spiders also reminded me of "Daddy Long Legs," but how could I possibly dream of being *two* spiders? I saw the two dream spiders so clearly in front of me that I could not resist

I DREAMT I WAS TWO SPY-DERS

"It is rare that I can use a picture from a dream for a drawing. But once I had a dream which really startled me: I dreamt I was two spiders in the zoo of Berlin. This really did not make any sense and my associations did not lead anywhere. Then I made a drawing of two long-legged spiders and when starting to write the caption, I stopped when I noticed that I spelled spider with a 'y'—like in Spy-der. It was then clear to me that I once more had to work on a conflict about being German born and an officer in the Medical Corps of the American army. The dream was activated through my first visit to Berlin after the war." From Martin Grotjahn, *My Favorite Patient*, 223; drawing reproduced from p. 228. Reprinted by permission of Mark Grotjahn.

> making a drawing of them during the day, hours after awaken-
> ing. Then I added the caption: The Dream of the Two Spy-ders,
> and then the interpretation of the dream was clear: the work
> with the German prisoners made me feel like a double spy-(der),
> or two spies, spy and counter spy, German and American, my
> brother Peter in one army, I myself in another army. (107–8)

One touchdown in the Prometheus complex deserves another, but this one takes off. Grotjahn's auto–case study overflows with the coordinates that *Nazi Psychoanalysis* will be getting into (as in "digging") for the longer time it takes for us (like in a session after a whole season in therapy) to "stay with" the links or juxtapositions that are there but otherwise so easily re-re-pressed. Grotjahn recounts how by the end of the war, he was able to quit smoking on the spot. It happened while Martin and Etelka Grotjahn were preparing for landing back in the U.S. of A. following their first trip to Germany after the war:

> During the slow descent from the sky down to Mother Earth, I
> extinguished my cigarette "for the last time" and said to myself:
> I never will smoke again when I put my foot on American soil....
> It is of symbolic significance that the entire incident happened in
> mid-air. The awareness of one's own ego is different when fly-
> ing: the ego boundaries become vague and seem to include the
> airplane, and perhaps at times the universe. This feeling is quite

pronounced in me and does not seem to get dulled on repeated travels. So to speak, I was suspended between Europe and the New World, the past and the future, and could feel and integrate both. The past, again symbolically speaking, went off in smoke and the experience of immigration was finally integrated and the rebirth became acceptable—actually fifteen years after it had happened. I had to immigrate a second time before it was definitely integrated. A new chapter of my life had started. Professionally it was expressed in a slow and gradual growth of my preoccupation with analytic group therapy. I did not replace psychoanalysis but completed it. (116)

Show of Resistance

We already know going into this that Nazi research-happiness is legend. It's Nazi Germany's equal time share in modernism. The Nazis were engaged in the all-out pursuit of whatever research project was out there, as long as it could be billed as a war effort promotional. But this proviso represents, within any history of modernism, no exceptional or additional restraining order, if, indeed, it offers any constraint at all. Wernher von Braun, for example, is not a stray, projected, single-case overlap covering Weimar, Nazi, and U.S. aerospace projects. In other words, a circuitous, discontinuous "Dialectic of Enlightenment" or "Case of California" is not the only way to test the endurance of Nazism in our own time. There's also the direct hit or fit of continuity. Within the limits and links of the one consideration given the total war service, Nazi research also mobilized psychoanalysis, and that means one of the most protected and progressive sources of "our" modernism. But on the wider range of a more eclectic or more reunified rapport with psychotherapy at large, it was the model of intrapsychic reality (in contrast, for example, to the one taken only interpersonally), the model we saw first with Freud, that was pressed by Nazi researchers into areas of scientific inquiry where no psychological model had gone before.

Nazi psychoanalysis is the place where a more complete range of Freud's theorems can be tracked beyond the ranging doubled and contained within the alleged compatibility between psychoanalysis and the sociopolitical administration of what's out there. When Chasseguet-Smirgel refused to dismiss Nazi psychoanalysis as the kind of contradiction in terms belonging only to the category of aberration and discontinuity, she was able to project theoretical consequences for the transference within greater psychoanalysis. But really every other fundamental concept of psychoanalysis must also line up for rereading within the missing continuity and context.

With a thank-you note up front, it's time to zap the historians of the Nazi era of German psychotherapy out of the running commentary and controversy, with one parting shot. Gudrun Zapp's groundbreaking 1980 dissertation, which was not replaced, for example, at least not item by item, within the later Lockot history, falls back again on the words and names that keep on getting in the way. It's the patch of resistance Zapp documented so well earlier, and much to the credit of Schultz-Hencke's more convincing auto-contextualization. When she quotes Bumke as he crosses this patch, his reactivity slips and slides until it opens up, down to the wiring, the force of the reception of psychoanalysis that is with him.

Bumke states "that psychoanalysis—even if its claims were correct—on account of its content would right away encounter under any conditions intense resistance, and that the intensity of this natural resistance in turn explains the very forms in which it is given to express itself" (Zapp, 215). But in her own introduction, Zapp leaves behind these chips from her workshop, which are, however, still on her shoulder when she counts out loud the degrees of relevance of her study: "Not only for an appreciation of the longer-lasting effects of National Socialism on the position of psycho-analysis in Germany, but also and especially because the motives leading to rejection of psychoanalysis which have crystallized in the course of this work are in part still valid today. The ability to accept psychoanalytic results presupposes an unusual degree of self-criticism. The insights mediated by psychoanalysis represent in the first place a lowering of self esteem, only in the second step or stage can they be received as helpful. But this cannot of course be expected when the resistance to self-discovery can base itself on prejudices that are distributed generally throughout society. The rejection of psychoanalysis during the reign of National Socialism cannot be grasped simply, therefore, as a historical error, but rather as an event that can—in modified form—repeat itself" (Zapp, 6). The contributions that the historical documentations of the decade before made to the excavation of this uncanny era are self-evident and, from now on, need no longer bear repeating. They fell for the curse of the secretly buried, before in turn being buried alive. In other words, their theorization fell short of the material, even and especially of the very insights that the Nazi compromise formations manage to articulate if only between the lines, always with the slip showing, or on some stage of acting-out.

Almost ten years after the Hamburg Congress, the representatives of New York and German psychoanalysis that were summoned to contemplate power surges in and around their science of the transference in the immediate aftermath of the reunification of the Germanys, did not address the docu-history on exhibition in the foyer, the 1985 souvenir, which thus remained out of earshot of the lecture hall. Passing references could be made in overview openers or, in one case study example, along for the transference. What passed for knowledge so current it could go right on without reading left an opening wide for the author of *The Case of California*. Your West Coast respondent went for full-time reintroduction of the missing era of Nazi psychoanalysis.

The diplomatic buoyancy of the 1994 Congress, which caught New York delegates coming out with the equal guilt of Americans for the genocide of the Indians, and thus the equal rights of protection (and projection) for the German colleagues too, was short attention span. When the Californian finished, you could hear the vacuum-packing suck-sounds of repression seal the very place or span of audition. Afterward, on the sidelines, members of the audience sided with the response and estimated the value of the reintroduction, even with regard to the "savings" psychoanalysis received, on all the sides of both world conflicts, following from Freud's original encounter, the first time around, with the mass epidemic of war neurosis. But when the letter of the broadcast was later read by one of those single-file cheerleaders, the feeling that now had to be shared was that the Californian response was really into blaming, first Freud, then the Jews. But it's appropriate to our age that excavation projects of this tall order must flash back to Freud's publication of *Moses and Monotheism*, which at the time of reception by the requiring mind of nonreaders was, simply, same time and station of a double cross that the Jews were made to bear. The charge of splitting or self-hatred always gets signed on the first line of defense taken up against uncanny work.

REINTRODUCTION

The Setting

To clear the static on the direct lines between reunification of the Germanys and the return of German nationalism, xenophobia, and anti-Semitism, Werner Bohleber tries to make the Germans a "presence of the past." But midway, he proposes a group-level intervention that responds to the world-wide recycling of World War II since the end of the Cold War. The outbreak of stray, projected hostilities in Germany after the fall of the wall were symptomatically in sync with the eternal rerun of total-war phantasms we watched during the Gulf War. From the German response to the opening shot of the war, which followed the leader, to the phantasm of portable gas chambers (made in Germany) strapped to the buzz bombs of the Battle of Britain, World War II was back on the air. But it wasn't only this media war that stayed tuned to receptions that were decontextualized and haunting precisely to the extent that, according to Theodor Adorno's reckoning (Taylor, 112), they referred to the recent past, the past that always flashes back as primal; on another channel, we found ourselves watching the old programs or pogroms that were rerunning all over Europe following the end of the divide between the two Germanys. Television was not the "liberator" of the Eastern European countries (which we had last visited, while they were still safely behind the Iron Curtain, in *Shoah*). In Eastern Europe the rise of group psychopathology issued its repress releases via live transmissions

This stamp, *Ungültig* (meaning "invalid" or "invalidated"), was branded over Third Reich stamps designating the reading material as military or state property. Most of the archival materials studied in the course of writing and assembling this book bore this stamp on top of the other stamp.

43

at once occult and techno-mediatic, morbid and immortalizing. Painting by the number of racisms and nationalisms that were going down in the missing place of the superego, portraits of the vampire were drawn into relations with the father-leader and (as with the AIDS-infected babies of Romania) from the blood bond with mother. The Gulf War too mixed receptions between something new and something (the same thing) that's ancient. Was it possible that in spite of the diversification of new multicultural tensions that took left wing during the anti–Vietnam War reunion, the only racism that was back on the air for all to watch (just follow the bouncing bombs) targeted the Jews? Both the renewal of Eastern Europe and the Gulf War tuned or turned into the at once technological and group-psychological reception of phantasms, phantoms, doubles still coming home from the Second World War.

But Is It Good for the Jews?

Within media-war contexts that keep coming complete with their own pop-psychological reception of just how to relate to gadgets (namely by following, from trauma to love, the beat of identification), anti-Semitism makes ghost appearances on the season finales of ancient history by taking a spin around the metabolism of modern psychological warfare, a spin cycle with its own recent and primal history. What the U.S. experts were soon referring to, in shorthand, as "psy war" was the group-sized legacy of an internalization, technologization, and metabolization of trauma that first stood to analytic attention case by case during the World War I outbreak of war neurosis. Just look at German expressionist cinema, the sensurround of shell shock and unacknowledgeable losses: where there's doubling, monstrosity, and other literal limits of "assimilation," of "becoming image," the Jewish cemetery (in *The Student of Prague*) or ghetto (in *The Golem*) can serve as backdrop for the final suicidal showdown.

The Jews were special-featured in the Rorschach Blitz of German total wars from the start, but on a continuum with philo-Semitism, which was the look the projection or propaganda had during the First World War. Before General Ludendorff's 1935 secondary elaboration of the German loss of the war as the melting plot of Jews and Catholics, his first second thought, right after the war, was that the British really beat the Germans when they jumped the gun and stole the fire from German propaganda initiatives by authorizing Jewish colonization of Palestine (Lasswell, *Propaganda Technique*, 176). The World War I phase of German propaganda or idealism can be tracked in the work of Hanns Heinz Ewers, whose overlaps with psychoanalysis began in 1913 when he wrote the screenplay for Stellan Rye's *The Student of Prague*, the cinematic breakthrough of doubling that Freud picked up on in studies of the uncanny and, in the first place, of war neurosis. Ewers's 1920 novel *Vampir* understands or follows the heartbeat of the war, the lust for blood that the philo-Semitic alliance uniting Germans and Jews against the anti-Semitic nations, America and Russia, had brought to consciousness. Under this double cover, *Vampir* also documents Ewers's own propaganda efforts on behalf of the German cause while landlocked inside the United States. The problematic blood bonding with vampirism was the line Ewers gave his public between the wars, which is when the novel appeared. But the portion that belongs to Ewers's stay in the States in 1915 gives evidence for a German propaganda move that protected, I mean projected, the Jews. That Ewers later befriended Hitler, who commissioned

Ewers to write the hit novel *Horst Wessel*, belongs to a metabolism of projection that isn't only historicizable within vaster eras of intolerance. What changes with World War I, with the German defeat in World War I, is a change of art, of the art of war: the German military complex was now convinced that war would henceforward be won or lost only on group-psychological grounds. While observing the German cutting of losses in preparation for the Second Coming of world war, Frankfurt school theorists recognized a specular reversal or disconnection between the psychoanalytic discourse and the culture of its resistance. In the German psy war, the live transmissions of psychological warfare were beginning to choose and pick up their frequencies where the more transferential work of propaganda had left off getting us off.

Bohleber framed the German postreunification return engagement with anti-Semitism as directed against the history of the-Germans-and-the-Jews: the Jews get set up, dead or alive, as in the way of the return of interest on a narcissistic investment in nationalism. The reruns that tuned in with reunification thus continued to broadcast the defense measures against guilt or guilt-*Geld* that the Mitscherlichs diagnosed in the West German administration and reception of the restitution to be awarded victims of Nazi persecution (81). The xenophobic attacks on asylum seekers, in particular the charge that they are bogus victims (in other words, simulators or malingerers), indeed reflect a radical lack of empathy, the intrapsychic shutdown of the ability to make reparations.

But when the charge of simulation meets its match and maker in internal problems of reparation, a series of psychohistorical contexts has also already opened up around the questions Bohleber was raising. Starting from the background on up: Bohleber claimed to have grounded his own understanding of anti-Semitism in Ernst Simmel's World War II essay on this special-interest-group psychopathology. Simmel identified anti-Semitism as one of the living ends of Nazi psychological warfare, one that would, if left unattended, continue breaking out, he predicted in 1945, among U.S. veterans returning to peacetime conditions. In this work of caution, Simmel located anti-Semitism within the uncanny cohabitation of psychoanalysis with National Socialism:

> The second Nazi teaching of significance for us was that the fundamental principles laid down by men like Freud . . . could by skillful misapplication be used, contrary to the intent of their discoverers, to create hate and destruction. Anyone who studies the book, *German Psychological Warfare*, will be amazed at the scholarliness and the attention to minute detail with which the

knowledge of dynamic psychology is employed in organizing for destruction, for clouding and disintegrating the collective and the individual human mind.... For this purpose, anti-Semitism became their most handy and terrible weapon. Anti-Semitism is the psychological robot bomb of the Nazis. They fired these bombs effectively long before the war started. (*Anti-Semitism*, 72–73)

The "flight into mass psychosis" Simmel attributes to anti-Semitism—"an escape not only from reality, but also from individual insanity" (49)—is on one continuum with the theory and therapy of war neurosis he developed for World War I, which he refers back to in his second take on war neurosis written during World War II, and thus at the same time as the essay on anti-Semitism, as follows: "I think my statement of twenty-five years ago that the soldier's ego saves him from a psychosis by developing a neurosis is still valid" (233). Reading between the texts, anti-Semitism would be one of the ways in which psychological warfare gives shelter from the individual breakdowns of traumatic or war neurosis. Could the rise in the popularity or nihilism ratings of anti-Semitism that followed reunification be seen, then, as registering the press of the war neuroses, which were significantly absent down the German ranks at the end of the war? Germany's doubling and dividing would then link up with deferral of the outbreak of war neuroticization, a breakup that Nazi psychological warfare had previously doubled and contained, and against which the post–Third Reich German populace was reinoculated (in the Western backside) through the series of emergency identifications with U.S. pop culture addressed by the Mitscherlichs in *The Inability to Mourn*. Back East the Germans were doing the limbo, as timeless as the repressed, slipping into the ranks of the eternal antifascists. These are the two or three psychohistorical contexts to show for this inside view of the loss or trauma that a reunified Germany was not able, not right away, to control release, not before the mass-psychotic self-help programs of anti-Semitism, nationalism, and xenophobia first filled in with surefire projections the blanks that the long-running split and leave-taking between the two Germanys had supplied.

Freud's observation that in his day anti-Semitism had become a popular outlet for resistance to his science opens up, along the stereo tracks of ambivalence, a "success story" of psychoanalysis that begins with the therapeutic encounter with war neurosis. The entry of Freud's intrapsychic model into all the adjacent departments of psychological therapy and theory was brought about through the acceptance of psychoanalysis by the military complex as treatment of choice for war neurotics. Freud opens his

1919 introduction to the proceedings volume *Psychoanalysis and the War Neuroses* with a flashback and near miss. In 1918 official representatives from the highest quarters of the Central European powers were present as observers at the Fifth Psychoanalytic Congress, which was completely devoted to the treatment of war neurosis: "The hopeful result of this first contact was that the establishment of psychoanalytic Centers was promised, at which analytically trained physicians would have leisure and opportunity for studying the nature of these puzzling disorders and the therapeutic effect exercised on them by psychoanalysis. Before these proposals could be put into effect, the war came to an end, the state organizations collapsed and interest in the war neuroses gave place to other concerns" (*SE*, 17:207). But what came too late for the war effort was right on time for the peace that everyone was out to win.

Covered!

In the newfound lab space that was World War I, analysis had seen that war trauma alone did not guarantee symptom production. The shell's direct hit tracked down the dotted line of predisposition all the way to childhood trauma, to problems of dependency or separation anxiety. But it doesn't really matter whether the psychoanalytic success story was based on actual cure-all. More important is that the healed war neurotic became the most potent myth underlying what I prefer to call "greater psychoanalysis" (and by which I mean that widest ranging of Freud's intrapsychic model through all the departments of therapy that was ready, set, and going with Freud's World War I engagement with war neurosis). World War I had provided large-scale uniform or uniformed populations for study under the laboratory conditions of total war. During World War II the insights into war neurosis were tested on the newest research resource, the children and adolescents evacuated from the target sites of total air war. The "Sceno-Test," for example, was originally devised at the Berlin psychotherapy institute for treatment of children whose separation anxieties were set to go off with the bombings. In England, on Emergency Island, hands-on work with children and adolescents became the latest specialization of analysis, both the Kleinian and Anna-Freudian brands.

That only greater psychoanalysis won the world wars doesn't cover the complete history. What's missing is that even or especially psychoanalysis (by which I mean greater psychoanalysis) could not be left out of the Nazi reunification of psychotherapies beginning in 1933. But therapeutic eclecticism or correctness wasn't a real imposition that just happened to psychoanalysis. A comparison shopping of approaches was how psychoanalysis expanded and shifted on contact, inside and out, with the newness of the shock. This consumerist perspective is evident throughout the 1919 volume that carried name-brand approval, the volume Freud turned up full blast with his introductory offer of the dynamic of doubling, which he saw going down in war neurotics between "peace ego" and "war ego" (or, as Freud would distill the formulation one year later, ego and superego). Two of the contributions (Simmel's and Sandor Ferenczi's) address the resistance and boundary blending between psychoanalysis and all the standard-brand bearers of shock treatment during the corridor wars waged over the massively presenting problem of war neurosis. Simmel, one of the psychiatrists to cross over to the side of psychoanalysis during his fieldwork with shell shock victims, could read between the front lines of denial. Even physicians who submitted war neurotics to a "system of tortures" in order to "black-mail" them into letting go of their symptoms "acknowledge unconsciously in the reversal of the Freudian principle its basic view": "they try to make the neurotic "flee into health'" ("Zweites Korreferat," 59–60). Indeed, the war was all fair, a trade fair for "the comparative study of the different so-called psychotherapeutic methods" (42).

With the pressure on to treat soldiers in two to three sessions, Simmel found he had to mix and match all the techniques occupying the common ground of all-round acceptance (or denial) of the psychogenesis of war neurosis into a blend that left out the interminable associations and direc-tions of peacetime analysis and kept sights trained on target problems. The personality disorder was left alone. Nor was sexual content the focus in session. Instead Simmel dealt with the affects born of war (terror, anxiety, rage) and their war-related mental representations. Unlike the sex drive, which serves the preservation of the species, the affects of war are along for a basic drive to preserve oneself. In the intro that established the value or rate of Simmel's contribution by volume, Freud gave his first and lasting formulation of the division of labor of love between ego libido or narcissis-tic libido and the object libido that had been the one-sided focus or frame of analysis before the Great War.

War, Simmel declares, brings up issues of *Selbstsicherung:* self-protection, security, insurance. But whether war or peace, all neurosis gets organized around splitting, which gives the basic "insurance" coverage. Thus the symptom-formational shift (also through splitting) from psychic to physi-cal registers already gives shelter or protection *(Sicherung)* to the beginning of healing. The first baby step in therapy is therefore to introduce the pa-tient to the "meaning of the neurotic healing tendency which lies in the symptom" (47). Hypnosis is the fast two-step that follows: war-neurotic symptoms are themselves "realized posthypnotic auto-suggestions" (49).

Same time, same volume, Ferenczi reviews the defense and insurance contexts of the wartime showdown between the neurologists and the ana-lysts. Already prewar, the diagnosis of traumatic neurosis (following, say, a train wreck or factory accident) had redefined neurosis at large according to the striving for security or insurance, which in turn promoted the con-tamination of the neurotic condition or conditioning by so-called simulation for insurance benefit. When during World War I neurologists transferred their view of "pension hysteria" to war neurosis, they recognized the wish fulfillment piece of the traumatic-neurotic symptom formation but did not include a place for unconscious psychic processes. But after several years of standoff engagement with shell shock, the neurologists had to *interpret* the neurotic symptoms that didn't want to go away and infer their unconscious content and discontent. Within the large body of neuropsychiatric investigations of shell shock victims that picked up following this shift in attention span, Ferenczi is able to point out the signs or symptoms of an acceptance of psychoanalysis so complete that it went without acknowledgment even as it almost went all the way: "So you see, Ladies and Gentlemen: the experiences made with war neurotics gradually led further than to the discovery of the psyche—they led the neurologists almost to the discovery of psychoanalysis" (19).

One year earlier, in 1918, Simmel had already published a monograph on his therapeutic combo of techniques and perspectives for the treatment of war neurotics, which packed into its mix and medley both the direct hits of analytic theory and improv-therapy enactments featuring a "stuffed phantom." Simmel analogizes his treatment of trauma with the mobilization of the freeze-frame that, spliced together again with the discarded or repressed frames on the cutting room floor, lets roll, lets go, within the "film" that comes on under therapeutic direction (*Kriegsneurosen*, 25). On the way to this reprojection, the war neurotic has already split into illness. Running on the reserves of predisposition, splitting peels its expanding protective layers off an equally expansive recording surface that stores in split level all the bad impressions "like on a gramophone record" (13). But where there's more and more likelihood of nervous illness, that's where more insurance coverage can also be extended. *Selbstsicherung*, protecting or insuring oneself, is what the neurotic organism is doing when it gets into battle fatigues (11–12). Contortionist or cramplike symptoms, which often "strongly border on psychotic expressions" (43), represent "the substitute action through which the split personality satisfied the need for physical activity in the service of self protection [*Selbstsicherung*]" (43). What Simmel already in 1918 brought to consciousness or theory as the insurance drive takes out its war neurosis policy against the threat of psychosis (83).

This view that the neuroses were safety catches or fuses that helped prevent psychotic blowout—which was just one self-help step away from Simmel's follow-up reflection (in the essay on anti-Semitism) that membership in mass psychosis or psychological warfare issues group protection against breaking down one by one—participates in an opening up of access for control of the internal splitting and doubling of the ego in wartime. Soldiers and civilians alike were to be sent to the borderline between neurosis and psychosis, a newfound no-man's-land that, from World War I onward, doubled as the place of "psy fi" expansionism into the outer spaces of psychosis. By 1918, German military psychologists saw in Freud's close encounter with war neurosis brand-new training grounds for the defense and offense industries opening up. That's why, again, when the psychotherapies that had split psychoanalysis by World War I were reunited after 1933 under the leadership of Göring's cousin, Göring, the Adlerian therapist, psychoanalysis could not be excluded.

Family Packaging

In session Bohleber sees the psychohistorical continuum that belongs to the institution of greater psychoanalysis (where, like the uncanny in Freud's wartime essay, it was to be forgotten but was in effect preserved) come out in the watch of the transference, but always at the one narcissistic remove or removal of the most immediate gap of generation. "In a painful process of remembering, German psychoanalysts had to confess to their own involvement in the Nazi regime. The silence had to be broken, idealizations had to be taken back and the truth recognized, before we are able to deal with the Nazi inheritance that is still transgenerationally effective in psychoanalytic treatments" (330–31). The "trans-," the "across" that every one-on-one unit or unity must bear, rebounds from the generation that is not the parental one. The grandparents are the "trans-parents," doubles of their grandchildren, who share the fantasy of tension-free relations somewhere over the reign and dread bodies of parents and offspring. This is the Oedipal articulation, played close to the family network, of a fundamental disconnection lying between (or rather across) the couple and the group, between the transferential relation and the psychology, the transparent bonding, of groups.

Bohleber touches down on the group-psychological trajectory of the phantasm delegations of National Socialism and on the specific genealogy of the Nazi and not-seen secret within the institution and history of psychoanalysis (and, in family packs, across the skipped gap of generation). Although the German reunification with phantasms (all but one accounted for by Bohleber) has been a big, bashing success, "The Presence of the Past" doesn't touch the homosexual question. The exclusion, I take it, is not to be taken interpersonally but is meant to pass as the discretionary policy of a kind of hypercorrect politesse. Right to the point and credit of Bohleber's discretion is his avoidance of the utter availability of applied-psychoanalytic interpretations of the fascistoid psyche in terms of the degrees of homosexuality secretly attained. Klaus Theweleit's *Male Fantasies* offered a stay against this automatism of analytic explanation that locates the origins of the acting-out and psychotic makeup of National Socialism now or ever within the toxic dumping grounds of ungraduated perversion. But Theweleit's corrective, which, when push came to shove, attempted to return the whole package deal of group psychology to a paranoid, controlling sender inside psychoanalysis, went too far by half, by the missing half of what Bohleber refers to as "the fantasy of the group as unitary entity or whole or as a mother's body" (337). Bohleber again shows discretion by not assigning homosexuals to the same lineup of exterminations that went single file for the Jews and Gypsies. Homosexuals who stumbled across the neuropsychiatric end of the corridor of treatment were indeed forced into the cure-alls of castration, sterilization, and extermination. But the protective wing of psychotherapeutic eclecticism that was on the rise throughout the Nazi era advocated for the talking cure of the pervert. Lines that were originally laid down to all the outer, narcissistic limits of the transferential model following the grand opening advertised by Freud's inside view of the war neuroses could be given in therapy to every behavior that could be (of course!) construed as neurotic and thus as treatable. For this reason, however, homosexuality holds the bottom line, seen from both sides now, of Nazi projections and science fictions. In turn, Nazi rewiring of the perversions and psychoses to the group effort of total war is unthinkable without the psychoanalytic intervention in shell shock (which was rapidly syndicated within Freud's thought as group psychology and inside the military-psychological complex as the new art of psychological warfare).

Panic of Influence

The compromise formation that was Arbeitsgruppe *A* at the Berlin institute is not necessarily the place to look to observe the extent of Freud's influence, which ranged throughout the Nazi military, psychological, and military-psychological establishments. Freud was there at the outer limits of Nazi research projects and projections, for example, in Paul Metz's work on the intrapsychic relations between the pilot and the flying machine with which he must merge. Yes, it makes a difference if you can't, even if it's only in public, published contexts, use the analytic vocabulary. In his introduction to *"Gift, das du unbewußt eintrinkst..."* Bohleber sees the Nazi takeover of analysis as its word-by-word eradication. But what's in a word, including the word displaced by the one that's been censored? Only by restricting the frame to a small group of "analysts" (or "depth psychologists") at the institute—and taking them at their words—can one derive this sense of shutdown beyond all displacement. But in the big picture, Nazi Germany was a pop-psychological culture of all-out healing that followed the intrapsychic model even into regions that had been declared off-limits, set aside for management by sociology alone. By the 1940s the military-psychological complex worldwide was following the lead taken by the German colleagues through Freud's analysis of group psychology.

Anticipating or projecting more double take, talk, think along the lines of resistance I have already tripped up and over, a preemptive warning label might fit in here: this genealogical recontextualization of phantasm delegations and their institutional relays is not about laying the blame on Freud (or, better yet, on the Jews). Nor do I subscribe to any of the brands of new historicism, whether the German revisionist kind or the kinder and gentler version practiced in U.S. English departments. It might be more to the point to reconsider Freud's early model of the transference neurosis in the contexts I am excavating as the emergency of a side effect of treatment that at the same time inoculatively gets the psyche reorganized for the cure. At this discursive or institutional intersection, the transference neurosis that my analysis-in-progress would construct covers contamination by, and containment of, the aberrant discontinuities and reactions that continue to give rise to the Nazi regime, the regimen to this day of "not seeing" the continuity that was there. Only the reconstruction of a "Nazi psychoanalysis" can lead to a resettlement of symptoms within the suffer zone of a future cure. In addition, then, to the application of psychoanalysis to those symptomatic returns of a Nazi past that keep coming under the category of

The Library of the German Institute for Psychological Research and Psychotherapy, Berlin, 1936–1945. Until the air-raid destruction of the institute in 1945, Freud's works were kept in a locked case but remained accessible to training candidates, who were required to sign in or out (Käthe Dräger, 264). Was this to keep a check on who was too interested in Freud, or was this because the volumes were just too rare and irreplaceable in book-burning country? Reprinted from p. 81 of *"Here Life Goes On in a Most Peculiar Way...": Psychoanalysis before and after 1933.*

Secretarial office of the German Institute at 41 Keithstr. in Berlin. Reprinted from p. 148 of *"Here Life Goes On in a Most Peculiar Way..."*

aberration and discontinuity, I propose staying with the direct connection between one of the most protected and progressive sources of our modernism and the outbreak of National Socialism, the connection lying therefore within the institution, discourse, and history of what I'm calling greater psychoanalysis but which precisely cannot be separated from psychoanalysis "itself."

FIRST PART

Another False Start

"Just like the Yankee press," he thought, "just the same!—It
shrieks: Germans! Therefore barbarians, Huns, traitors, bomb-
throwers, robbers, and murderers of children. Kill them! Just
like the Czar and his gang, exactly the same! Jews, they scream,
Jews, they crucified the Lord and drink the blood of Christian
children—kill them!—Fusilar a esos carajos!" He was leprous,
the German, like the others—like the Jews, like the Catholic
priests: thus fate welded them together.

—HANNS HEINZ EWERS, *VAMPIR*

There are continuities and contexts missing from any history of modernism
that subsumes, under the category of discontinuity, all tension between its
most protected or progressive sources and the aberrations on a mass scale
that, via symptomatic or dialectic connection, still belong to modernism,
but modernism beside itself. But there are direct hits of continuity, too.
What's missing or not seen is always the side effect of what psychoanalysis
calls identification, which originates in trauma. Not to see or to "Nazi" is
what fills in the missing-continuities-and-contexts report. The histories of
these missing entries, which are ultimately always into war, never really
leave the corridor wars between different departments of psychological interventionism.

At another end of this corridor, in 1992, Judith Herman's *Trauma and
Recovery*, which signs the war record of psychoanalysis onto the label of the
at once eclectic and reunified band of the psychotherapies, is a giveaway
covert operation. Yes, the book nonphobically recognizes Freud in history,
but for right now it remains in the ready position to admit not only the
same old links to Freud but also, and most freely, the limits back there in
Freud's science that psychotherapy continues to pass beyond. But right
down to its intrapsychic model, which, before everything is taken interpersonally, is the bottom line of its theory and therapy, psychotherapy, whatever else it may be, still falls in with greater psychoanalysis, that widest
circulation of the intrapsychic model within psychotherapy, psychology,
psychiatry, you name it, which was first set in motion through the success
story of Freud's engagement with war neurosis. Now, there are two reasons, occlusions, or even fronts that keep the direct line to this expansionism of Freud's model from entering consciousness.

Lecture at the German Institute. Lecturer unidentified. *Back row,* J. H. Schultz (in uniform); *on his right,* G. R. Heyer; *far right,* W. Kemper. The portrait of Hitler faced a portrait of Freud (off camera) until 1943. Reprinted from p. 154 in *"Here Life Goes On in a Most Peculiar Way..."*

In Herman's history of trauma treatment, for which her how-to book serves as After picture, two features can only be found—missing. First, while everyone else misses the foundational impact of Freud's inside view of the World War I epidemic outbreak of battle neurosis for the formulation of his second system, on Herman's dating of trauma history, she goes all the way and completely evacuates Freud from the combat zone in order to leave him hanging over his desertion from the first stand on the seduction theory and, thus, from all real-time tracking of trauma. Second, she leaves out the complete picture of war neurosis theorizing and practice in and between the world wars. By carrying only one Anglo-American line of research, the one that culminates in Abram Kardiner's World War II study of war neurosis, Herman gives a double dose of inclusion and antibody-style diffusion of psychoanalysis inside the psychotherapeutic management of trauma. But what remains on the sidelines is the context, I mean contest in which U.S., British, and Nazi German military-psychological establishments raced to toe a finish line where the intrapsychic ingredients of war neurosis that Freud unpacked could be folded forward onto prophylactic preparations against its outbreak on one's own side and, on the other side, onto the same preparations only in reverse, in the service of neurosis production across enemy lines, via what the Germans were the first to name psychological warfare. What gave this therapy competition its race character was the lead the Nazis held thanks to their early takeover of the psychoanalytic core and advance front of what Herman in 1992 still thinks is something else again, namely psychotherapy's successful match with traumatic neurosis. But in 1941 we can watch the Anglo-American establishments doubled over with the all-out effort of keeping up with the Nazis, which at the same time meant catching up with Freud's second system, the one that started somewhere over the pleasure principle over the body of the psychological casualty of World War I. So what Herman's book not sees during the station break of identification is, one, Freud on war neurosis and, two, Nazi psychoanalysis. Freud's science, at once expansionist and self-reflexive, and therefore not in any position to generate all its terms out of itself, went to war and won—I mean the corridor war against all institutional resistance. In the forgettogether that followed, psychotherapeutically correct eclecticism was established first in Nazi Germany.

Faust, Freud, and the
Missing Entries—into War

There's a legacy of Goethe's *Faust* that suffuses and distends through high and pop literature, aesthetics, psychology, you name it. Between two book-ends of this effect, between Marx and Freud, a conveyor belting out of quotations advances the specter of a failed paternal economy that in *Das Kapital* is rereleased, for example, as "paper money ghosts" and at the Freudian end sinks its vampiric quotation fangs into the corner of every scene of the superego's introduction. Certainly by the time of Paul Valéry's and Thomas Mann's retakes of Goethe's *Faust,* the delegation of direct connections between political projections and their internal or eternal preprograms had gone into overkill. But at an earlier point of entry, the *Faust* effect takes us all the way into the secret history of Freud's second system or, as we should also address it, greater psychoanalysis. Picking up where the direct effect leaves off, one can still follow it going without saying right into the psychic reality or technology of war trauma, which gets psychoanalysis where the war effort wants it and leaves it there. The staying power of this leftover could not be interrupted, not even for the station break brought to us by Nazi Germany. Or in other words, as far as the history of psychotherapy goes, the Nazi era marked an unprecedented triumph in the struggle for recognition and acceptance of the standards of therapeutic correctness. One focus to fix on in this polymorphously reopened account of modernism, one in which the Nazis have an equal time-share, is the survival in Nazi Germany (or was it the arrival?) of the intrapsychic view of homosexuality (as opposed to the one taken only interpersonally). But again, what remains basic even or especially to the activity of helping homosexuals out is the internal reading of war neurosis, internal, for example, to the development of Freud's thought from World War I onward. It's the overdetermined beginning toward which a couple of Faustian footnotes not included in *The Standard Edition*'s index can nevertheless get us going.

In the transitional place occupied by "On 'the Uncanny'" where the conscious versus unconscious structures of Freud's first system meet the repetition compulsion and other undisclosed messengers of the second system coming soon, Freud drops a note to Goethe's *Faust,* which covers two souls, alas, in Faust's breast or, as Freud prefers to address it, the internal doubling of the ego. The one-stop researching advertised by the index to *The Standard Edition of Freud's Complete Psychological Works* nevertheless leaves out this and the other reference to Goethe's *Faust* that's packed into a pair of double footnotes. The notes get dropped just after Freud has brought up in his essay "On 'the Uncanny'" a different way of doubling, the one rebounding between the ego and the special agency that gives self-love shelter in self-observation, self-criticism, and self-censorship.

That's right: what would be along for the drives inside Freud's second system is already marching to the same beat as this other double. It's a second phase of narcissism, too. Freud has already assigned ancient Egyptian doubling of the body to the unbounded self-love he calls primary narcissism. But this is also already the place where doubling can be turned around into division along its own cutting edge. Beyond this reversibility along the cut of doubling, beyond double or nothing, there's the next stage of narcissism that's no longer body based but now recircuited and recruited for the long-distance relations of control.

In the essay "On Narcissism," Freud saw this shift to the next stage as lying between unbounded self-love and the bond of supervision with an ego ideal that always measures just how short the ego falls of that perfection of childhood, which has been lost. Even as the ego ideal's replay of parental criticism berates the ego, ego feels fine: in this roundabout way, some relation at least (at last!) to the original perfection has been retained. Another way Freud sees it (for example, in *Totem and Taboo*) is that omnipotence of thoughts, the audio portion of our narcissism, must first assert itself as the death wish. Since absence happens, little one makes sure that, anyway, he wished the one who's not there gone, that is, a goner. Because your death wish cannot be accepted or brought into focus in close-up, it gets projected in long shot. That is, you have to share it with the goner; the long-distance haunting that keeps you two in touch is the death wish victim's time-share in your omnipotence. So in this funereal account of self-esteem, it's the death wish bond with the other's absence that shifts us into narcissism part two.

It was the difference between the two narcissism stages that inspired Hanns Sachs in 1933 to explore the shift from the Greek use of machines as playthings only, with their technological potential kept under body wraps, to the modern or Faustian relationship to technological expansionism and interventionism. But one stage always also contains the other one. Ask any psychotic who's hallucinating influencing machines: the technological relation switches on as a kind of emergency projection in the face of the uncanniness of body-based narcissism. According to Freud's study of the Schreber case, the psychotic, whose break with reality represents withdrawal of libido down the escape chute from trauma and trauma's total mobilization of repression, indeed must make it from stage one (wipeout of the ego and end of the world) to stage two, the sadomasochistic coupling of ego slave and its mastery. The psychotic creates a new delusional and hallucinatory world in the place of the one that was lost. In thus giving stage-two shelter to the narcissistic destiny of his libido, the psychotic brings his delusional order, the one that externalizes the psychic apparatus in order to bring in the new world, so close to auto-analysis. As he's getting ready to give us the good news about psychosis, Freud introduces into the background the Chorus of Spirits from Goethe's *Faust*, who mourn the world Faust has just destroyed with his curse and who cheerlead him to build it up brand new inside himself (*SE*, 12:70). For his part, Schreber makes it via the internal reroute of traumatization to a stage of self-healing that is the techno-delusional order that he must follow with Goethe's *Faust* as one of his guides (*SE*, 12:44). In the new order that Schreber calls "soul murder," the psychotic has a stage-two future in the auto-technologization of self-observation—the inside job of keeping the ego in line. All this, then, sets the stage of narcissism that goes with the other idea of the double:

> The idea of the "double" does not necessarily disappear with the passing of primary narcissism, for it can receive fresh meaning from the later stages of the ego's development. A special agency is slowly formed there, which is able to stand over against the rest of the ego, which has the function of observing and criticizing the self and of exercising a censorship within the mind, and which we become aware of as our "conscience." In the pathological case of delusions of being watched, this mental agency becomes isolated, dissociated from the ego, and discernible to the physician's eye. The fact that an agency of this kind exists, which is able to treat the rest of the ego like an object—the fact, that is, that man is capable of self-observation—renders it possible to invest the old idea of a "double" with a new meaning. (*SE*, 17:235)

The new double would, as superego, coming soon, serve as sponsor for the new organization of Freud's second system. But he passes quickly over what he could not yet fully admit into his system. Following the premature articulation, he buries the new double fast inside the footnote underworld alongside the unindexed reference to *Faust*.

> I believe that when poets complain that two souls dwell in the human breast, and when popular psychologists talk of the splitting of people's egos, what they are thinking of is this division (in the sphere of ego-psychology) between the critical agency and

> the rest of the ego, and not the antithesis discovered by psycho-
> analysis between the ego and what is unconscious and repressed.
> It is true that the distinction between these two antitheses is to
> some extent effaced by the circumstance that foremost among
> the things that are rejected by the criticism of the ego are deriva-
> tives of the repressed. (*SE*, 17:235–36 n. 2)

Back in the main text, Freud comes again with the new double, which is so far removed from the old one that it keeps crossing the limits of visibility to meet Faustian striving: "There are also . . . all the strivings of the ego which adverse external circumstances have crushed, and all our suppressed acts of volition which nourish in us the illusion of Free Will" (*SE*, 17:236). At this point the new Faustian double drops out of sight into a footnote that's right next to the one that saw through Faust's internal double or divide: "In Ewers's *The Student of Prague*, which serves as the starting point of Rank's study on the 'double,' the hero has promised his beloved not to kill his antagonist in a duel. But on his way to the duelling-ground he meets his 'double,' who has already killed his rival" (*SE*, 17:236 n. 1). *The Student of Prague* counts (down) as the first film version of the Faust legend. Along-side the drop to his footnotes to signal that a division of doubles stood already mobilized in Faust's breast, Freud dives down again to show that division's first assignment on the big screen of doubling.

   The Student of Prague recycles the shadow or double of the Faust legend into or as the new medium of cinema. In *War and Cinema* Paul Virilio characterizes the story of the film as the anticipation of, or preparation for (in other words, as the psychologization of), total war. *The Student of Prague* is, in Virilio's words, "the premonitory tale of a student who sells his reflected mirror-image to a wizard. This image begins to act in the student's place, 'dishonoring' him and forcing him to remain a war-fixated conqueror. The student shoots at this irksome double in the hope of destroying it, but it is he who dies as a result" (30). Virilio's otherwise enigmatic replay is not out of sync within Freud's reception, where it toes the line of the double footnotes, which, in the uncanny mode of dismembered motion, guide us back to where they came from: Freud's first public/published encounter with the double or doppelgänger over the body of the psychological casualty of World War I, the war neurotic. Same time, same station as the essay "On 'the Uncanny,'" Freud's "Introduction to *Psychoanalysis and the War Neuroses*" characterizes the central conflict of shell shock in terms of the internal doubling that pits one ego against the other one:

> The conflict is between the soldier's old peaceful ego and his
> new warlike one, and it becomes acute as soon as the peace-ego
> realizes what danger it runs of losing its life owing to the rash-
> ness of its newly formed, parasitic double. It would be equally
> true to say that the old ego is protecting itself from a mortal dan-
> ger by taking flight into a traumatic neurosis or to say that it is
> defending itself against the new ego which it sees is threatening
> its life. (SE, 17:209)

War neurosis already mobilized the difference between doubles and narcissisms that the techno-Faustian footnotes in "On 'the Uncanny'" were on their way to, and which doubles as the difference or transition at once internal to Freud's thinking right from the start and then between the two systems of his thought. The wartime research was pulled up short by the end of the war—just as the centrally powered war effort was preparing to send psychoanalysis to all fronts. Just a few years later, in *Beyond the Pleasure Principle*, war neurosis, or as Freud now preferred to generalize it once again, traumatic neurosis, plays an at once central and extraneous role. It's the repeater dreams of these neurotics that show Freud the way to a traumatic breakthrough that goes beyond the defense of anxiety where it starts from scratch (like the scratch in the war record) over and over again. It's a form of auto-healing that rerecords, in other words, erases, and builds up out of the groove of repetition the bottom line of all defense, namely anxiety, or, better yet, preparedness, that is, trauma or war preparedness.

> These dreams are endeavoring to master the stimulus retrospec-
> tively, by developing the anxiety whose omission was the cause
> of the traumatic neurosis. They thus afford us a view of a func-
> tion of the mental apparatus which, though it does not contra-
> dict the pleasure principle, is nevertheless independent of it and
> seems to be more primitive than the purpose of gaining pleasure
> and avoiding unpleasure. (SE, 18:32)

On the way to completing an argument ultimately about the bottom-line defense of war readiness, Freud folds into the dream material of traumatic neurosis the child's play of *fort/da*, Freud's update of the frontline status (within narcissism or omnipotence of thoughts) of the death wish. It's the same game Freud had already analyzed in his wartime reading of Goethe's one-time-only recollection from early childhood, in which the ejection of pots out the window puts the arrival of sibling rivals into reverse. But with *fort/da,* after all is said and done—the mother, whose body and absence are at the remote control center of the game, was Freud's daughter Sophie, who died in 1920—there's still Freud's follow up, one year later, within the time frame of the close study: "A year later, the same boy whom I had observed at his first game used to take a toy, if he was angry with it, and throw it on the floor, exclaiming: 'Go to the fwont!' He had heard at that time that his absent father was 'at the front,' and was far from regretting his absence" (*SE*, 18:16).

Is it possible to argue that Freud only turned to current events and casualties to illustrate or analogize a theory that had its own history? No: Freud and his immediate colleagues were brought to an enormous breakthrough not only in practice but also in theory by their encounter with war neurosis, which, with all factors accounted for, amounted, at least, to a double internalization of war. First off, the laboratory conditions of the war literalized Freud's 1909 notion of the "flight into illness." That's why Freud stood up for so-called malingerers: their wish to desert is unconscious, at odds with their conscious sense of duty. Yes, their symptoms go away upon removal from the war zone. But that only proves the psychic status of the symptoms, which are not accessible to punishment but can only be treated in analysis. And treatment is indicated because not every traumatized soldier develops symptoms; the proportions of actual trauma and major symptom formation are mixed not on the battlefield but in early childhood. And then, and most important, once Freud figured out war neurosis, he was out from under his major peacetime embarrassment, the seemingly contradictory evidence that his opponents claimed traumatic neurosis supplied against the libido theory. It was at this point that everything inside and out was opened up to psychoanalysis.

With traumatic neurosis, the psychic backdraft of natural catastrophe and techno-accident, psychoanalysis had already been backed up against the wall of the scientific community's resistance. How could the sexual etiology or libido theory of neurosis hold up when the shock of catastrophe was enough, in more or less real time, to produce neurotic symptoms? War neurosis showed Freud the way shell shock detonated down the dotted lines of predisposition to neurosis or psychosis which always time-travel back to conflict in the ego, in other words, to the earliest stages (one and two) of traumatic developments. War neurosis diversified the holdings of psychoanalysis by dividing or doubling the libido theory between the drive toward the outside and the drive inward. Only psychoanalysis won the war, a corridor war among the different departments of psychological

Two war-neurotic soldiers from World War I diagnosed as simulators of deafness and dumbness. Reproduced from p. 545 in G. Alexander, "Die Simulation von Ohrenkrankheiten," *Wiener klinische Wochenschrift* 29, no. 18 (4 May 1916): 541–47.

interventionism that would one and all have to accommodate themselves to the trend the military first set.

In *Group Psychology and the Analysis of the Ego,* Freud kept right on giving the German military psychological advice. The home front of Oedipus should have been kept in a special place in the art of war:

> The Commander-in-Chief is a father who loves all soldiers equally, and for that reason they are comrades among themselves. . . . The neglect of this libidinal factor in an army, even when it is not the only factor operative, seems to be not merely a theoretical omission but also a practical danger. Prussian militarism, which was just as unpsychological as German science, may have had to suffer the consequences of this in the [First] World War. We know that the war neuroses which ravaged the German army have been recognized as being a protest of the individual against the part he was expected to play in the army. . . . If the importance of the libido's claims on this score had been better appreciated, the fantastic promises of the American Presi-

dent's Fourteen Points would probably not have been believed
so easily. (*SE*, 18:95)

But in his "Introduction to *Psychoanalysis and the War Neuroses*," Freud
scored the war record of psychoanalysis according to the internal advances
analytic theory and therapy had made on the narcissistic front (between
neurosis and psychosis):

> The theory of the sexual aetiology of the neuroses, or, as we pre-
> fer to say, the libido theory of the neuroses, was originally put
> forward only in relation to the transference neuroses of peace-
> time and is easy to demonstrate in their case by the use of the
> technique of analysis. But its application to the other disorders
> which we later grouped together as the narcissistic neuroses al-
> ready met with difficulties. An ordinary dementia praecox, a
> paranoia or melancholia are essentially quite unsuitable material
> for demonstrating the validity of the libido theory or for serving
> as a first introduction to an understanding of it. . . .
> It only became possible to extend the libido theory to the
> narcissistic neuroses after the concept of a "narcissistic libido"
> had been put forward and applied—a concept, that is, of an
> amount of sexual energy attached to the ego itself and finding
> satisfaction in the ego just as satisfaction is usually found only in
> objects. This entirely legitimate development of the concept of
> sexuality promises to accomplish as much for the severer neu-
> roses and for the psychoses as can be expected of a theory which
> is feeling its way forwards on an empirical basis. The traumatic
> neuroses of peace will also fit into the scheme as soon as a suc-
> cessful outcome has been reached of our investigations into the
> relations which undoubtedly exist between fright, anxiety and
> narcissistic libido. (*SE*, 17:209–10)

In *Civilization and Its Discontents* Freud continued to draw the line
through his World War I reintroduction of narcissism and beyond: "The
concept of narcissism made it possible to obtain an analytic understanding
of the traumatic neuroses and of many of the affections bordering on the
psychoses, as well as of the latter themselves" (*SE*, 21:118). The concept of
libido, however, was, in exchange, "endangered." Was there one instinctual
energy after all—as had all along been Jung's prime desexually suggestive
corrective? But how could there be one of anything? In theory, the death
drive "was there" when one war neurotic kept repeating his traumatic moment in his dreams. Narcissism was instinct with death to the extent that

Hospitalized soldier allegedly suffering from shell shock during World War I, diagnosed as simulator of deafness in both ears. Reproduced from p. 545 of "Die Simulation von Ohrenkrankheiten."

the mono record of philosophical resistance was a big hit. The doubling of the ego in war neurosis started over with narcissism from scratch in the stereo record of drives beyond narcissism's prewar personalized license (that went to homosexuals, women, and children first).

During the great wartime *Introductory Lectures,* you can see Freud still giving an exceptional status within his libido theory to war neurosis, as though caught in a flashback loop with the seduction theory. Even in *Beyond the Pleasure Principle* that ready-made structure of psychic disturbance put on display by traumatic or war neurosis was an exception to the other neuroses, but this time around the exception it took was way back in the prehistory of defense. But out of these two different exceptions came the new rule of the sexual etiology of neurosis and psychosis that had been following the two directives of libido flow into the second system. There the new sadomasochistic administration energized them for the life-and-death struggle of the drives. But the new order was, as a rule, already forecast with commanding clarity in the "Introduction to *Psychoanalysis and the War*

Neuroses" in terms of the clash between egos in the establishment of an "internal enemy," public enemy number one.

One connection in Freud between Moses and Goethe's Faust turns on the sight in the end of conflict and flight of the promised land of recognition bearing his own name brand. To explain, in *Moses and Monotheism*, the long stalling during installation of Mosaic doctrines in his people of choice, Freud draws on analogy. First he points out the slow acceptance of Darwin's theory of evolution owing to emotional resistances that had to be overcome. The lengths of time such a process has to go to should not take us by surprise. "We probably do not sufficiently appreciate that what we are concerned with is a process in group psychology" (*SE*, 23:67). Freud's second analogy may seem especially incongruous, he warns us. But because what must have been crossing his mind as he contemplated the delay in Darwin's recognition—which nevertheless caught up with him, Freud underscores, in Darwin's lifetime—was his own science's breakthrough to following, it is after all congruent that traumatic neurosis should come up (in particular, behind the lines, in its wartime manifestation as war neurosis). "It may happen that a man who has experienced some frightful accident—a railway collision, for instance—leaves the scene of the event apparently uninjured. In the course of the next few weeks, however, he develops a number of severe psychical and motor symptoms which can only be traced to his shock, the concussion or whatever else it was. He now has a 'traumatic neurosis'" (67). But if traumatic neurosis and Jewish monotheism end up by analogy strapped to the same tracks, it is only, Freud rushes to add, with regard to the factor of latency or incubation (68). In the next section dedicated entirely, even in title, to "The Analogy," we find that every neurosis develops symptoms following a period of latency linking and separating symptomatic outbreak and the early pathogenic trauma. Thus Freud indeed jumped the gun when, hot on the tail end of identifying (with) Darwin's delayed acceptance, he just had to bring up traumatic neurosis as a specific case of latency when, after all, every neurosis exhibits this structure. The childhood trauma that awaits neurotic developments probably overrides traumatic neurosis anyway, since what shocks the adult must, in theory, travel back to early childhood trauma to get the running start to form symptoms. The death drive is the shorthand placeholder, first, for this trauma at the core of every neurosis, even when meltdown is always to some extent deferred, and, second, for traumatic neurosis at the turning point of theorization of the borderline between neurosis and psychosis.

The paternal relation that, according to Freud's free postwar advice, the group psychology of armies requires externalizes or personalizes an internal license. As witnessed by the stockpile of *Standard Edition* index entries, "What thou hast inherited from thy fathers, acquire it to make it thine" was Freud's all-time favorite *Faust* quote. It comes up in the second system each time Freud sets forth the regime of the superego, and it pops up one last time in the posthumously published "An Outline of Psychoanalysis," where it brings to a close the final section, which is all about the "Internal World" of the superego and how, in other words, "the present is changed into the past" (*SE*, 23:207).

The inheritance of *Faust* accompanies Freud's discovery of the psychotic war economy that doubles (internalizes and technologizes) the ego's rapport with the other. The ego-superego relationship is modeled in turn after the internal conflict between peace ego and war ego, the uncovered structure of war neurosis that would double on contact down the whole dimension (or dementia) of internalization and technologization that goes with the ego libido. That covers the analysis of the ego. The group psychology part of the title and project completes the system. Ever since there's been an art of war (see Sun Tzu's primal manual) there has also been psychological warfare. But as Freud points out in "On 'the Uncanny,'" aesthetics at large is another word for pre-psychoanalytic psychology. Under the influence of the treatment and theorization of the war neurosis, which was shooting up Freud's science into the mainline of military and psychological establishments, psychological warfare keeps right up there with psychoanalysis between the wars in Germany. In other words: group psychology *is* total war *is* psychological warfare. It's the collapse, war economy style, of one crisis or survival onto another one.

The Faustian couple ends up covering, in *Civilization and Its Discontents,* the ultimate couple in Freud, that of love and death drives:

> In Goethe's Mephistopheles we have a quite exceptionally convincing identification of the principle of evil with the destructive instinct. . . . The Devil himself names as his adversary, not what is holy and good, but Nature's power to create, to multiply life—that is, Eros. (*SE*, 21:120)

In "Analysis Terminable and Interminable" Freud dismisses any etiological impact of shock and stands by his system: "It is impossible to define health except in metapsychological terms: i.e. by reference to the dynamic relations between the agencies of the mental apparatus" (*SE*, 23:226 n. 2). A moment ago Freud had summoned, with Goethe's *Faust*, the assistance of the witch, who is beamed up into the system as "the Witch Metapsychology" (*SE*, 23:225). But which metapsychology? That purely theoretical dimension to which Freud consigned such features of his science as the model of a psychic apparatus divided into separate agencies and the model of the drives, both of which he thus kept separate from empirical, experiential realms of verification? But these were the models coming down the runaway success of Freud's science following the hands-on, mega therapeutic encounter with case after case of war trauma. Twenty pages later Freud is willing to give Empedocles of Acragas precursor credit for the dynamic due theory of drive power; as a new theory attached to his own name it could be but the effect of over-reading and "cryptomnesia" (SE, 23:245). But when Freud tries to pass on the recent (primal) past of this piece of his metapsychology he at the same time cites comparison of Empedocles with the historical Dr. Faust, whom Freud however can describe only by modifying a line from Goethe's *Faust*. Goethe's *Faust* contains Freud's expanding inside view by preserving, ultimately, a moment or notion of contact, even of first contact, of "influence," as therapeutically necessary but theoretically untenable distinction.

The Cinema of War Neurosis

The internalization of war over the theory and therapy of war neurosis was syndicated symptomatically in phantasms or projections brought to us by the occult and the technical media, phantasms that colonized or bounced back from relations of long distance that not only keep us in touch but also follow out that inner course of ego libido Freud discovered and charted inside war neurosis. The leaders of the post–World War I media sensurround of German mass culture were (forget about fiction) in fact war neurotics: not only Fritz Lang and Carl Mayer, among others, but Hitler, too. On the World War I front, they were buried alive in blasts and blinded by gas; the shock turned on the psychotic self-help program that double featured, in Hitler's case of gas attack, a flashback of blindness and the hallucination of mother Germany appointing him to the position of her savior. His double vision goes down in Riefenstahl's *Triumph of the Will*, where the Nazi slogan for the future of a new or true Germany that's been evoked above, around, and inside those present (from the techno-airspace Hitler's plane crossed with Christianity all the way to the audio columns rising up from the chorus that's funereally reciting the place names of the battles of the lost war) is ultimately pitched to the war dead, who, we're told, are not dead. As we get ready to take off for a Germany that's part crypt, part airspace, we still hear the vanishing point that's made in Germany: the lost warriors are undead. (Even George Bush went untreated for a war neurosis that broke out after his plane was shot down. Wasn't he thus locked onto the beam of the mediatic retake of World War II in the Persian Gulf?)

If the joint account of war and cinema that Virilio has opened up seems, while spectacular, somehow nihilistic or positivistic, in any event, unconvincing, it's because the war record of internalization has been skipped. The external or thematic connections between war and the media were already superseded, in other words, by the psychoanalytic inside view of where the trauma of war goes.

"On 'the Uncanny'" scopes out an occult habitat of dismemberment and twitchings that could be relocated directly to the war zone, right down to the uncanniest phantasm of all, live burial, which regularly accompanied shell blast, and which, according to survivors, turned on the video portion of hallucination and hysterical blindness. Ernst Simmel's work with war neurotics unearthed the primal scene of expressionist-film physiognomy:

> While the patient was lying unconscious under the rocky ruins
> and images of his homeland rose up before him as in a dream,

Two soldiers from World War I allegedly afflicted with shell shock diagnosed as simulators of deafness in both ears. Reproduced from p. 547 of "Die Simulation von Ohrenkrankheiten."

he was constantly forced to grimace to clear away and keep the breathing passages free from the masses of sand lying on his face. ("Zweites Korreferat," 49)

In the uncanny terrain of war to which both the "Introduction to *Psychoanalysis and the War Neuroses*" and "On 'the Uncanny'" reassign each other, the scenario of peace ego and its double, the war ego, gives the primal screenplay of German cinema. Stellan Rye, the director of *The Student of Prague*, gave the advance preview of doubling down the technologization or internalization of war before he died one year later on the French front. The film's scriptwriter, Hanns Heinz Ewers, is best known as the author of occult fiction that was always at the same time propaganda for the German side of both world wars. In a trilogy that counts down as *The Sorcerer's Apprentice*, *Alraune*, and *Vampir*, Ewers mixes legacies of Faust (including the syndications of Frankenstein or Golem) and then turns to vampirism to camouflage the account of his own psychological warfare activities in the United States in 1915. The German cause, the philo-Semitic one that must be defended against the outright anti-Semitism of America and Russia, is championed by German and German-Jewish psychological warriors. Their leader, Frank Braun, the leading man in all three novels, is at the same time a vampire whose blood lust can be traced back down the same bloodlines that feed the world war.

Ewers introduces *Vampir* through a war-torn preface, the document of its delays in getting to the war effort on time. He concluded the novel in 1916 in Seville. But getting it back to Germany was another story—and, yes, he tells it. The captain of a Norwegian ship took it along for the ride of neutrals through the blockade around Germany. But when the French stopped him, he destroyed the manuscript before the search could bring it up. A copy was then sent in 1917 from New York. At the same time, a series of house searches of the author's apartment resulted in yet another copy traveling along a relay of safe houses. At this copy's final rest stop, the Irish hostess had to burn *Vampir* in the back of her place before the agents searching up front could seize it. In the meantime the author was in prison. All interrogations led to the question of the whereabouts of *Vampir* (a few advance preview chapters had appeared in Spain). By 1919 Ewers was out of prison in New York, not only under surveillance and house arrest but even under the prohibition to publish. But then he made it back to Germany after all, and the book (the second copy had survived), which was largely written in 1915 and 1916, could appear in 1920 with a few emendations added at the late date of its publication. "The French, the English, the Americans have done their best to destroy this book—and the one who wrote it. That their attempt failed—that was fate."

Set aside inside *Vampir* there is, in the I of protagonist Braun, a field of representation that is frankly projective, hallucinatory, haunted. When world war begins for Germany, Braun is on a German ship traveling up the west coast of South America. But even the British won't board it, not even as an act of war. Yellow fever monopolizes all on board to go directly to death without docking. Braun steals off the ship at San Francisco but goes not free of the haunting recollections of all that dying and disposing of the dead. Together with two fellow Germans, Braun travels by train to the coast closer to the European theater of war that all three hope to enter on the stage left of the German cause. But as they depart Salt Lake City, Braun's attention is grabbed by a figure sitting up the aisle from him who keeps on spitting into the spittoon without once missing. He is a hole in one, a sight for sore Is. Braun goes Rorschach Blitz: he thinks the stranger could be his long-dead uncle who also always spit hit his mark. Then the spitting image admits another ghostly occupant: it is the Chinese whose body Braun sewed into the sack for a dump at sea. But when the body in a sack went overboard, it wouldn't sink—Braun, not able to wait, hadn't weighted it down properly—but rather kept right on bobbing alongside the ship. Next Braun sees that the buoyancy of the spit is really the arc of black mice—more uncanny spitting images. On the sidelines of Braun's hallucination, a fellow traveler runs war commentary on the same figure, as though giving the alternative to—or other side of—Braun's more personalized reception: "The guy should be a submarine! And his spit a torpedo. And the spittoon an English cruiser" (41).

When the screen figure gets up and leaves, Braun follows him—just in time to vacate the one unsafe place in the train in the accident that happens. The axle of the carriage that someone put before the train at the crossing pierces one window and kills on the spot the German who took Braun's projection seat. In *The Interpretation of Dreams* Freud put on ears to overhear as stowaway in *Spucken*, "spitting," another word, *Spuken*, meaning "haunting" (*SE*, 4:248 n. 1). Although always in some other place, "haunting" appears in *Vampir* to denote how a thought won't stop crossing one's mind. The connection between spitting and haunting—way more than the more official-looking sideline of references to "unconscious" behavior and even "drives"—marks the spot of influence Ewers is in, in this book, with Freud.

The haunting hallucination medium stays on trauma tracks. But in addition to uncanny doublings, the medium also serves to protect Braun, even physically, as we saw. Otherwise the medium of occult beliefs or superstitions, which Braun's haunting track traverses and draws on, is monopolized and mobilized by the English and the French as propaganda against the Germans.

The border between the occult transmission and the propaganda industry becomes a happier medium in the discourse of Braun's lover, Lotte Lewi. It inspires her to inspire him to commit himself as propagandist for the German side in the American diaspora. Lewi shows Braun Aaron's priestly breastplate (as shown in the Old Testament), which has been in her father's family for hundreds of years and across the whole of Europe. "What would the Eastside say if it were known that this is now on the Hudson: Choschen Hammischpath! Can you imagine: two million Jews live here and not one knows anything about it" (98). This priceless jewelry, which countless nations stole but which always and again returned to the Jewish people, Lewi dedicates to the German cause. Braun: "You? A mixed breed—Lotte Lewi!" Lewi: "I feel it all twice over. I feel for my father's people, horribly martyred to death in Poland and Russia—and for the people of my mother now fighting life or death against the entire world" (101). This transmission of the legacy of jewelry is not a hand-me-down: her father always hated all things Jewish. Frank Braun first called her Jewish, awakened the Jewess in her. But, he asks, did he also make her German. "No, that the war accomplished. I am what I am: a half breed. But I have a fatherland, have my people—two nations, if you will" (101).

She will awaken the German in him, cure his apathy, his inability to love, to believe. Before she gives him what she alone knows he needs, she offers (him and us) a circumlocution for her unnamed blood sacrifice to his unconscious vampirism. "I am your bride and your mother, I am your lover and your sister in these difficult times. And I am also your prophet. I will make you strong and great—and I can do it if I make you German. For I know very well: that will raise you—far, far above and beyond yourself" (104). The future belongs to the Germans and the Jews. The Lewis were originally the priestly tribe among the twelve. The only tribe not granted a territory, the Lewis held instead the position of prestige over all the other tribes and thus held them all together. Their flag: black-white-red. This passing of the flag across centuries is the sign or omen that Lotte Lewi alone among the Jews and the Germans can identify and interpret on the mark, already set to go to war. The Jews and the Germans will rule the world. Total world domination is the promised land (105).

Braun now sees it her way. Back on the street he recognizes that only the Eastside Jewish press admits German victories into the headlines (107). And indeed, rabble-roused support for England, France, and Russia against all things German reminds Braun of the anti-Semitic mass that he once observed the Slavs in Bohemia attend, in communion with charges of Jewish blood ritual and well poisoning. He remembers how the Germans in Prague—largely students attending the oldest German university—were for the most part German Jews hated by the Slavs as Germans. "All Slavic hatred of Germans was at bottom nothing but anti-Semitism" (109). Lotte Lewi was right: the Jews already were a tribe of equal standing in Germany, like the Swabians or the Pommeranians. Her dream was already in production—her mix was the guarantor and model. Israel would be mixed up with the bloodlines of all the German tribes, uniting them all that much more strongly. Braun dismisses the race question as outmoded. "Germany was Israel's Zion—and the promised land—was the world" (110).

The unconscious conflicts that Braun's hallucinations metabolize are tagged in the time-out before and after the projections. Braun watches a giant polyp emerge from a fat man whose metamorphosing arms double as women writhing, reaching out to suck his blood (307, 436). At a fundraiser Braun initiates da capo applause for a consumptive who has just finished performing onstage as Jumping Jack, his second number after the one before as female impersonator. Unstoppable applause makes him hop along till he drops. On the inside Braun admits identification with the man's suffering; on the outside he knows he wears the mask of ruthlessness in the face of the man's collapse. "What did it matter. A female impersonator, a castrated queen, who would never slime his way up out of the gutter, vomit, consumptive, a complete pervert. There were only three ways out for him in this life—by way of the hospital, the prison, the insane asylum" (350).

Insight gets closer to the truth the further away it stays from Braun's recognition. Before he discovers at the end of the novel—on the cut person of Lotte Lewi and all over his own bloodied mouth and shirtfront—that he is the vampire, one former victim of his unconscious bloodlust who had filled in while Lewi was away gives him the diagnosis. Braun, like most people, by the way, is a citizen of Sodom. In other words, the soul or psyche of an animal lives in him as in almost every human body (412). The transmigration of souls guarantees, given the animal majority, that only few human forms bear human souls. "The sexual psyche," she continues, "is nothing more than such an animal—and the animal seeks its own kind. . . . The higher a creature stands—the more souls find room in him. Two souls, according to Goethe, dwelled in his breast—but if you read him, you will find that it was not only two, but rather two hundred, at least" (412). The soul, she says, is *Geschlecht* (sex, genus, stock, generation). Consequently two drives determine human behavior and thought: the drive of self-preservation and that of reproduction (413). The soul is the bearer of the sex or reproduction drive. The body is driven by what it wants: self-preservation. She closes by pointing out (in passing forever out of his arm's way) that he, for example, packs the suck soul of a flea, mosquito, spider, tick, or bat (418).

The streets of New York overflow with the fallout from the boundary damage done to his segregated projection space. The theater boys hit the streets in makeup. A heartbeat later, Braun notes with approval, strong sailor boys come out—also for sale, only cheaper (427–28). The female prostitutes in the district are all Jewish. They drove out their German competitors, who now walk the streets uptown (428). Inside this projective medium (which also plays the field of propaganda), Braun's bipolar disorder, right down to the hallucinations of blood flow, finds a context in the charge that gets pieced together against Lewi, the bloodsucking vamp. Behind the projections there is an identification of soon to be axed ex-colonies as object losses capable of inducing the hunger that preserves even as it destroys.

His condition is most likely neurological or nervous ("probably psychic genesis—the war"). But whenever he feels and looks ill again, "something very alien" has taken control of his person (432–33). There is a corollary diagnosis offered by the German Jewish physician Dr. Cohn, whose second opinion Lewi had urged Braun to consider in the first place. Braun's symptoms fit a newly uncovered symptom picture endemic to the South Seas: it is a strain of malaria transmitted by bats that spreads as symptoms of cannibalism. Braun did visit the German colonies in the South Seas. But he suddenly remembers that Lewi, too, had traveled not far from there not so long ago (227–29). That he always assumes that the vampire is the other is part of Lewi's self-sacrifice plan. Only if he is kept unconscious of the blood lust she feeds until death do them part does the vampirism get the rise out of him, not only out of his intermittent apathy but right to the heights of a kind of speaking ecstasy that he shares with his audiences and that counts as the only psychological weapon on the side of the Germans in the United States during World War I.

When Germany surrenders, Braun drinks his fill (still without knowing it)—drinks himself back to health and puts Lewi finally on the brink of death. Once he realizes the way things were, he is already healed. Lewi assures him that with her lifeblood she made him more German and joined him in the blood supplies of this healthy excess. Braun's unconscious vampirism was what the world at the same time was up to its years in blood. But what about Germany's bleeding defeat? What cure is this? The bloodbath administered the beginning of the cure. Lotte Lewi prophesies on her deathbed the resurrection of Germany, which won't get even but will get it all.

The resounding suck-cess pooling of phantasmatic bodily resources that is *Vampir* mobilizes and affirms the literal insides of the German and Jewish (or German Jewish) "symbiosis" for an ultimately all-out psychotic last stand of Germany to the end of the world. As World War I nears the finish line, Braun contemplates a trip to Mexico to stir up another war front for the diversion of Yankees—but then he gives up on all further earthbound attempts to reverse the course of the world war. Only the Martians could save Germany now (457).

When Hitler was on his way up, he commissioned Ewers, who was already hailing this chief as Germany's long-lost resurrection, to write a book celebrating Nazi martyr Horst Wessel, which was Ewers's last big hit. His decadent past soon kept him busy diagnosing himself as typical neurotic affected by the international sickness of that period, which he sucked in like the successful author he was. Hitler had figured it out: Germany owed guilt-*Geld* for assimilation of and with the Jews. Philo-Semitism was the curse onto which who better than Ewers, one of those afflicted by the melting plot, could up the anti. "By this means the Germans were enabled first to admit the guilt they clearly felt and then to free themselves of it. Germany was guilty—yes—guilty of moral corruption and selfishness. But the guilt did not belong to true Aryan Germans, it belonged solely to the Jews and could therefore be remedied by the simple expedient of expelling them" (Durbin and Bowlby, 138).

At the time that Ewers's vampire novel was hitting the top of the charts (between the wars), Murnau was tuning in the video portion of the same hit parade. Murnau directed the first film versions of *Dracula* and of Goethe's *Faust*. In between he came up with *The Haunted Castle (Schloß Vogelöd)*, in which the loss of the war is recycled as death wish mismanagement on the home front, and Weimar cinema as the projective demonization of the same affront. That's right: it was four years ago, according to this 1921 film, that a brother, who was also a husband, was murdered back in the castle. And now, four years later, the other brother, who was under suspicion but not charged, has returned an unwelcome guest who's back to clear his name. The other guests ask him to demonstrate his gift of prophecy that has beamed back with him all the way from India. Can he forecast the outside chance that shots will be fired in next day's hunt? One shot will be fired, says the unwelcome guest or ghost. Posing as priest, he obtains his brother's widow's confession. And once his identity is out from under the priest's cover, the murderer, the widow's second husband, releases the one prophesied shot that has been held back for four years. With this suicide, the hunt or haunt goes down and out.

Four years ago there was, then, a loss that was not put to rest—and a false marriage, a false comradeship, a false peace. The murdered husband had sought his pleasure back then in so-called unworldly pursuits, notably reading and research. He entered an auto-relation that left his wife behind. Suddenly the wife cries out that she wants to see something evil, a murder, and in a heartbeat, her husband has been shot. The brother, the true comrade, didn't kill his brother in unworldliness. It was a death wish on the home front that betrayed them both. Arriving from India, on the Aryan track, with the special powers of prophecy he acquired there, the other brother assumes the position of priest or father and clears the name of the unworldly alliance.

Before making the haunted movies, which, in *Nosferatu* in particular, are all about the image, its empty circulation, and both its power, just the same, and its concealment packed inside its open display, Murnau made propaganda films for the German World War I effort. A few months after his true love died on the eastern front, Murnau took to the skies of the new air force. There he discovered artificial flight as a new manner of perception tried and tested in the lab experiment of the Great War. He now knew that film would realize this motion through and across the image. Whether on purpose or by accident, Murnau landed in Switzerland. It was while he was in this spot of neutrality, having descended there from the plane's-eye view, that he changed the guard of his war effort and became propaganda filmmaker.

While too late for the immediate upward mobilization of psychological warfare, German expressionist cinema from *The Cabinet of Dr. Caligari* to Lang's *Dr. Mabuse* films reports firsthand on the condition of war neurosis. The report comes in loud and clear from the outside of exile in Edgar Ulmer's 1934 *The Black Cat*. Former officers of the losing side of World War I, an Austrian architect and a Hungarian psychiatrist meet in the Bauhaus villa that the architect built postwar on top of the ruined fortress he betrayed to the enemy. It is now the largest cemetery in Europe. Above the funereal site, the Austrian and the Hungarian agree that they, in a sense, in Schreber's sense of "soul murder," died here fifteen years ago: "Aren't we both," one asks the other, "the living dead?" In the villa's basement we find the encrypted loss of the war: the fortress gun turrets and rotating drum-like cell already recall the cinematic apparatus. But the chambers of a double shoot also feature embalmed women, encased in Snow White coffins, who have been downed along the same lines of internalization and long distance that hold back (until the crypt blasts open at the end) the gunfire of the lost war. Down in the crypt of the war, there's no outwardly directed libido. The libido directed inside, narcissistically, gives the ego the high of slavery or mastery over look-alike mummies holding the place of earliest relations with the body, the mother's body, your own.

Sandor Ferenczi's "Two Types of War Neuroses" includes the advice that the contradictory twitchings and joltings (electrocution style) of war neurotics can (like the lurching mobility of the vampire's carriage in Murnau's *Nosferatu*) be captured only on film (125). The internalization of trauma meets its match and maker in media technologization. That's why in his report on war neurosis, Simmel recommends, given the rate of pileup and turnover of cases at the front, that the analytic intervention be fast-forwarded through hypnosis. The forgotten memory of the instant of war trauma can be pulled up under hypnosis, which means that "the experience can be repeated. The 'film' is let roll once again; the patient dreams the whole thing one more time, the sensitized subconscious releases the affect which in turn discharges in an adequate emotional expression, and the patient is cured" (*Kriegsneurosen*, 25). In Pabst's *Secrets of a Soul*, the first film designed to illustrate psychoanalysis, the patient (who was played by the same actor who performed in the double role of Dr. Caligari) suffers the deadlock of a compulsion and a phobia, the workings of which Ferenczi claimed war neurosis displayed. In *Secrets of a Soul*, the only way the film can illuminate the lifting of radical forgetting or repression of trauma is the only way Simmel could, by way of analogy, do it in writing about his treatment of war neurotics. The psychoanalyst in *Secrets of a Soul* is something of a film director or film critic who plays back and analyzes the film up to the point of his intervention. The film freezes around a photo shoot in order to bring back from out of the family album the primal scene contained in a photograph. But the more unconscious material (which goes without the analyst's interpretation) includes the shoot that the patient's cousin, in military uniform, directs at him. The shoot of the camera and the cut of the editor's knife head the patient off at an impasse that Karl Abraham had learned to recognize through his treatment of war neurotics as that of unresolved same-sex relations ("Psychoanalysis and the War Neuroses," 34–35).

These unworldly relations of comradeship keep on switching back and forth, war economy style, between loyalty and betrayal. This can be watched in such movies as *Mädchen in Uniform*. But it can also be tracked on a larger scale of continuity. The war economy inside Weimar cinema covers or symptomatizes war neurosis as a crisis in same-sex relations or, same difference, in auto-relations. The elusive beam of sexual-identity crisis that is so often brought up and dropped in the scholarship on Weimar cinema and, in equal but separate measure, on Riefenstahl's films (or on Nazi art in general) was in fact strapped to the tracks of the intrapsychic view of war neurosis in a Nazi culture of total healing from 1933 onward, soldiers.

The knife held down in *Secrets of a Soul* is let go in *Pandora's Box*. *Büchse*, "box," can also mean rifle. The cutting that will finally transform Lulu into a motion picture is neurotically contained in the father-and-son warfront-versus-home-front fantasies that, while not given a war record or history, observe the external frame of military display. The cabaret revue that the son (Alwa) creates as vehicle for Lulu on her way to becoming image is crowded with military formations; the movie closes in a terrain crisscrossed by the Christian soldiers of the Salvation Army. Backstage in

the cabaret sequence there's a primal scene, an inside view of the apparatus behind the spectacle, shared by Lulu and the father-and-son team of Dr.
Schoen and Alwa. It's a technologized primal scene repeating automatically
like a rifle. On the way to the first retake of the scene, a gun threatens a
phallic-funny little man or Sandman (Schigolch) originally introduced as
Lulu's illicit friend but who now at gunpoint turns out to be Lulu's father.
It's the gun offered Lulu as instrument of suicide when Dr. Schoen returns
to their honeymoon suite—to the repeater scene of home-front betrayal—
to see son with head on Lulu's lap. But when the gun goes off, it kills the
father. When she accidentally kills Dr. Schoen, Lulu has been made (over)
to share a fantasy of fatherlessness that has put Alwa masochistically at the
disposal of father figures or Big Brothers. He shares his masochism with
Lulu, with whom he identifies, and on whose person it all gets acted out at
the end.

When Jack the Ripper looks past Lulu's smile, her image, he sees a
knife; in the meantime Lulu has been turned in the flickering light into a
motion picture. But first the editing must be performed. Certainly Ripper,
as surgeon-collector of private parts, is the snuff-film father of the kind of
fetishism that's in evidence in Pabst movies (the butcher cutting his meat
in exchange for looks up skirts in *Joyless Streets* is classic). Lulu's murder,
which doubles as the transformation that gets her into pictures, belongs to
the series of fantasy makeovers of women into machines or androids. The
technologization of the woman's body from the inside out puts in reverse
the direction of the cut. It's Ripper's penetration of the body that's barely
veiled in a techno-transformation that needs to start on the inside. Here too
an image of unacknowledged loss is carved out of home-front bodies.
We're getting the point of the back-knifing legend with which the military
blamed the home front for defeat and which cuts along the death wish
edge of an inside-out editing. The Jews to whom German World War I
propaganda appealed (at least according to the postwar fantasies about
the kind of propaganda that should have been tried out) found loyalty
turn around into betrayal. They were part of the horror of a loss that became
the horror shows of home-front diversions. The remobilization of the internal affront under the cover of demonization and exorcism (often including
suicidal sacrifice, as in *Nosferatu*) dares the world war to come again.

Suckarama

Before war investments joined his rank vampiric interests, and before their mutation into *Ants*, and before they final pulled up short inside the Third Reich (in Hitler Youth shorts) for *Horst Wessel*, Ewers took his occult straight (with just a twist of androgyny and cross-dressing). At the end of *Alraune: The Story of a Living Creature*, Ewers dates its writing 1911. Framed, like Shelley's *Frankenstein*, by the correspondence from brother to sister, the central conflict or war in *Alraune* is, as used to be the case quite regularly before World War I, between the sexes. Frank Braun, the leading man in all the novels of Ewers's trilogy, visits his uncle, who shows him a gnarly wooden fetish called Alraune and tells his nephew the legend that goes with the name: when a hanged man shoots his final load, it falls to earth, inseminates on the spot, and up pops another Alraune, "a male or female" (52). Frank convinces his uncle, who is forever performing scientific experiments involving artificial insemination, to go for something bigger than just skipping one of the players. They stick to the posthumous seed of the original recipe but improvise when it comes to mother earth. Instead they select a prostitute as surrogate mother: "Her womb will be just like that of the earth" (65). But before they finally convince the woman whom they've chosen to go through with it, she has to be told a whole story about unmournability, how she's won the look-alike contest, and that only she can serve in the place of the missing woman (she dies giving birth to Alraune).

Alraune grows up into a regular Lolita, who destroys all the men she attracts. But then she meets Frank Braun, who's back for another visit.

> He drank her kisses, drank the hot blood of his lips which her teeth had torn. And he intoxicated himself, knowingly and willingly, as with bubbling wine, as with poisons from the Orient. (408)

> "I bit you," she whispered.
> He nodded. She lifted herself up, embraced him, and drank with glowing lips the red blood....
> They looked at one another—now they knew that they were enemies unto death. (424–25)

When he sees her sleepwalking the upper-story window ledges late at night, the death wish crosses his mind that if he called out her name now, she'd lose her balance with the wake-up jolt that would push her over the edge.

But the call comes from someone else, standing by below, who also gets crushed by Alraune's fatal fall. He's beside himself with self-recriminations. A witness reassures him that he wasn't the one who called out to her. "He laughed shrilly: '—Was it not my wish?'" (454). It's at this point that he decides to relive the old wounds and write this book for his sister's consumption. The blood that fell to the earth at this reopening has fertilized the artificial creation, his book. The creation of Alraune was all along felt by Braun—at least this is what the writer Braun tells his sister—to "have sprung from the illicit pleasure of absurd thoughts" (5). A thought gave the incestuous object a murderous life; Braun's death wish, on second thought, took it away. Following World War I, Ewers would be more plain-text in the scheduling of his occult symptoms (which would, from this time onward, be joined by the new war-sponsored gadgetry that entered the work). But *Alraune*, like prewar occult fiction in general, must be read in reverse if you want to cut to the crypt. It was the death wish that was at the beginning. And it transformed the loss that at the same time could not be acknowledged, at least not up close, into a seductive but murderous creature, who can only begin to be put to rest by putting the occult metabolism into reverse.

Ewers's first book in the trilogy to put in an appearance, in 1917, was *The Sorcerer's Apprentice or the Devil Hunters.* Frank Braun is hanging in there, in a Mediterranean spot, which gets blasted by the arrival from America of a star evangelist who converts everyone in hypnotic sight. Braun's local girlfriend becomes the star of the new culture of conversion: she's got the stigmata to prove it. Through their intimacy, Braun figures, he opened her up to suggestion. But the suggestion slid into the posthypnotic mode, which means no further suggestion could ever change the program.

> A miracle?—No, that it surely was not. Of course she was now the equal . . . of all the holy women he had told her about. And in fact the displacement was minimal: just one little word had to be changed.
>
> Auto-suggestion rather than alien-suggestion. That was all.
> (321)

Braun's study of the local ecstasy-through-conversion fad leads him through science fictive speculation and sensation right to the arrival, with the Lewi family (Lotte is Braun's partner in vampirism for the third novel), of currently realized alternatives to or improvements on American conversion psychology: the airplane and the movies. Before he experiences hovering and flying sensations that defy gravity (366–67), he solves the evolutionary scheme of ecstasy, picking up *Faust* along the way to discover his missing link.

> If in the development of billions of years protoplasm grew up into man, if bones and muscles, blood and nerves, were formed, then the form of consciousness must have become something different. That's the kernel of all ecstasy: that the consciousness of the ecstatic human was a different one. Was it possible to find this other form, somewhere on the long step ladder of development.
>
> Then he thought of *Faust* . . .
>
> That was it! But not just two souls that separate: one soul only, that becomes another one. One soul that is homesick for the filth of the fathers, that yearns to go back, away from the clear air, down into the musty cave depths of the lower ancestors. . . .
>
> The human soul in this sense was the consciousness of the separation of ego from the external world. (364)

When the Lewis arrive, Mr. Lewi updates and upgrades Braun: "Today I'm an enthusiastic aviator" (501). Then Braun takes Lotte to the movies:

> "A cinema!" he cried out with pleasure. "Shall we go, Lotte? Oh how long it's been that I haven't seen a film!" . . . They saw Blériot flying over the channel with his bird. . . .
>
> "Oh the cinema!" he exclaimed with enthusiasm. "It is the most glorious invention that our era has created! . . . Cinema . . . is the best historian, a fanatic for the truth, one that knows no error. And at the same time cinema is the true alchemist, it breaks apart what reason preaches and is the world's only magician." (505–7)

Braun gadget-lovingly instructs Lotte Lewi: "Imagine a cinematograph accompanying you through your whole life" (509). The book counts down to the kind of ending, in midmetabolization, that can only signal that work is to be continued. Frank Braun has graduated from his solo close encounter with conversion ecstasy, made in America but at the same time suggestively in sync with the hypnotic history of Freud's science, all the way to gadget love. The channel crossing by plane he sees in the movies is like the moment of personal airspace invasion Freud saw as already the advance previewing that World War I was coming soon. "In the moment at which Blériot flew across the Channel in his aeroplane this protective isolation [of the U.K.] was breached; and in the night during which (in peace-time and on an exercise) a German Zeppelin cruised over London the war against Germany was no doubt a foregone conclusion" (*SE*, 22:178).

In Love and War

Freud was aware that in its practical application analysis must undergo dilution. This is but the natural fate of every great ideology: it loses its noblest characteristic, its splendid isolation, and acquires practical value only in its dilution, alteration, adaptation. This is necessarily the destiny too of analysis because as an empirical science it serves practical ends wherein the immediate result must be of permanent value. Thus of the genius-given gift of Freud humanity will acquire its fullest social value only when it becomes by this dilution a common property, even indeed divorced from the name of its creator.

—HELENE DEUTSCH, "FREUD AND HIS PUPILS: A FOOTNOTE TO THE
HISTORY OF THE PSYCHOANALYTIC MOVEMENT"

During the formulation of Freud's second system, the number of claims made on psychoanalysis in Nietzsche's name were, on all sides, on the rise. Will to Power and amor fati went along for the death drive while the model of the psyche was changing into id and superego inside Superman's booth. Nietzsche's inside view of life as self-affirming joy or as suffering that says yes scored big time inside the second system's alternation of takes on female sexuality, group psychology, and the death and destruction drive (the sadomasochistic distribution of pleasure). Like Nietzsche, like Freud: it's the experience of women that has a group-psychological moment.

The same pull tugging inside and between Nietzsche and Freud (which collapses group-psychological concerns onto a question of woman raised together with that life-and-death issue that comes complete as drive) can be found stretching and marking the reception of the Nietzsche-to-Freud connection. Women caught the connection and were admitted into the theoretical discourse that turned on sexual difference: it was the first discourse (some call it misogynist) to give gender politics shelter.

The wish to equalize in theory what was pressing for equal rights in practice (a shift in register from politics to thinking that Freud diagnosed as psychosis compatible) counted in such followers as Adler and Jung while counting them out of psychoanalysis. The couplification of repression around the bisexuality thesis—the opposition or the equalization of sexual difference—brought us the grand opening of the psychotherapies, which, already by 1914, flourished in the afterglow of their breakup with psychoanalysis. The breakaway Adlerian and Jungian movements were, by 1933

A hospitalized soldier allegedly suffering from shell shock during World War I diagnosed as simulator of deafness and muteness. Reproduced from p. 588 of "Die Simulation von Ohrenkrankheiten."

at the latest, much more popular than psychoanalysis. It was at the time he was reinscribing the traumatic origin of identification within the psychopolitical contexts introduced by World War I that Freud issued the warning that his science must not be confused with those new and improved therapies and theories. But psychoanalysis too was making the headlines with its interventionism in the military complex: "When I knew Professor Freud in Vienna in 1922, he was aged 65 and more or less at the height of his career. Soon after 1910 the solitary obscurity which had surrounded him and his work for something like 20 years had begun to lessen, while the war neuroses in Europe had generated, both in the medical profession and in the general public, an interest in the psychological approach to such disorders" (Riviere, 128).

The triad of group psychology, female sexuality, and the death and destruction drive was admitted into the second system with the serial dreams of traumatized war and accident victims. The traumatized dreamers' compulsion to repeat rather than remember had shot up through the shock's

Two soldiers hospitalized for war neurosis during World War I, diagnosed as simulators of deafness and muteness. Reproduced from p. 589 of "Die Simulation von Ohrenkrankheiten."

penetration beyond pleasure or before defense: it "was there" at the starting point of all absorption, preparedness, or first-line defense. With catastrophe you start all over again from first scratchings of the breach of defense: but once you have the catastrophe where you want it (down inside identification), it leaves you there, in the state of catastrophe preparedness that's *über alles*.

Before World War I, Freud was still figuring out the death wish fulfillment at the vampiric heart of identification. As self-evidence of such a thing as symptomatic synchronicity, the pre-world-war era was at the same time the danger zone of the first departures from, or improvements on, psychoanalysis. Led by her auto-analytic and endopsychic insights into the groupified position of female sexuality, Sabina Spielrein didn't so much split psychoanalysis as give the advance preview of Freud's second system. The "psychotic Hysteric" started out as Jung's bedside discovery: their transference-love affair gave her the cure. Which is why she became a Freudian analyst. But Spielrein was still riding out the countertransferential current of Freud's resistance when she decided to be Freud's disciple but Jung's best friend. That's why even though he knew she was giving him a bad case of the ct's, Freud had no choice but to defend his underworld exploration of delusional systems against Spielrein's premature acceleration of death wishes onto the death drive.

In 1912 Freud could write Jung that he found Spielrein's destruction drive not to his liking because it was "personally conditioned": "She seems abnormally ambivalent" (21 March 1912). It was too much ambivalence—too soon. (What's more, Freud had already written to Jung, she was hooked on biology [30 November 1911].) But by the time he admitted the death drive into his system, Freud was also admitting the very measure (beyond pleasure) of personal conditioning and ambivalence overload, indeed, a strong dose of biological (or biographical) dependence: it was the time of his daughter Sophie's death. It was only at this point that Freud accepted life insurance (i.e., the death drive) into the system: it was a group protection plan that granted female sexuality equal coverage. It was only then that Freud took in Spielrein's inspired or dictated anticipation of the death drive—at the time, then, of Nietzsche's increasing claim on psychoanalysis. And it was time for psychotherapy to grow an influence that in the name of the precursor was already in World War I outflanking psychoanalysis. Thus in 1917 Jung interrupts his all-out attack on Freud to give Spielrein some sound advice: "You must read Adler or Nietzsche" (Carotenuto, 215). Women were getting the reading lists on the pathologies they modeled. Their counteroffensive contribution or reading exhumed the pre-Oedipal mother. Spielrein's 1912 *Destruction as the Cause of Becoming* dropped inside its preview of Freud's second system a case study of Nietzsche as matricentric schizo.

Nietzsche Baby

Spielrein had, then, already in 1912, diagnosed Nietzsche. His lifelong soli-
tude (especially when it came to libido) was too much for the poet: he created along the group-psychological trajectory the imaginary friend Zarathustra (with whom he identified). "The yearning for a love object brought
about that Nietzsche became in himself man and woman and both of these
in the shape of Zarathustra" (30). The celebration by Nietzsche/Zarathus-
tra of a natural rhythm method of mergers (for example, between the sun
and the sea) strikes up an internal depth inhabited ultimately by the mother:
"If the mother is his own depth, then the union with the mother must also
be seen as autoerotic, as union with himself" (31). What goes around comes
around: in the series of Nietzsche's displaced mergers, the finale transforms
Nietzsche into "the engendering, creating, becoming mother" (31).

This maternal bond scores an almost perfect regression on a large scale
of identification. But, says Spielrein, it's just the radical feminine mode of
destruction and self-destruction control: the internalized distribution of
desire between the sexes puts man in the position of subject loving the object projected into the outside, and woman in a position to love herself as
his object (32). In the feminine position of identification with a masculinist
mother (who penetrates him), the dementia praecox patient living in autoerotic isolation tends to pack a homosexual component. But both woman
and child hang out with even stronger homosexual, incestuous, and autoerotic tendencies: "she must imagine how she is loved and accordingly put
herself in the role of her parents" (33).

"But if, through identification with the loved individual, the object
representations grow in intensity, then the love reserved for oneself leads
to self-destruction" (34). That's why even the act of procreation follows the
beat of self-destruction (the other fact of life Nietzsche's imaginary friend
calls "self overcoming"). The destruction drive may make you come and
go, but it also has you covered: the eternal returns on identification keep
schizo Nietzsche in business.

According to the coverage Spielrein gives the psyche, you get what you
ask for: one's relation to one's ancestors *(Ahnen)* embodies a resemblance
or likeness *(Ähnlichkeit)* that, whether downing identification or doing sex,
one likes—to be like. That's why reproduction is a merger with one's ancestors through the lover that looks like you. The death that follows on the
Oedipal heels of incest is not just punishment and prohibition; incest real-

izes one's desired restoration to the engenderer and subsequent dissolution in him (39).

This ancestral likability bond pervades all experience—which can never be in the present tense. "Every content of conscious thought is a product of differentiation from other, psychologically more ancient contents" (40). By making the content fit the present moment, we personalize it and give it the character of an ego connection. But when we share the fantasy (with the other), that is, when we start talking, then we dedifferentiate and depersonalize back to the generic that goes for the species. This move travels the second opposing tendency in us, the beaten track to assimilation and dissolution. "I" no longer speaks for a unity that has been transformed into a larger unit for which "We" is the spokesperson or talk show host. This is how art, dream, and the pathological symbolicity of dementia praecox form an alignment on parallel tracks. The creation/dissolution of the ego-connection goes with the upsurge of pleasure or unpleasure. Whenever the personal experience has been transformed into a generic one, we relate to it as members of the audience to a staged event in which we participate only if we get into it. That's our role when we're unconscious: dreams are our time-shares in the complete conglomerate or complex called dementia praecox.

Ambivalence is along for the generic drive (the one that's out to preserve the species): this is where each positive component releases a negative counterpart, and likewise, I'm sure. The ego drive is the static one that tries to defend the egoic or individual status quo against foreign influence. The differentiation tendency is along for the drive to preserve oneself. The drive to sustain the species is a reproductive drive that goes the way (down) of dissolution and assimilation. But here another differentiation of the primal material comes up: it's the one called love. Dissolution of the ego in one's lover is at the same time the strongest self-affirmation; it means in the person of the lover a new lease or policy of life for the ego. Without love, the change that comes over the psychic and physical individual from the outside (as in sex) gets represented as death and destruction. That's why resistance to life is *the* neurotic symptom (there is no other symptom).

In the case of Nietzsche, the schizo solo course of libido alone contains eternally the same tension between the sexes. Drawing current from the interchange or charge between annihilation phantasms and autoerotic satisfaction loaded into her Nietzsche diagnosis, Spielrein plugs in the ultimate connection—all the way into the future—between groupie psychology and war neurosis. To read between the dreams (in which girls see themselves

knifed), she activates the psychoanalytic decoder: dreams contain no negation and thus no negation of life.

> In accordance with the fact that the woman gets penetrated in
> the sex act, the girl sees herself, as does the woman, as the victim
> in the dream of a sadistically colored sexual act. That's why the
> events of warfare are so suited for the outbreak of neurosis, which
> at bottom has its source in the disturbances of the sex life. It is
> war that goes along with ideas of destruction. Now, since one
> idea calls up other related ones, so the ideas of destruction in
> war excite ideas associated with the destructive components of
> the reproductive instinct. These latter ideas can ruin existence as
> something outright transitory and pointless even for normal peo-
> ple and especially for the neurotic, in whose thoughts the ideas
> of destruction outweigh those of becoming and who thus only
> has to wait for appropriate symbols for the representation of
> these destruction fantasies. (26–27)

Spielrein goes on (down) to interrogate in these contexts the teen girl
fantasies of lying in graves. These open onto womb fantasies right down to
the interchangeability of grave digging and penetration (and birth). For
the neurotic this is the same as the live burials and aftershocks brought to
us by shell blast: "For a normal girl the idea of being buried gives rise to
ecstasy as soon as she thinks of dissolution in her lover. A young girl told
Binswanger, 'the greatest happiness for her would be to be held inside the
body of her lover'" (28–29). In Spielrein's reading (as would also be the
case, on the other side of World War I, in Freud's "On 'the Uncanny'"), the
womb covers all the testing sites of uncanny repetition—in particular, the
dream series in which many eternal returns of the traumatic incident must
be watched by the traumatized soldiers.

The womb is the bottom-line guarantee that the war bond of neurosis
(the bonding of group identification that scored an origin in trauma) can be
converted back to the treatable effects of a sexual disturbance that made
the one predisposed to neurotic outbreak always on the lookout for destruction symbols: what already had the stranglehold (on the inside) on sex or
reproduction reaches the outside and gets the upper hand in war neurosis.

In her analysis of Nietzsche, Spielrein thought she was doing Jung and
Freud. In Geneva when she was doing Piaget she thought she was doing
Jung and Freud too (two). (Yes, Spielrein analyzed Piaget and conducted
her research on children with him.) She was the first psychotherapist. Her
eclecticism was born of the spirits of unresolved transference (the one that

crushes love into adoration). In short, she was the loyal type. (Which means every thinker she followed she stabbed in the back.) The eclecticism or reunification of the collected psychotherapies that had split off from psychoanalysis (which included psychoanalysis as one more therapy to borrow from in treatment) was already part of the destruction manual Spielrein shared with analysis in 1912. Already part of the primal preview we find parallel treatments of war neurotics and homosexuals, of girls and schizos, against a backdrop of their interchangeable theorization in group format.

Adult Hood

If, down these pages, I collapse Nazi and Jung, then this serves as short-hand for the nit-picking and knitting together the middlebrow that indeed can complicate Jung's case in the spirit of historical understanding. But I am preparing neither a legal brief nor a history. I speak before the court of mourning. And I am tracking Jung's negative transference on its terms. To understand Jung is to forgive him. That's not even therapeutic. It is certainly not analytic. We must interpret for the transference. Historical understanding, too, especially when personalized, can be just another mode of not seeing.

Jung's skipping around Freud's emphasis on early childhood as the preprogram of all development to the process of growing out of adolescence into adulthood (during which development happens not because it recurs but because it occurs here and for the first time) underlies to this day both linear and dialectical theories of adult development (one of the required parts of the curriculum in Californian psychotherapeutic eclecticism). But these theories of development can come into their maturity only by first locking in their investment in Jung's resistance to Freud's theory, his repression of (the theory of) repression, and his own unresolved transference. In the case of Jung, the turn away from childhood (in other words, from sexuality) to the growth potential of adolescence has a history that packs a psychopolitical charge.

In accepting the international leadership of Nazi psychotherapy, Jung just the same came into renewed contact with Freud's science, which was represented by a prominent component of the now reunified eclecticism of German psychotherapy. So in 1934 Jung again takes on Freud, and he does so via a contrast of their views on *Faust*. The Freudian view, says Jung, is that Faust is neurotic, since the devil doesn't exist:

> Consequently his psychic counterpart doesn't exist either—a mystery still to be unriddled, born of Faust's dubious internal secretions! That at least is the opinion of Mephistopheles, who is himself not altogether above reproach sexually—inclined to be bisexual, if anything. This devil who, according to *The Future of an Illusion*, does not exist is yet the scientific object of psychoanalysis, which gleefully busies itself with his non-existent ways of thought. Faust's fate in heaven and on earth may well be "left to the poets," but meanwhile the topsy-turvy view of the human soul is turned into a theory of psychic suffering. ("The State of Psychotherapy Today," 172–73)

The real issue is Jung's discovery in 1931 of adult development, which pre-
supposed the onset of development in adolescence and thus the relative
unimportance of childhood. The tension of adolescence that precedes the
psychic development of midlife turns on the same scenario of doubling
Freud first dedicated to war neurosis.

> Psychic birth, and with it the conscious distinction of the ego
> from the parents, takes place in the normal course of things at
> the age of puberty with the eruption of sexual life.... The state
> induced by a problem—the state of being at variance with one-
> self—arises when, side by side with the series of ego-contents, a
> second series of equal intensity comes into being. This second
> series, because of its energy-value, has a functional significance
> equal to that of the ego-complex; we might call it another, sec-
> ond ego which in a given case can wrest the leadership from the
> first. ("The Stages of Life," 99)

Jung summarizes how a neurosis, because it is a growing, developing
process in real time and not a mere fixation or remainder from the past,
gives a cross section of human development from adolescence to midlife
(and back again). We're back at the front lines of war neurosis: "In the neurosis is hidden one's worst enemy and best friend. One cannot rate him too
highly, unless of course fate has made one hostile to life. There are always
deserters, but they have nothing to say to us, nor we to them" ("The State
of Psychotherapy Today," 169).

Jung's automatic dismissal notwithstanding, the psychology of the deserter, which was drafted for the psychopathology unit of war neurotics,
would be high up there on the agenda of Nazi psychotherapy. How to fortify the German war effort (on all fronts, including the home front) against
neuroticizing or psychoticizing shocks? And how to prevent the soldier
from succumbing to the "perversion" (as it came to be diagnosed) of desertion and, most important, subsequent betrayal of information to the enemy?
But even if Jung felt he could afford to miss the historical change and chance
that psychoanalysis afforded, not even Nazi psychotherapy could take such
a chance and ignore a method that had intervened so successfully in the
cases of World War I war neurotics.

The Faustian coupling that accompanied Freud over the top of war's
internalization shoots up symptomatically in Jung's perpetual state of unresolved transference, which began, in the beginning, with his psychotic
break in childhood (which gives him a break in theory *with* childhood). Jung
symptomatized or thematized this legacy of war as the perpetual psycho-
tension and attraction between teen self-esteem and the midlife crisis.

Look at any case of adulthood: the development that got you there was way more discontinuous than it was, overall, sequential or dialectical. As set down by Freud, childhood is the defective cornerstone of life's co-herency, which unravels along the dotted line of early conflict. But with the intervention of psychoanalysis, one's childhood can also give bottom-line order (and no longer self-destruct orders) to the life coming at you, grow-ing incoherent. If we follow the bouncing ball of the development of per-sonality traits (or of symptoms), it's hard to see development being awarded equal opportunities in distinct ages or stages of life. Only in some general and thematic sense (that is, in a pre-psychoanalytic sense) are there, for ex-ample, new developments in adulthood that grow (dialectically or sequen-tially) out of adolescence. Adolescence, seen as group psychology, pres-ents a strong case against any continuous view of development. Adolescence is the place of development's arrest. Faustian "striving," the metathesis in German *(Streben/Sterben)*—and the denial in theory—of "dying," accom-panies Jung's view of an ongoing development that continues beyond death.

In the 1931 study that's the acknowledged precursor of current adult-development theory, Jung doesn't want to add adulthood (and, in the first place, adolescence) to childhood. He's out to make a clearing for the new and improved view by wiping out the role of childhood in psychic devel-opment: "when normal, the child has no real problems of its own" ("The Stages of Life," 100). A human being can only be at variance with himself by first growing up, which for Jung begins with the teen age. So childhood doesn't count; the countdown of development via the dialectic of self and other begins with the second stage, that of adolescence. Next comes the middle age or stage of development, which represents "significant change in the human psyche" (104). For Jung it's a question of accepting or denying that one has entered not just a new stage but the stage of aging. With accept-ance of the fact of life that one's vital direction and metabolism have shifted down (indeed into reverse) there comes a new internalizing emphasis on one's self-care, which turns from the world to illuminate the self and turn on insight. But if you don't accept, you still have to face the consequence of denial. "Instead of doing likewise, many old people prefer to be hypochon-driacs, niggards, doctrinaires, applauders of the past or eternal adoles-cents—all lamentable substitutes for the illumination of the self" (109).

This perfectly fine description of middle and old age could have come from many places (for example, from a *Gymnasium* student's paper on Goethe's *Faust II*). For Jung there's division in adolescence (see *Faust I*), and then there's culture, the resolution of division, in adulthood. Childhood (and that means the sexual etiology of all development) is missing, and

Freud's got to go. He's the father whom the perpetually teen Jung wants dead, but only in the name of the significant change of adulthood, which is the dimension of development that he marks as his own discovery. No wonder Jung summons religion to close the circle and seal the deal. To develop means to look forward to a goal. (Somehow insight was not enough.) That's why the belief in the afterlife helps us out of a morbid experience during the closing stages of life. Thus old age joins childhood on the common basis of being "the stages of life without any conscious problems" (114).

In his 1934 "The State of Psychotherapy Today," Jung openly situates his new view of development within his dispute with Freud. He sets up the dispute as a three-sided contest in which he can include himself in the eclectic spirit of equal rights for all theories and therapies. Freud's view (just one of three equals!) reveals a one-sided emphasis on desire and greed. In the other corner there's Adler, who theorizes always only the power urge or surge that puts one "on top." Now, both Freud and top-man Adler go at development from the infantile angle. And that's why Jung's view, which he modestly introduced as but an equal third, is really the better half: he introduces the "will to adapt," which liberates development from the fixation on infancy. The infantilism Freud and Adler cling to could be genuine—but it could also be symptomatic, in which case it reflects an excess of adaptation. There has to be a difference between the state of remaining infantile and another state that's in a process of growth. Rather than always track back to the cradle in the face of so-called infantilism, the therapist should go for the creative content even of the "infantile-perverse" fantasies. What's more, Freud and Adler are only diagnosing themselves while maintaining the authority of their neurotic selves—in theory and in their practices. The theory of infantilism serves to keep the analyst on top through the reductionism of "nothing but" claims. But this is "nothing but" Jung's Adlerian reading of Freud's science: the two one-sided sides he set up neatly fold up to shut up Freud. "Psychoanalysis is evidently a technique behind which the human being vanishes, and which always remains the same no matter who practices it. Consequently, the psychoanalyst needs no self-knowledge and no criticism of his assumptions" (163).

So psychoanalysis packs the projections of a teenager who confuses the sex on his mind with what Freud has in mind when he refers to sexuality. "Freud, of course, thinks that the thing concealed is the thing these fantasies more or less openly allude to, i.e. sexuality and all the rest of it" (170–71). It's "the adolescent smutty-mindedness of the explainer" (167) that the psychoanalytic interpretation advertises. "The psychoanalyst's every second word is 'nothing but'—just what a dealer would say of an article he wanted to buy on the cheap."

Because the article is man's soul, Jung must remind his audience of German psychotherapists that they have "quite other forebears than Mesmer... and the rest," in other words, than Freud (172). Forget infantilism, forget the past: "The true reason for a neurosis always lies in the present, since the neurosis exists in the present. . . . It is fed and as it were new-made every day" (171). Tracking back into the past does not take us back to a wrong turn—it *is* the "wrong turning." Psychoanalysis not only undermines the present tense of neurosis; the continued presence or existence of the neurosis—which is in fact the neurotic's "own self, the 'other' whom... he was always seeking to exclude from his life" (169)—comes under the attack of Freud the hunter, the bargain hunter. Punch lines are reserved for the living end. The *Zentralblatt für Psychotherapie,* the official organ of the new German psychotherapy, in which all the psychotherapies (including psychoanalysis) were reunited, was proud to publish Jung's 1934 reckoning with Freud. Although the leader on the German front, Göring's cousin, Göring, was the one to follow, Jung as the new leader of the international outfit, which had been kept on to give the German developments credibility, was responsible for all the internationally circulating headlines.

When the transference goes unresolved, the neurosis indeed keeps to the present tense. "To lose a neurosis is to find oneself without an object; life loses its point and hence its meaning" (167). What the "Jews have... in common with women" is their analytic "technique" (which is the compensation for their physical weakness) whereby they tear down their adversaries by bringing unconscious impulses to consciousness: "The Jews themselves are best protected where others are most vulnerable" (165). But that's why the Jews have missed out on the future; as far as the future goes, they're history: "The average Jew is far too conscious and differentiated to go about pregnant with the tensions of unborn futures" (166). Jung's seeming right-to-life allegiance to what is unborn remains the other side of his undead or perpetually teen tendencies.

Jung's directives for Nazi psychotherapy are the sentiments fitting for (and into) a figurehead. The "business," as usual, of a theory and therapy of the "Germanic unconscious" is "to treat the whole man and not an artificially segregated function" (166). Jung's thematization, desexualization, and repression of Freud's contributions kept him so radically prepsychoanalytic that he was outmoded even or especially within the overall Nazi mobilization of the psychotherapies that had split psychoanalysis.

Jung Hitler

The antithesis is clearly one of apeman and superman. How
much this imagery from the funny papers means to adolescents
is well known.

—ERIK H. ERIKSON, "HITLER'S IMAGERY AND GERMAN YOUTH"

The way Jung back in 1912 suddenly turned to mythology gave Freud advance signs of their break coming soon. The distinction Freud drew up short before mythology between psychoanalytic rereading and Jung's receptivity also goes for their different takes on psychotic delusions, the occult, technology—on all the contexts, in short, of Freud's discovery and delegation of the unconscious. "Consequently I hold that surface versions of myths cannot be used uncritically for comparison with our psychoanalytical findings. We must find our way back to their latent, original forms by a comparative method that eliminates the distortions they have undergone in the course of their history" (Freud to Jung, 17 December 1911).

Jung's 1936 current-events essay "Wotan" met latent latest standards when it still met, in all its alleged ambiguity, with Nazi approval. Wotan is the divine trendsetter for German youth movements that in 1933 followed Hitler's beat and thus signaled that "Wotan the wanderer was on the move" (180). On this forward march, everyone's a stand-in for some precursor: "The German youths . . . were not the first to hear a rustling in the primeval forest of the unconscious. They were anticipated by Nietzsche" (181). Wotan thus is "an elemental Dionysus breaking into the Apollonian order" (187). Breaking in with Wotan into Nietzsche's opening of the origin of the community spirit brought to us by music, Jung brings Nietzsche up to date: "The maenads were a species of female storm-troopers, and, according to mythical reports, were dangerous enough. Wotan confined himself to the berserkers, who found their vocation as the Blackshirts of mythical kings" (185).

In "After the Catastrophe," Jung claimed (in 1945) to be picking up where he had left off in 1936. This time around, he developed a diagnosis of the German modeled after Nietzsche's case:

> Inferiority feelings are usually a sign of inferior feeling—which
> is not just a play on words. All the intellectual and technological
> achievements in the world cannot make up for inferiority in the
> matter of feeling. . . .

This spectacle recalls the figure of what Nietzsche so aptly calls the "pale criminal," who in reality shows all the signs of hysteria.... A feeling of inferiority... can easily lead to an hysterical dissociation of the personality, which consists essentially in one hand not knowing what the other is doing,... and in looking for everything dark, inferior, and culpable in others.... Therefore all hysterical people are compelled to torment others, because they are unwilling to hurt themselves by admitting their own inferiority. (202–3)

Nietzsche was German to the marrow of his bones, even to the abstruse symbolism of his madness. It was the psychopath's weakness that prompted him to play with the "blond beast" and the "Superman." ... The weakness of the German character, like Nietzsche's, proved to be fertile soil for hysterical fantasies. (212)

But Jung admits that in 1933 or 1934 the "information" he was receiving, had it stopped short then, could have called for a different judgment: back then it was, after all, a "refreshing wind" (205). But the show of dementia praecox was nonetheless in place. Jung is not reviewing only Hitler's maenadlike "shrill, grating womanish tones," which cheerled "the power fantasies of an adolescent" (204). Jung is interested in the fantasies that were shared: "The nation of eighty millions crowded into the circus to witness its own destruction" (204). However, when Jung concludes that the Germans in their "hysterical twilight-state" followed their "mediumistic Führer... with a sleep-walker's assurance" (208), he is repeating (without the more open, even upbeat, conclusion) the commentary on German events he ran by us on Radio Berlin in 1933. Why stop there: both times, he's quoting Hitler's description of his own automatic-pilot mode.

Jung's 1945 diagnosis of German hysteria as the exciting cause or first run of what must issue in collective guilt takes the diagnoses of women made by Nietzsche, Freud, and Jung and contains them in the one-sided reception of Nietzsche as German time capsule. Between the (at best) ambiguous reception of the Nazi libidinal upsurge and the postwar thesis of collective guilt (which, before everyone else gets body-counted as innocent bystander, counts in Nietzsche as one of the in-group of hysterics teleguiding the emergence of the Nazi symptom), Jung was capitalizing on the rapid turnovers in Germany. Between 1934 and 1936 many articles by Jungians were special featured in the central organ of Nazi psychotherapy (*Zentralblatt für Psychotherapie*), and its second issue (after the 1933 takeover) was completely devoted to Jung's analytical psychology. In his introduction to the December 1933 issue of the new *Zentralblatt* (which had just been brought back under a new name for the new era), Jung concluded: "The difference between Germanic and Jewish psychology, which has already been long recognized by genuinely solid and insightful people, will no longer be blurred, which can only be of benefit to research" (*Zentralblatt für Psychotherapie* 6 [1933]: 139).

Going Out for Business

In 1945 Jung's conception of "collective guilt" extended the coverage he had given himself in 1933 when he tried to run down Freud on those unresolved transference tracks that happened to traverse certain externalizable or political effects (the ones Jung in 1945 still chose to disown). He extended coverage even to his fellow collaborators by sharing the blame for the special effects with everyone (else). "They should realize that the German catastrophe was only one crisis in the general European sickness" ("After the Catastrophe," 214); Germany remains, after all, "the nerve-center of Europe" (213). Didn't it all already start with maenadlike Nietzsche and his shrill, womanish invitation to the Superman to replace the dead God? Jung asks.

> It is an immutable psychological law that when a projection has come to an end it always returns to its origin. So when somebody hits on the singular idea that God is dead, or does not exist at all, the psychic God-image, which is a dynamic part of the psyche's structure, finds its way back into the subject and produces a condition of "God-Almightiness," that is to say all those qualities which are peculiar to ... madmen and therefore lead to catastrophe. (214–15)

With Jung's charge of projection there's also a double or group projection—I mean an all-out group protection. "If collective guilt could only be understood and accepted, a great step forward would have been taken" (217). "Psychological collective guilt is a tragic fate. It hits everybody, just and unjust alike" (197).

Jung nevertheless turns in industrialization and massification as the other collective guilt that's ultimately the guilty party. It's his party—so he can pretend he was only crying wolf, I mean Adolf, if he wants to. It's the line of argument or defense that the reunified psychotherapists and psychoanalysts used during the Third Reich to "save" their line of work and their otherwise Aryan but just the same neurotic clientele. Different time, same station: public intelligence and morality are automatically undermined by the devastating "psychic effects of living together in huge masses" (200). How could it be any other way, even today, and even in another setting: "We, who have so many traitors and political psychopaths in our midst?" (200). The condition of this "state of degradation" "is the accumulation of urban, industrialized masses—of people torn from the soil, engaged in one-sided employment, and lacking every healthy instinct, even that of self-

preservation" (200). The loss of this instinct is a liability covered by overde-
pendence on the state. "Dependence on the state means that everybody relies on everybody else (= state) instead of on himself. Every man hangs on
to the next and enjoys a false feeling of security, for one is still hanging in
the air even when hanging in the company of ten thousand other people.
The only difference is that one is no longer aware of one's own insecurity"
(201). Hanging with Jung, then, on the airwaves, we have the insurance
coverage of collective guilt. Cut off from the self-preservation drive, man,
in Jung's words, "becomes the shuttlecock of every wind that blows." At
that point of sickness (Jung was there), "nothing short of catastrophe can
bring him back to health" (201); nothing, that is, short of insurance.

Between the Wars

One could characterize the Jew as the repressed inferiority
complex become flesh.

—GOEBBELS, *DER KAMPF UM BERLIN*

Adler had all along championed in the name of Nietzsche a holistic socialization approach against Freud's insatiable working of sex and transference.
He coupled his therapy with Marxistoid politics and was thereby able to
introduce his real-time counseling into schools and other institutions of
the everyday. While the Nazi socialists had to strike out against the completely external and recognizable labels of political groups that had competed with them, the assignment was considered complete with the shutdown of left-wing-sponsored programs in Vienna and Berlin. But since
Adler's conversion to Christianity did not, not for the Nazis, tame the brute
issue that he was a Jew, the name, too, had to be forgotten. But individual
psychology remained popular in Nazi Germany, where its Nietzschean
and Vaihingerian therapeutic attitude—the "as if," the testing rapport with
risk—was fixated. As in: what if psychoanalysis had been invented by Nietzsche, which, in a sense, was Adler's question all along. That the head of
Nazi psychotherapy was Adlerian is therefore not extraneous to what was
all along part of the Adlerian challenge to Freud; it's the same difference
that is getting displaced here, too.

In 1934 Nazi German psychotherapist Leonhard Seif (another Adlerian) turned to Nietzsche and Clausewitz as the two authors of the notion of
a psychologically conceived community feeling that was congruent with
the war effort. Politics would continue to provide the institutional frame of
community, but pedagogy and psychotherapy would lube the tracks guiding each child to his or her life tasks within the national community. As Seif
put it in 1940: "Education or psychotherapy is the task of forming a vital
community, a 'we' relationship" (32).

Adler too made neurosis psychosis's distributor: "The neurotic tendency
toward security...is always the effective cause of the psychotic construction" (*Neurotic Constitution*, 241). Indeed, it is often enough a "buried feeling of humiliation" that demands "over-compensation in the psychosis"
(422). Thus what Adler calls "insurance" covers the progression from normal, conscious use of a fiction (a "useful safety-device"), through neurotic
attempts to realize the fiction, all the way to the psychotic's conviction that
his fiction is a reality (169).

The psychotic, at the nonnegotiable extreme of the insurance phantasm, Adler counsels, "acts under the most intense urgency. . . . In a similar
manner he simultaneously feels himself to be woman and Superman" (170–
71). Adler recycles Nietzsche through the psychotic's endopsychic perception and replaces Freud's theory of anxiety with Nietzsche's philosophy of
power (and of war between the sexes). Where there's war, there's also equal
coverage.

> It is only to this fixity of the uncertainty that Nietzsche's asser-
> tion is applicable, namely that every one carries within him a
> portrait of womankind which he has derived from his mother,
> and which makes him honor woman or despise her or entertain
> a total indifference toward her. (79)

> That along with this the mother serves in a certain sense as a
> model for the boy has long been known and has been mentioned
> by Nietzsche. [The child] even goes so far as to entertain sexual
> wishes in regard to the mother, a proof of how boundless is the
> Will to Power. (114)

Inferiority, compensation, guiding fiction, insurance: these are the terms
of a constitution of neurosis that trades in pleasure for securities. Thus
Adler was empowered to look beyond Freud's "imperfect and one-sided
theory of dreams": "The dream . . . always drives towards security" (399).
Adler holds equally displaced views of sexual etiology and transference,
both of which can be explained (away) by putting repression back in its
place as "byproduct" of "the striving towards a fictitious goal" (6). The
"neurotic desires to insure himself" by clinging to what appears "to him to
be useful for his security" (150). Thus a "guiding principle" requires "an
insuring anxiety" (181) and related "security devices" (192). One can also
obtain "security through neurotic anxiety" (272) or even cop the "security
of the feeling of self-accusation" (273). The stress is on "when a renuncia-
tion without adjustment is demanded" (155).

Nietzsche's Will to Power walks down Adler's runaway notion of the
guiding principle as model (with "the insuring anxieties" dragging Nietzsche's Eternal Return of the Same, in the fine prints of their tread, to the
front of the line). By relying on Vaihinger's "philosophy of as if" as guide,
Adler can expand on Nietzsche's "will to seem" and underscore the ficti-
tiousness of the guiding goal (all the way to the Will to Power) (30). This
intertextual project is repeated or rehearsed within Adler's notion of mas-

culine protest, where, at the latest, a one-way or phallic sense is a given: the tendency to gain security is the same one that's out to conquer woman and, at its strongest, takes out the insurance policy of homosexuality (249).

"The sexual feature of the psychology of the neuroses which Freud looks upon as a cardinal point is in this wise explained as the effect of a fiction" (62). Instead, following Vaihinger as if Nietzsche, Adler sees neurosis, including neurotic sexual conduct, as craving for, and pursuit of, security or insurance. "I have discussed the reasons for the marked prominence of the sexual guiding principle in neurotics, first, because it, like all other guiding principles is considerably accentuated in the neurotic, and so to speak, felt as real instead of what it was intended for—namely, as a protective guiding line—and second because it (the sexual guiding principle) leads in the direction of the masculine protest" (158–59). Thus Freud's libido theory is just another fiction, one of the "bad sort" (69).

There is, then, a certain symptomatic correspondence between neurotic thinking and Freud's theory: "It is no wonder that in the psychoanalysis of these cases with the male-female manner of apperception which belongs to the foundation of the neurotic psyche, one hits only upon sexual relations" (293). But in Adler's view, "every perversion and inversion," indeed "all sexual relations in the neurosis are only a simile," "a symbol" (368 n. 2, 303). They reflect the guiding fiction's eternal negotiations for security, insurance, compensation, masculine protest, preparedness: "Repressed or conscious perverse tendencies . . . are . . . detours, . . . symbols of an imaginary plan of life whose purpose is self-assurance" (63).

"The 'recurrence of the same' (Nietzsche) is nowhere so well illustrated as in the neurotic" (17, translation modified). Even when the neurosis is in open competition with the influence of situations or events, Nietzsche leads Adler to see through the current event to the larger pattern of guiding fiction, compensation, and insurance. "The 'return of the same' (Nietzsche) leads to the belief that the patient must have had her part in the play since both times she helped herself out of the situation by a neurotic arrangement so as to break off at the same moment" (397, translation modified).

That's why the break in the place of a boundary concerns transference. "Freud's hypothesis of transference . . . is nothing more than an expedient of the patient who seeks to rob the physician of superiority" (225). It's true that intimate contact or anticipated contact is a catalyst, but what it releases is a "heightened tendency to gain reassurance" that "causes the outbreak of that which is ordinarily termed a neurosis or psychosis" (252). Thus the onset of a neurosis can also be "such symptoms as fear . . . of a test" (254) or of "danger of death" (28). And the neurosis then "continues in its construction of assurances" (258).

"The neurotic carries his feeling of inferiority constantly with him.... His fear of the new, of decisions and tests, which is usually present, originates from lack of analogy for these new conditions" (18). But the neurotic is also always just testing: "The insatiableness with which the neurotic tests his partner is an indication ... of his lack of self esteem" (380). "In the relation of the sexes there arises nearly always an obstinate and selfish feature, a tendency to put to test" (215). Thus "a premeditation and testing of difficulties carried on in accordance with the patient's own peculiar scheme" provides "a protective way for the ego-consciousness out of a situation which threatens a defeat" (148).

One of the ways to "seek security" is to make "preparations for security" (235). Adler unpacks the mode of catastrophe preparedness organizing one neurotic's "insurance" policy:

> Whenever he used an automobile, the thought that a collision might take place came to his mind.... Yes, even when he used the tram cars for an extended trip, the thought occurred to him, upon reaching the point where the cheap fare terminated and the more expensive one began, that a collision might take place, or that the bridge which had to be crossed might collapse, so that he would always pay the cheaper fare, save a few pennies and cover the rest of the distance on foot. (145–'6)

But beyond the ego-driven reading of the taxi meter of accident protection and compensation there's the generic neurotic preparedness, at once futural and visual, projecting a psychic-mediatic model of total conflict.

> The gaze of the neurotic ... is directed far into the future. All present existence is to him only a preparation. (21)

> But with neurotic strivings of "anticipatory thinking," attention approaches problems and arranges them in accordance with the neurotic's antithetical mode of apperception, which values a defeat as death, as inferiority, as effeminacy, and victory as immortality, higher values, masculine triumph, while the hundreds of other possibilities of life are annihilated by withdrawing them from attention. In the same manner the way is entered upon to the anticipation of future triumph and terror as well as an hallucinatory reinforcement for the sake of security. (389)

In our sort of neuropsychology one always gains the impression
that the visible neurotic conduct is directed straight to the final
purpose, to the fictitious goal, as if one were examining one of
the intermediary pictures in a cinematographic film. (232)

The ready position of "neurotic preparedness" (29), "neurotic preparedness to attacks" (361), or "anxiety preparedness" (233–34) requires (for lack
of any other analogy) an all-out mobilization of defense, "somewhat like
our modern states conducting war preparations without even knowing the
future enemy" (134).

The already existing preparedness for the symptom becomes
embodied in the web and woof of memory as an insuring agent
against the fear of being under-estimated or neglected.... The
whole army of neurotic symptoms ... may well be traced to
these ready-for-use psychic attitudes. (*The Neurotic Constitution*,
213)

A number of neurotically acquired adaptations and certain traits
of character assume prominence, so that the individual remains
in close touch with the enemy. (216)

A certain manifestation which one frequently observes in the
neurosis was likewise present here, and in an especially accentuated form, namely, the strong emphasis of a pedantic character
trait, which, not unlike the "crack regiment" in war time, took
over the task of coming in touch with the enemy. The enemy
was first of all the mother. (194)

The projective identification via the feminine (which goes back and
forth between Nietzsche or Freud and Spielrein, Anna O., or Dora) creates
an antagonist who observes pathology while exercising a transparent Will
to Power over that pathology in the name of a born-again truth, the one
called true love. But this adoration, which must find maxi protection against
the ambivalence that created it, collapses (down unresolved transferences)
onto the death drive. The group-formatted ambivalence of female sexuality
(in other words, Spielrein's transference love affair or her theorization of
the failures and betrayals that get downed with loyalty-or-identification
transferences) redeveloped the death wish and paid or paved the one way
to death drive. It was no accident that Spielrein packed a case of Nietzsche
into this introduction and thus at the same time contained him (the mascot
of her preemptive scoop of Freud's second system) in observable scenes
of therapeutic interventionism. The Eternal Return of insurance is at the

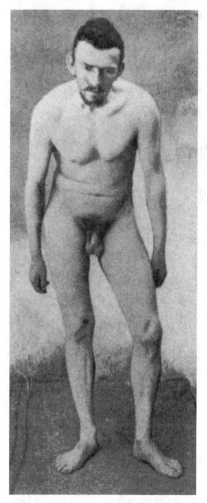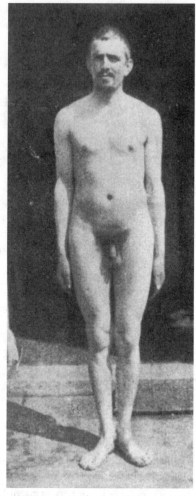

Before and after pictures of 29-year-old soldier suffering from war neurosis, successfully treated during World War I. The case was titled "Limping of the Hip-Disease Type and Forward Curvature of the Trunk, of a Year's Duration," and these photographs were accompanied by this description:

"Wounded by shell in the left flank and buried on 29th July 1915; loss of consciousness, embarrassment of respiration and mutism. Walked bent forwards and limping since 5th August 1915.

Several times in hospital and six months at the depot. Underlying mental deficiency. By one séance of electrical treatment the vicious posture of the trunk was corrected. Limping persisted and necessitated prolonged daily treatment by re-educative methods.

Discharged cured on 20th October 1916, without limp or curvature; slight lumbar pain persisted. Given sick-leave.

Left: Posture of patient on admission. Right: Eight days later, cured."

From G. Roussy and J. Lhermitte, *The Psychoneuroses of War*, 44. Images reproduced from top of plate 7, next to p. 44.

matricenter of group protection or projection. The insurance system promotes the rise (so what if it's, at first at least, only the equal opportunity) of women's involvement in observing. Mother is transformed into the (uncanny) measure of correct observation and intervention. In a letter to Freud dated 15 March 1916, Lou Andreas-Salomé fixes the focus on the camera inside a paranoid delusion analyzed by Freud: "Also in the case of the supposed camera, I am reminded of the mother's eye, which like God's eye 'sees everything,' which has always seen the child all alone, naked and stripped." Margaret Mahler's subsequent view of mothering as the unconscious of relations would fold out a military network complete with "refueling" stops all the way back to home base. But first psychoanalysis had to be diversified and reunified.

Lay analysis covered the interests of mother and the group, which were acted out after 1933 between the reunited psychotherapies and psychiatry over the prize of insurance coverage and, on the winning side, in Nietzsche's name. At the central institute of psychotherapy in Berlin, adjunct or lay psychotherapists were able to overcome global resistance to their inclusion. With their admission, an overall affirmative action balance between men and women throughout the institute was created.

The preponderance of women therapists in the Adlerian and Jungian groups was established already by the twenties. Notwithstanding the overt bias of the "masculine protest," Adler set himself up as defender of women's equal rights against Freud's unfair practice. (Freud had already argued, however, in "A Child Is Being Beaten," that the way Adler had lined it up, masculine protest could be successfully realized or overcome only by women.) The neurotic giveaway on Adler's checklist or questionnaire was the estimation of the opposite sex (i.e., of women): "It will become apparent that every stronger denial of the equality of the sexes, every detraction or overvaluation of the opposite sex is invariably connected with a neurotic disposition and neurotic traits. They are all dependent on the neurotic tendency to obtain security" (*The Neurotic Constitution*, 263).

On pp. 166–71 of *The Psychoneuroses of War*, the use of electricity or faradization, for example, is explained as highly suggestive and thus as the best support, in the short term, for the psychotherapy conducted with the isolated patient. "When the case has been diagnosed, one tries to explain to the patient the nature of the disorder from which he is suffering or believes himself to be suffering (the result of a mental or physical shock, fear, fatigue, etc.), to show him how it has arisen, to reassure him as to its gravity, and lastly to promise him a cure" (166). Reprinted by permission of Masson et Cie.

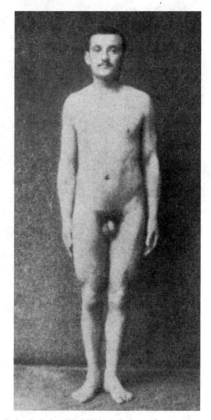

Before and after pictures of soldier afflicted with shell shock during World War I. Before: "Contracture of the right knee of eighteen months' duration." After: "The same patient cured after one séance of treatment." Reproduced from the top of plate 8, between pp. 54 and 55, in *The Psychoneuroses of War.* Reprinted by permission of Masson et Cie.

In essays scattered across the extent of his independent career, Adler came out big time on the side of equal rights for women. The other side of the same agenda was his cure-all for homosexuality, which he also promoted. "In times when women step more vigorously into the foreground of public life, a large number of men prefer to increase the distance from the female sex and resort among other safeguards also to homosexuality" (*Cooperation*, 155). Indeed: "Every sexual deviation is the expression of an increased psychological distance between man and woman" (159). That's the way it was in ancient Greece, says Adler. Women, who were on the rise, deprivileged and insecurized men, who had two optional coverages to choose from: either depreciation or idealization of women. The homosexual trend was set. But even if Greek pedophilia prepared the boy for the package deal of heterosexuality-cum-comradeship, still Adler finds this approach as incorrect as the one masturbation represents (157–58). (That's right: Adler's community spirit didn't approve of the for-him-related diversions of homosexuality and masturbation. As Freud saw it in "On the History of the Psychoanalytic Movement," it was because Adler was so freaked by sexuality that he promoted aggression over love.) Thus Adler baits the master as pro-homosexual. "Why must people take an actually hostile attitude toward homosexuality," Adler rhetorico-strategically asks. "Freud and his followers are satisfied with the answer: because they have repressed their own homosexuality or have sublimated it." But Adler then counters: "This explanation is not only improbable, it also can certainly not be verified. It is derived not from facts but from psychoanalytic theory" (149–50). Adler's faith in everyone coming out to be cured gave the upbeat to Nazi psychotherapy's sympathies with all-out healing:

> We expect from the future first of all a more correct attitude toward this problem, a voluntary decision of the offender to be treated. (150)

> Cure and improvement are possible through psychotherapy. (167)

> As for many other ailments, so also for the neurosis of homosexuality, treatment should be mandatory. (170)

Adler doesn't want to criminalize homosexuals; he just wants to reintroduce them into the community through consensual treatment, a laying down of neurotic arms and the canceling of neurotic insurances, but not the laying down of arms or the cancellation of coverage. It's still lay analysis. The ex-homosexual, who had come under Adler's treatment and was in the meantime an impotent heterosexual, talks to Adler about the current war: "He had at once registered as a volunteer. But the closer the date of his call approached, the greater his fear became and the desire to get out of it. From this attitude, I could easily guess the present phase of his sexual development" (230). The extraneousness or curability of homosexuality is the camouflage its centrality to the military-insurance complex assumes, a complex that outdoes the Oedipus one in universality, in coextensivity with everything else. In the policy fine print to *The Neurotic Constitution*, it was already granted that militarization participated in the kind of acceleration of norms that characterizes neurosis (with homosexuality, that umbrella policy of neurotic insurance, opening and shutting on the safeguards against women, at the front of the line):

> For the benefit of psychologists of a keener insight, I note here the prevalence of examples which have been taken from military

life have been chosen by me with an especial object in view. In military training the starting point and fictive purpose are brought into closer relation, can be more readily noted, and every movement of the training soldier becomes a dexterity which has for its purpose the transformation of a primary feeling of weakness into a feeling of superiority. (77 n. 6)

In *The Problem of Homosexuality* Adler drops into the ditch of a footnote a connection that announces homosexuality to be to neurosis what desertion or flight is to war. "In the first edition of this study, which appeared during the World War, I noted at this point that the increasing understanding of war neurosis had strikingly shown the validity of the Individual Psychology view" (*Cooperation*, 161 n. 11). In this applied-Nietzschean or psychotherapeutic view, equality of (or, same difference, war between) the sexes is the policy of group protection; it shifts the couple outside the personalizable policies of neurotic insurance into the global zones of war and diplomacy. The danger of sameness (and thus of bilateral violence or suicide), which a vote for the community at the same time brings into closer range, is embodied (in this context of emancipation) as homosexuality. So that the mobilization of defenses can proceed along the lines of equal coverage, homosexuality must not so much be defended against as "transcended" (as the SS prescribed for the Wehrmacht) (Cocks, 206).

Policy

In theory, insurance covers funeral arrangements; in practice its coverage extends via catastrophes and wartime mobilization. When Pascal was commissioned around 1654 to figure out the chances of a certain number recurring at roulette, he at the same time introduced the notion of calculable risk, which became the basis of modern insurance (and of the new and improved self-other bond or group psychology that insurance also applies). Thus it was gambling, the first of the modern causes or explanations of out-of-control group behavior, that promoted, in its calculation as risk, the modern mass formations of catastrophe preparedness. Wherever Freud's second system can be located for certain, the first one isn't far behind. One of the first applications of Pascal's symptomatic or side effect discovery was the calculation of life expectancy (in 1671, for example, Johan De Wit applied the theory of probability to the value of a life annuity). Indeed, primally speaking, life insurance began with the burial clubs of Rome, into which the members paid down payments and fixed monthly fees to guarantee the funding for their proper funerals. "That club members did not always intend these entire funds to be used for burial purposes is clearly evidenced by Roman rulings which forbade men from joining more than one burial society at a time" (Maclean, 5).

But with risk calculation, insurance shifted from speculation on down payments to coverage of risk in the mass format of catastrophe survival. By the end of the seventeenth century, marine underwriting and fire insurance were available. In 1683 the "Friendly Society" was the world's first mutual fire insurance association. By the end of the nineteenth century (with railway passenger insurance and workers' compensation already in place), the insured bond with the other via risk had grown a group psychology that displaced class interests.

The move in the United States to set up compulsory health insurance, which began revving up in 1912, lost its momentum by the time it extended into World War I, all the way into the U.S. war effort. At that point, as Roland Numbers documents, Germany was targeted as psychologically programming the world to accept its Kultur through the spread of its insurance system. The reception of society-wide insurance (in other words, the German brand of group psychology) was staggered within the shifting takes on propaganda and war psychology, in which now the Entente and the Allies, now the Germans, took the lead.

In 1935 Charles Baudouin's contribution to the central journal of Nazi psychotherapy was an analysis of risk that psychologized calculations that began with Pascal. Baudouin opens by conjugating risk through Jung, Adler, Freud, and Rank as follows (and respectively): introversion, inferiority, castration, birth trauma. The risk of mutilation was controlled through the invention of consensual mutilation (in other words: sacrifice). Thus the risk with which, Baudouin argues, every action comes complete must be managed over and again: a veritable "action drive" is matched on the other side by a sacrifice drive (which permits or controls the risks you end up wanting to take). This drives the notions of risk and security into interchangeable places. A couple is formed (that of risk and security) that leaves us with the one alternative to alternation "between loss of will power and the frenetic course headed towards catastrophes" (113). Baudouin thus gives a strict metapsychological accounting of the insurance effect or impulse on a society-wide scale of the psychic balance still to be paid.

In 1939 Matthias Göring, an Adlerian by training, explored the insecurity complex prompting the neurotic to split present tense and tension for insurance coverage or catastrophe preparedness in an article entitled "The Significance of Neurosis in Social Insurance." Göring had already appointed psychoanalyst Gerhart Scheunert as head of the outpatient clinic; they both agreed that short-term therapy would be most effective, particularly in solving the time-is-money problems that had kept psychotherapy outside the state health insurance system. The neurotic tends to live in the futural mode of preparedness only; he must be confronted with the quick results of short-term therapy, which lock him into a short attention span as "if" he thus inhabited the present.

In the positive reception of psychoanalysis as in outright resistance to Freud's science, phases and phrases of *Versicherung* (insurance) or *Sicherung* (security, safety catch, fuse, or, in English translations of Adler, even insurance) are sparked by the about-face in the status of traumatic neurosis, which before the world war was exhibit A in the defense against Freud's charge of the sexual etiology of neurosis but by 1919 became the cornerstone of the interdisciplinary foundation of Freud's unstoppable influence. The common cynical linking of so-called traumatic neurosis to the subvention benefits obtainable through insurance or pension was in turn psychologized to model an internal structure or motor running neurosis. The discourse of insurance and the discourse of nerves thus came to occupy interchangeable places. Wartime testimony from an insurance professional with an informed knowledge of psychoanalysis (which bears the extra weight of coming from the author of the world war fiction "In the Penal Colony") documents the crossover discourse of nerves from the other side of the insurance complex:

> The world war, which contains the accumulation of all human misery, is also a war of nerves, more a war of nerves than any earlier war ever was. Too many have already fallen victim to this nerve war. Just as in peacetime over the last decades the intensive activity of machines has endangered, disturbed, and sickened the nerves of workers, so the increased machinic aspect of current war operations has introduced the most severe dangers for and afflictions of the nerves of the combatants.... The nervous trembler and jumper in the streets of our cities is just a relatively harmless delegate of a monstrous mass of sufferers. (Kafka, *Amtliche Schriften*, 295)

Before the onset of war-neurotic symptomatization of the unconscious significance of insurance, philosopher Josiah Royce, from the other other side, sought, right at the onset of war over there, to raise to consciousness the insurance coverage that is uniform in the military formation as a mutual form of violence control at the art of war. In California at the start of World War I, Royce proposed international mutual insurance coverage among nations as setting a limit to total war. (Royce conceived the plan as an extension of workers' compensation, which was Germany's contribution to the history of insurance.)

"Modern wars may, as we now know, become more widespread, more democratic in spirit, more ideally self-righteous, than ever they were before" (Royce, 10). But first things first: there are "positive virtues" backing the militant spirit that cannot be reduced to a hatred exclusive. War's appeal is its appeal to nonimmediate, noncouplified others or authorities. The relation to immediate neighbors is covered by hate. But the relation to honor, to one's own country, but also ultimately to humanity, is what puts war on the side of "fearless faith in life" (19). The danger grows in the more immediate relationships, in the one on one: "A pair of men is what I may call an essentially dangerous community" (30). When one neighbor says to another (out of love for his fellowman and for his own voice), "Listen! Don't interrupt. I've got something to say to you," that's the start of war. "A certain social tension is therefore a perfectly natural accompaniment of any concrete social relation between two people" (31).

> We hate not merely because we remember injuries. Many of our sources of antipathy seem to be, in the single case, much more petty than is a desire for revenge; but are actually deeper in their

meaning than is such a desire. Very often we tend to hate simply because there are so many of us, and because we are so different one from the other; and so because, when we are taken in pairs, we thus appear in each pair as interrupters and intruders, each member of the pair annoying his fellow even while trying to express whatever love he chances to possess for the other, and each emphasizing his own hatred when he feels it, by dwelling on these dual or bilateral contrasts. (38)

Family ties and other bonds of solidarity or loyalty (such as the ones recycled in war) are readily available alternatives to the violence of the couple. "Love, when it is a merely dyadic relation between a pair of lovers, is essentially unstable and inconstant. For the two tend in the long run to interrupt, to bore, or collide each with the other" (35). "In those communities which are mere pairs, time is the consumer of love but the nourisher of hate" (41). To counter couplified conflict, Royce introduces the third person (excluded from the couple through peer pressurization, ongoing groupification, invasion by the group's one on one of mutual identification). There are a few social and commercial institutions still around that promote triadic relations. Insurance, which tends to take the form of mutual insurance, promotes formation or coverage of larger social units: "It tends, in the long run, to carry us beyond the era of the agent and of the broker into the coming social order of the insurer" (64). This new world order of insurance will keep wars "progressively less destructive and less willful" (66).

In World War I the U.S. selective service act ruled that acceptance for service guarantees that the soldier upon entry was physically and mentally sound. If a disability nevertheless emerged, then the soldier became beneficiary of what was later called the United States Veterans Bureau, but which started out under the name of Bureau of War Risk Insurance.

Theodor Adorno, the first philosopher to admit psychoanalysis as the force that will be with you when you're thinking, gives a reading of the group psychology of Nazi Germany that borrows Simmel's bottom lines about the control-release relationship of war neurosis to psychosis. According to Adorno, the psychotic delusions that were everyone's collective share in the Third Reich kept many individuals from going, one by one, psychotic. Adorno modeled his view of the split-level distribution of the psychopathology continuum on Simmel's 1919 work on war traumatization. We saw the relationship of *Sicherung* between war neurosis and war psychosis pull up a continuum or continuity between war and "insurance" (or "safeguard," "security," "safety catch") that fit squarely within the psychologization of warfare. War readiness was Adler's favorite "analogy" (in other words, model) for the constitution of neurosis; *Sicherung* was Adler's key term for the pathogenic fantasy, desire, and repressive mechanism free-ranging from neurosis to psychosis. Simmel: "The war neuroses are in essence switched-on *Sicherungen* which aim to protect the soldier against psychosis. Whoever has mustered such a large patient population for a year and a half with analytic focus, must come to the realization that the relatively small number of war psychoses is only to be explained through the relatively large number of war neuroses" ("Zweites Korreferat," 45).

While the German insurance policy thinkers cannot but reside within the ambiguity of *Sicherung*, H. D. Lasswell, a U.S. first-generation psychoanalytic sociologist, picks up on the security (and insecurity) shaping policy, bottom line, in the new discourse (made in Germany) of psychological warfare. In the background of "The Psychology of Hitlerism," Lasswell addresses a context or contest among interest groups and individual members of a newly extended class of professionals, which already the invention of modern propaganda, for example, right away doubled in size. Lasswell thus introduces National Socialism into the setting of the discourse through which he is given to read, locate, or project it. Although he ultimately has too easy a time reinventing history or coming up with new historical subjects, Lasswell gives endopsychic proof in his reading (by the fact of his reading), and if we keep the displacement to one side, of the discursive kinds of networking that are the haunt of "Hitlerism."

> In some measure the use of the Jewish scapegoat is an incident in the struggle for survival within the intellectual class.... Postwar Germany abolished many limitations upon university training, and German universities pumped an increasing volume of trained talent into an overstocked market.... The growing complexity of modern civilization has created a vast net of reporters, interpreters, pedagogues, advertisers, agitators, propagandists, legal dialecticians, historians and social scientists who compete among themselves and with all other classes and sub-classes for deference, safety and material income.... The tremendous growth of symbol specialists in The Great Society suggests that we have to do with the emergence of a potent social formation with objective interests of its own, some of which can be fostered, paradoxically enough, by encouraging symbolic warfare among its members. (376–77)

Less professionally, it seems, or really just more profoundly inside one of the main coordinates giving us a new mass specialization in symbols, Lasswell evokes the bloodsucker projections that, complete with blinders and one-way focus, went after Jews in lieu of capitalists, and vampires in their own stead (375). A maternal channel (with, perhaps, mainly son subscribers) resonates with the cry that the blood of the dead soldiers "shall not have been shed in vain," but will flow back, feedback style, in, through the veins of the savior: "There is a profound sense in which Hitler himself plays a maternal role for certain classes in German society" (379). In his 1935 *World Politics and Personal Insecurity,* Lasswell globalized the Hitler effect for his book-length appraisal of the insurance drive, one that resonates with the backfire of World War I. In the essay on Hitlerism two years earlier, he had found the politics of projection internal to his own field, which had reproduced itself in National Socialism as its own, inside, side effect. But what is called politics was also seen to be most political when it took the form of therapy, a support-grouping around the suicide we defend against and control release. In 1935 his inoculative perspective opens worldwide: "The flight into action is preferable to the torments of insecurity. The flight into danger becomes an insecurity to end insecurity. The demand for security takes the foreground" (75). The balancing act Lasswell has in mind in the alternation between security and insecurity extends from the level of reserves and resources to emotional states and demands. The world war represented an insecurity crisis among parties believing themselves to be "substantially equal in resources"; what had to follow was "the balancing process where the expectation of violence prevails" (80).

> The analytic basis has already been laid for considering the insecurity crisis as a delayed reaction to the changes which modify the fighting effectiveness of various participants. The uncertainties connected with the balancing process generate the emotional insecurities which culminate in the overwhelming demand for security. (80)

DSM3Rd Reich

The divisions and doublings (and double crossings) that we have visited inside and around psychoanalysis beginning already before World War I were following the trajectories of new and improved directions, no turning back. But these trajectories also showed the way to eclecticism, which doubled them back onto psychoanalysis under the peer-pressurized command that in a Great War soldiers with incapacitating neurotic-to-psychotic symptoms get a quicker fix. As eclecticism, however, the difference between Freud and Adler, for example, became conceivable as difference within psychoanalysis, back home, home on the wider range of greater psychoanalysis. Eclecticism mixed and matched different methodologies, or rather their part objects and objectives (and not, not any longer, all those part objections) within "depth psychology," code word for greater psychoanalysis. The road to eclecticism is also the way toward reunification or synthesis. But in each case of a united front in the German establishment of depth psychology there is also a distinct quirk that symptomatizes the on-location task until it all takes on an independent, even overriding, existence. In this regard, consider the case of Fritz Künkel. His task in hand was to give Jung in the more perfect union the upper and. "The point of view of Jung needed to be changed least" (xi). That can also mean that this POV is not metabolized in the blend. First it is not enough to claim it, but then this claim takes up a life of its own that drives the corpus. What sets Künkel's blended theory apart is the leap of faith we all require in concluding with Jung.

The next-best place to start is at a point of crossover between languages and from the specialized discipline to the mainstream of self-help manuals. According to the author's inscription, "For Dorothy and Henry," Künkel composed the dedicated book as "'Practical Psychotherapy' written for doctors, 1935." In 1936 it bears the title *Conquer Yourself: The Way to Self-Confidence*. The book announces on an opening page the existing English-language titles "by the same author": *Let's Be Normal* and *God Helps Those* . . .

According to Künkel, in everyday life there is a lot of psychotherapy to go around that must only be raised to consciousness. Every physician, social worker, educator, and parent "must practice psychotherapy, whether he wants to or not. For if he happens upon an unconscious resistance, which is opposed to his treatment, all his efforts and skill are in vain." In their consultations and family visits, every physician and social worker, in particular, must practice "minor psychotherapy" (which has to hand the "severe cases of neuroses and hysterias" to the majors). "Like minor surgery, so minor psychotherapy is part of the daily bread of general medical practice" (ix).

Künkel's minor goal is therefore to compose an easily understandable psychotherapy handbook for nonspecialist consumption (which by referral serves "major psychotherapy," too). The polemical field of differences between competing brands of depth psychology maintains an unbreachable specialization of difficulties. "The names of Freud, Adler, Jung still have the effect of a war cry." But because fundamental attitudes to life underlie these war cries (a giveaway Adlerian approach to the establishment of community and communication), Künkel proposes getting rid of the attitude and getting what counts across to the relay of figures of authority who need to know all the psychotherapy that fits the formulation of an "exact diagnosis" and "proper directions" (viii).

The change in attitude is given a laugh track of conviviality in passing through the example of

> "shock syndrome," a group of symptoms occasioned by a shock. A mental stupor, verging on silliness (similar to that occurring in severe cases of hysteria), or else a catatonia with a complete mental and motor obstruction suddenly sets in as the result of an accident or natural catastrophe. These phenomena are observed quite frequently after a bombardment at the front or after mine disasters and great conflagrations. Usually they pass over without permanent results. In such cases, as in other psychoses, the psychotherapy can only administer to the comfort of the patient and wait. His real work begins when the opportunity presents itself to help the patient to a clear understanding of the disease through which he has passed and to free him from any fear of a relapse. (138–39)

War shock gets the passing-over nod of therapeutic closure and assurance while advancing in psychopathology to the status of psychosis. Even psychopathology gets a historical chance for a change. Although certain "dramatic scenes" and related symptom pictures once associated with "classic hysteria" have all but disappeared, it is not the case that the population of hysterics has decreased. "The methods used by patients have merely changed somewhat—apparently because popular tastes have changed. Complicated intrigues, insidious physical ailments, hatred, scorn and sullenness have taken the place of sensational blindness, muteness and other paralysis" (107).

It is time to overcome Freud's materialism and Adler's rationalism (or idealism). It's also time to remember that Nietzsche is our pioneer of depth psychology. Here Freud is credited with serving as "pathfinder who first made practical application of the depth-psychological interpretation." This credit, which in being given assumes a debt, lets something slip in the English: "But Sigmund Freud was doubtedly the pathfinder" (142). Undoubtedly Freud is admitted on the transference beam Künkel will not remove from the I of the patient. He thus breaks ranks with Adlerian dismissal of transference when he reformulates in Adlerian terms what he, for one, has to admit as so basic that we basically owe its discovery to Freud. Transference, both negative and positive, is a neurotic habit, one of the "'rules of the game,' as Adler calls them," whereby the patient, "afraid of dangers," strives for "complete security above all things" (182). "Here not only the experience of the infraction of the 'we' is transferred upon the treatment as an anticipated danger, but the securities are also applied which developed later as protection against such catastrophes. This is the 'negative transference'" (184). In submitting to the doctor, as in openly struggling against him, the patient tries to be in control of the therapeutic relationship. "Toward him the patient assumes a similar double role as Faust toward Mephistopheles" (183). But the therapist must take control: "The control of the transference, a timely recognition of it and its thorough elimination, constitutes an essential part of the psychotherapeutic task" (184). If this task is relinquished, the patient's life will go on—ex-static-cling—in a "pseudo-original-we" form or forum that can be held only in production with new symptoms. The formation in the therapeutic relationship of a "maturing we" is the site set for the successful conclusion of depth-psychological treatment. But you can't start out there. "Adler's way consists in the frank consultation between equals. . . . But the deeper connections and especially the transference, which is theoretically denied by individual-psychologists, often produce very disagreeable attendant results" (165). The understanding of transference as habit tagged for elimination, however, precisely sets limits to interminable analysis, in which "continued treatment itself has turned into a neurosis. The patient no longer is suffering from headaches or insomnia, but from 'analysitis.'—Pseudo-cures of this sort must be interpreted as serious professional errors" (181).

What also rises to consciousness in Künkel's manual is the institution of reception and of received ideas: "Wherever possible the familiar theories of older investigators are described, but with the changes that were necessary for the sake of unification" (xii). One way Künkel goes about forming his trinity (which according to the right of last say, which by rights goes

even to the synthesizer, gives rise to his own theory, that of "dialectic characterology" [xi]) is by staggering each method, beginning with Freud and
ending with Jung, as "consecutive stages of a unified comprehensive treatment, in accordance with those many therapists who are bound to no definite schools, and in agreement with the latest researches in this field" (xii–
xiii). In the larger setting of polymorphously or practically eclectic therapy,
depth psychology holds down the fort of recognizable positions. Thus in
Künkel's example of therapy and theory of compulsion neurosis, our first
orientation is Freudian or causal: "One must conclude, as Freud did, that
the compulsion symptom presupposes the repression of a desire and that
the symptom itself must be understood as a return of the repression in a
distorted form" (117). But one must proceed from consideration of cause to
consideration of the effect by asking oneself the Adlerian question "What's
the purpose?" (118). The question raises the treatment above preoccupation
with suppressed eroticism to address instead the suppression of freedom,
vitality, and life (120). It's about the we, not the little we-we. "If all neurotic
symptoms are in the last analysis direct or indirect results of the original
fear of life, then the cure must consist in the elimination of this fear. Therefore the task of the psychotherapist consists in developing courage, confidence, and an inner security. . . . In this way the after-effects of the original
fear, the exaggerated provisions for security and the heightened distrust,
which lies at the basis of these symptoms, are to be made thoroughly su-
perfluous" (168–69). By putting purpose where cause was, Adler gave a
better understanding of nervous symptoms: "Fear especially and anticipation of future dangers (on the basis of previous unfortunate experiences)
became more intelligible. 'Anticipation,' 'tendential apperception,' 'inferiority complex' are concepts that psychotherapy can no longer forgo" (145).
In the Adlerian phase of therapy, phrases are earmarked to show the patient
(and the reader) that he cannot be rid of his disagreeable symptoms "without a change in his fundamental attitude against life" (177).

The force that is with Adler is "popular sound sense" that "has always
rebelled against the psychoanalysis of Freud, not only because he tries to
make sex the predominant force in life, but primarily because he made all
psychic life appear mechanized and built up of impersonal energies" (144).
But first Künkel gave to the utility of the concept of resistance what was
due to Freud. Next Künkel must part company with Adler, that is, make
him part of a company in which Jung figures as boss. Although Adler pro-
gressed beyond Freud's limits to a "view of the whole," the location of the
hole in one was still too individualistic (145). What exactly is the personal

relation of part to whole? According to Jung, the person "is the whole and everything else parts of him" (148). Many of the instances of Jung's improvement, say, over Freud, take the form of desexualizing and uncanny-proofing the discourse of interpretation. For example, whereas Freudians speak of "a desire for the 'return to the womb,'" "the school of Jung shows a deeper understanding by speaking of a desire for submersion in the 'undivided unity' which lies at the basis of all life" (73–74). Thanks, school of Jung, for that demo of the yawning abyss.

The final Jungian stage in the triadic approach to compulsion neurosis is a leap of faith superseding all therapeutic stages: "A compulsion neurotic is in the serious situation that he must either remain incurable or get to be truly religious" (125). He hits bottom by establishing contact with the collective unconscious. In less difficult cases, the higher-power approach serves as adjunct to the Adlerian reeducation of the we generation: "Only slowly and very gradually will he arrive at the conviction that comparisons and the whole matter of evaluating is merely being misused as a security against the vital life. He must not only be told, but it must be proved to him by his own attitude, that the question of the value of a person can never be answered excepting provisionally and within a very limited field.... Somewhere every person fails.... The religious conviction of the insufficiency of all men here proves to be a therapeutic remedy of the highest order" (173). First find self, then the "we," and finally God (252).

Before Künkel tells the compulsion neurotic to find God, the one extended case study example he gives, that of a woman who can't stop washing herself, indicates that he still has a Freudian grasp of his patients. The washing represents and represses an illicit preoccupation with her own body. "Therefore the activity is really forbidden and, if she does it in spite of that, she can do it only in the form of an act for which she does not feel responsible. Therefore she does not say: I want to wash, but I must do it. On the other hand, the washing signifies the purging away of a defilement which is caused by the very washing itself. The more one washes oneself, the more one is indulging a forbidden pleasure. The greater the sin contracted, the greater the need for cleansing and consequently the greater the compulsion to sin." Then he restates the spot she is in, but on the upbeat and as though it were the third-position alternate interpretation (which accordingly begins with the big "but" of resistance). "But in the third place, the tortuous labor of washing also has the significance of penance, of the submission to punishment, and consequently an attempt at atonement" (123). The p-unitive intricacies and combos folding in and out of such a severe case of compulsion defy treatment. "A fully developed compulsion neurosis can be cured only if in place of it a very deep and very religious experience develops" (125).

Jung is able to have it every which way because he joins the opposition. Jung already constructed the "discoveries of both Freud and Adler" "into a unified picture" based on his own "fundamental idea that life is always built up of equally valid opposites" (146). The collective unconscious, which is Freud's unconscious only with an ancestral spin, is the oppositional setting for the psychic balancing act beyond neurotic conflict (which is always one-sided). "A neurosis represents the over-development of one conscious psychic function while the one of the opposite pole unconsciously degenerates" (146).

The good therapist must fulfill three preconditions:

> He must have gotten rid, in the individual-psychological sense, of his sensitiveness and irritability (which is present in every human being) to such an extent that he no longer hesitates to admit his errors, limits and mistakes even to his patients. His repressions and his inabilities to experience must be freed, in a psychoanalytical sense, until he has learned to feel directly, if he was a thinker, and has mastered valid thinking, if he was an emotional person. In the third place, the depth of his inner life must not only be revealed down to the strata of the collective unconsciousness, but must also be put into action—otherwise he will not be able to do justice to the distress of his patients. (275)

The good therapist is the guarantor of the spread of an accessible psychotherapy that is still in for the skill (the interventions of major therapy are as "serious as surgical operations" [164]). "Only thus will we succeed beyond the variety of present contending schools to a unified psychotherapy" (276).

The good therapist is Künkel who, describing himself in the third person, "has proceeded from the researches of Alfred Adler."

> His "dialectical characterology," tries to establish the theory of what C. G. Jung had already begun in practice, namely a significant unification of the deterministic views of Freud and the indeterministic views of Adler. According to him the only conceptual formula in which causality and finality can be consistently united is the dialectic.... Man is determined in so far as he is object, and at the same time he is free and consequently responsible as well in so far as he is subject. In steadily recurring crises he must maintain his freedom against his persistent danger; the hardening into an object. Neurosis is a special degree of harden-

ing, halfway between health and psychosis. But the subject that
conquers the neurosis is no longer a separate individual, but a
"we." The concept "we," which divides dialectically into the original "we" of childhood and of primitive people and into the maturing "we" of the cultured, also makes possible a more significant interpretation of Adler's idea of the community and a further
development of Jung's collective unconsciousness. (150–51)

I guess it's dialectical that Aryan psychotherapy gravitated toward Marxist
psychotherapists, not only Adler but even Wilhelm Reich (whose hard sell
goes totally without attribution). The dissociation from the politics and
ethnicity of both therapy founders doubtlessly splits the psychic receiving
area of their ideas, too.

Jung's politics didn't need to be washed down the brain drain. "In the
course of his researches Jung pointed out that the collective unconsciousness must vary with different races. It actually seems that the investigation
of collective unconsciousness . . . is the only means toward an understanding of ethnological characterology by way of depth psychology" (36). The
most fundamental archetype according to Künkel, who thus gets back to
his share, "is the picture of the group or the 'we' which produces its effect
within the individual in the form of longing, expectation or demand. This
'we,' in the form of a religious wish-picture, may lead to the founding of a
sect, as a political program it may change the world, it may lead some people to sacrifice themselves almost joyously; but it may also degenerate in
time and be distorted to an egotistical desire for help" (36–37). In time, in
our modern time, this wish picture, which insofar "as it belongs to the collective unconsciousness . . . is not yet spoiled or degenerated," is often frac-
tured at first contact, namely, with the mother, whose persona is bound to
be found wanting under "modern" conditions (38). Here the original fear
("the origin and the nucleus of all aberrations of character") is most likely
"still healthy. It is the experience of the curtailment and limitation of life accompanied by an increase of alertness and mobility" (57). In the aberrant
mode, fear "means the fear of the repetition of the infraction of the 'we'"
(63)—the faulty first contact with Mother. Therapy must break the vicious
circle, for example in cases of drug addiction. "But it cannot be broken unless the 'minus of disease,' against which the patient is now struggling, is
reduced to the 'minus of childhood' from which he originally escaped into
indulgence. Not until he learns to overcome the original minus and learns
to shoulder it will he be really cured" (95). In other words (fighting words),
"the original distress and anxiety, which is to be avoided at all costs, is not
only hidden beneath a striving for enjoyment and autointoxication, but it is

covered over again by a new distress and anxiety against which one now consciously goes to war" (94).

On the plus side, Künkel's big minus, the necessary inclusion and top billing of Jung in his therapy medley, becomes his guiding light postwar. *In Search of Maturity*, which first appeared with Charles Scribner's Sons, New York, was published in 1962 in German as *Ringen um Reife*. Its agenda is billed as a new "religious psychology" based on "we psychology" and embracing "religious life and the life of the unconscious" (vii–viii). "There are undeveloped, primitive tendencies in the unconscious of every individual (tendencies that contribute to the release of wars, revolutions, passions, crimes, neuroses and madness). It is only possible to approach and influence them to a significant degree when we have the insight and courage of the religious life. The need is so great, as the reader will see, that we gladly accept the charge of being mystics" (viii). Künkel has added to his precursor list religious thinkers such as Reinhold Niebuhr. But on the psychotherapy side, he maintains the same old trinity (in the dialectical order of his 1935 reflections). And as was also always the case, whenever the case material becomes hands on, and Künkel must formulate his application at once therapeutically and theoretically, it is apparent that he learned most from Freud, even in the course of his Adlerian resistance and return to Freud. In fact only Freud is cited beyond the 1962 book's opening ceremony. And yet Künkel continues to keep company with Jung (or God), whose inclusion heads him off at the impasse where, taken on faith, as faith, it also gives the only way to write it all up against the wall of untreatability. In *Conquer Yourself* the author described such a (technically neurotic) balancing act as running like a machine that is precisely not on the fritz: "One must understand clearly that a neurosis always has its reasons; that its construction may be compared to a costly equipment; and that the patient, because of a habit of many years, has been bound to a bad but nevertheless very familiar equilibrium which has developed within him between accomplishment (respectively failure), peace (respectively restlessness), adjustment to his fellow men, interpretation of life, physical health, etc." (175). Künkel (like Adler according to Freud in 1914) wanted his place in the sun. But to cut into the trio a piece of his own action, he ended up with "Peace Within and Without" (the title of the *Conquer Yourself* chapter dedicated to Jung's method), a place not of a son but, religiously, delusionally, of faith (in oneself) with God the Father on one's side.

Shot Shocks

That was European: German and Jewish.

—HANNS HEINZ EWERS, *VAMPIR*

Analytic engagement with war neurosis began, just for the public record, with the collection of essays that Freud introduced and cosigned. But even this close circle of followers working in the new war neurosis field was styling with eclecticization and improvisation. In large part this diversity began with the inclusion of Simmel, a recent convert to analysis while under pressure to treat shell shock victims. But even if Simmel seems to give analysis only short-term attention, his acceptance by the inner circle yielded PR returns down the corridors of treatment. In the sections that follow from this closed circuit of insiders, through the more distant relations (including those on the other side of the world war), all the way to the resisters who on second thought sure looked like they had accepted what they took to be analytic perspectives, which they otherwise more often than not dismissed or at least reinvented on their own terms, it's important to feel the symptom pressure build and witness the emergency of the symptom of Freud's unstoppable influence. In what follows, all the shocking conditionings of the opening wide of worldwide paths of least resistance to psychoanalysis must once again stand to our attention.

In his contribution to the psychoanalytic war neurosis effort, Simmel opens the new world-war lab space of human subjects available for study under conditions of mass treatment to "the comparative study of the different so-called psychotherapeutic methods" ("Zweites Korreferat," 42). Analysis, for one, shows "that the bodily symptoms are in their mute expression struggling to give evidence of the personality-destroying elements, which are imprisoned and buried in the unconscious" (46). In 1918 Simmel had already published a substantial monograph on his eclectic but analysis-based hypnotic treatment of war neurosis. By the end of his wartime crossover to psychoanalysis, Simmel situated war neurotics between the two extremes and norms of healthy egoism: the superhero and the shirking violet (31). In between or on "the reverse side of the medal," the war neurotic splits into illness. Split means predisposition, means more recording surface for bad impressions, which get stored on both sides "like on a gramophone record" (13).

The media war neurosis that Simmel analyzes is on location in the subconscious, which he sets apart from the rest of the unconscious as the receiving area for the "feeling complex" that the ego represses or secures as a condemned site harboring unpleasurable and indigestible feelings (12). Déjà vu is Simmel's everyday example of this subconscious service. The feeling that we were there (but when?) is an impression that was received from the external world by the subconscious at a time when the intellect was otherwise occupied on behalf of the ego complex and had no time to make a report. But the impression was nevertheless received and held fast as on a gramophone recording. Only an association was needed, which then, like a needle reading down along the impression, let it resound (13).

Everyone does splits into audio and video tracks on which affect finds release. Somnambulism, which turns you into a medium, is a transitional form or forum in which stronger feeling complexes use the dropping of personality in sleep to achieve motoric release and enactment (15). In one video example, Simmel borders on the original story of *The Cabinet of Dr. Caligari* (written by two world war neurotics). A soldier dreams of injustice and insubordination and, following a transitional phase of sleepwalking, tells his barracks neighbor all about it: the good listener then develops a war neurosis (34). In analysis, the association network has the tracks covered. The narrative that association lets roll opens the subconscious and issues the repress release. But under rapid fire, hypnosis must be used as the direct hit or fit that skips the circuitous routes of the association method.

Often the treatment of war neurosis must aim in the short term at enabling the neurotic to benefit from the one year of sick leave he has coming to him. The war neurotic is no hero, but he is also not a malingerer, deserter, or coward. He falls short of the healthy choices. Instead "he 'flees' — to use a Freudian term from 'peace neurosis'—into his illness" (31). The war had caught the world up with Freud's peacetime terms.

When the symptom relief of hypnosis has left the soldier seeming like a mechanically run doll, then the net of association must be cast wide. In any event, the hypno-cured patient soon develops yet other physical symptoms. Only psychoanalysis can answer, given time, the question why this one goes neurotic and his comrade in arms does not. The neurosis sticks to a person who is stuck—and all the rest is "grafted" onto this stick figure (56). For example: the death of a child on the home front (57).

War neurosis introduced Simmel to psychopathology's sliding scale. Specifically, he could see clearly now how the development of neurosis, as a self-securing or insuring of the organism, ultimately defends against the threat of psychosis (83). It is the ultimate balancing act. "Whatever in a man's experience is too powerful or too horrible to be grasped and assimilated by his conscious spirit sinks to the subconscious ground of his psyche.

There it lies like a mine prepared to detonate the whole psychic formation above it. And only the here described self-securing mechanism, with its sliding to the side of waves of affect, its attachment to specific organs, to external symptoms and symptomatic behaviors, prevents an ongoing disturbance of his psychic balance" (83). On the sliding scale of psychopathology's continuum, psychoanalysis, psychiatry, and the psychotherapies balance each other out as eclecticism. Simmel is on the side of psychoanalysis and warns his colleagues that the quick turnover treatment of symptoms via hypnosis leaves the underlying psychoneurosis intact and the psychic formation mined. But Simmel also admits (in the name of psychoanalysis) that hypnosis not only is a necessary adjustment of treatment schedule to the mass metabolism of the total war effort but is moreover in fact a better fit with war neurotics whose disturbance originates in the forgetting of a recent catastrophic war scene it, done it. Hypnosis gets the neurotic to relive the experience and relieve the repression—until he, too, can remember to forget. Simmel compares the process of this hypnotherapy to the rewinding and rerunning of a film (25, 27). Taking the neurotic to the movies is an "acceleration and simplification of the therapeutic process" (23).

In 1919, the same year as his contribution to the psychoanalytic documentation of the war neurosis effort, Simmel followed up his case-by-case work with the war neurotics by going into the full shipyards of striking workers. "As the party leaders continue to fight about which is at fault for the hopeless conditions of our fatherland, the war or the revolution, the masses are only too happy that everyone is still under the war's influence" ("Psychoanalyse der Massen," 36). The masses have "strike fever," by which Simmel does not want to second all the commotion about this being a new illness by its own rights, not some "revolution psychosis" "but a degree of heightened nervousness which we would diagnose in the individual as the pathological consequences of war in the form of war neurosis" (36). Simmel refers to the rise in mass appeal of the occult sciences as part of the same symptom picture.

All the bad side effects of the hunger blockade of Germany during the external war are now being reproduced and prolonged internally and self-inflicted interpersonally among striking Germans. When Simmel reviews the unhappy troopers whose condition lives on in the so-called revolution neurosis, he, like Freud, highlights the psychological aspects of Germany's war effort, such as the negative transferential overdisciplining of soldiers, as being at fault. Down these fault lines, the breakdown of individual soldier egos continues aftershocking within the group's psychopathology. "Thus the signs of our times, which we are accustomed to see as manifestation of unalterable decay take on the aspect of war damages to the psyche of the *Volk,* as neurotic detours and emergency exits which, in the individual, can make use of the body and in the masses must take over the economic organism in order to achieve the balancing act of tension release" (40).

Sandor Ferenczi begins his 1919 contribution to the united analytic front by having his fun and hating them, too: predictions of upcoming revolutionary activity failed because the Marxists overlooked psychic factors. This is precisely what happened to neurologists during World War I. The new group psychology of insurance coverage had recalculated class warfare in terms of psychological advantage and risk. But these same specialists continued to take this opportunity to reproach psychoanalysis for overreliance on the sexual etiology of neurosis. Ferenczi points out, however, that even in terms of strict sex, the high incidence of impotence symptoms in war neurotics already marked the spot they were in with the unconscious giving the orders. But the disorder's advertisement of nonsexual messages, as in such standard symptoms as loss of motor coordination, really reflected and refracted the infantilization going down to the blanket order of narcissism, in which the greatest pleasure was taken—away from us. "Someone already narcissistically predisposed will of course more likely sicken of traumatic neurosis; but no one is completely immune since the stage of narcissism forms a significant point of fixation in the libido development of every individual" ("Die Psychoanalyse der Kriegsneurosen," 27). That's why traumatic neurosis is often accompanied by paranoia and dementia. Narcissism is the answer: it reinforces the analytic view of sexuality as eros, which is not always into genitality.

Ferenczi's earlier "impressions on observing war neuroses in the mass" ("Beitrag zur Tic," 124) included, first, the Blitz-like freezing and photo finishing (over and over again) of the moment of impact that the explosion casualties speak of in terms of "air pressure" (125): "fixation of the innervation predominantly at the moment of the concussion (of the shock)" (126). Analogies from everyday life: "In a sudden fright one can often notice that one's feet become 'rooted' in the position accidentally assumed at the moment, that indeed the last innervation of the whole body—the arms, the facial muscles—remains rigidly fixed for quite a while. Actors know this 'gesture of expression,' and employ it successfully for the representation of the emotion of fear" (126).

The flash of fright catches the soldier off his guard or defenses, bolting him down to his riveting experience in the manner of conversion hysteria: "The sudden affect that could not be psychically controlled (the shock) causes

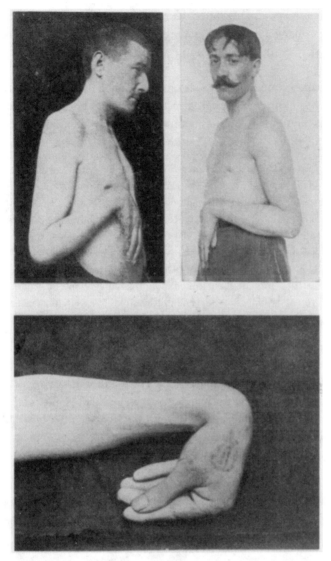

Three examples of symptoms of contraction and paralysis of hand and forearm in three shell-shocked soldiers treated during World War I. *Top left,* the soldier's symptoms fully developed within two weeks after he was wounded in combat in August 1914. *Right,* battle wounds that required amputation of the index finger in May 1915 preceded the emergence of the psychoneurotic symptoms, which were fully developed one year later. *Bottom,* soldier developed the documented symptoms following wounding in combat in August 1914 (his arm was broken at that time). All symptoms were fully developed and accounted for by 1916. From J. Babinski and J. Froment, *Hystérie-pithiatisme et troubles nerveux d'ordre réflexe: En Neurologie de guerre* (Paris: Masson et Cie, 1918), plate 4, next to p. 112.

the trauma; it is the innervations dominant at the moment of trauma that become permanently retained as morbid symptoms and indicate that undischarged parts of the affective impulses are still active in the unconscious" (129).

The controlling interest the trauma has taken in the shell-shocked soldier belongs to an unconscious structure that does not leave open slots in conscious daytime programming for turning intention around and peeling it off simulation.

> The suspicion of being "misled" by the patient, and the distrust of his statements, were the causes of the profound ignorance prevailing until recently among doctors concerning all matters pertaining to the psychology of the neuroses. Only since Breuer, and more particularly Freud, began to listen to nervous patients was access discovered to the secret mechanism of their symptoms. Even in case the patients had subsequently invented the situation present at the concussion, this "invention" may have been determined by the memory traces of the real circumstances which have become unconscious. (130)

This gets us away from the script and stage into the method of the neurotic acting: "The blast of air from the shell... may well have shaken their self-love to its foundations" (136). This bottom line overlaps with the evolutionary time travel of "neurotic regression, that is, the relapse into a phylo- and ontogenetic stage of development long outgrown" (137). But the evolutionary scheme of random, shock-driven development or selection begins in the photo labs of technologization:

> It is probable that consciousness generally automatically shuts itself off at first on contact with the overpowering stimuli. We may take it for granted that after the trauma a certain discrepancy exists between consciousness that has been relatively protected from the shock and the rest of the neuro-psychic apparatus. An equalization is here possible only when consciousness too becomes aware of the source of pain; this is then achieved by a certain "traumatophilic" attitude—the hyperaesthesia of the senses which in small doses gradually allows just so much anxious expectation and shock to reach consciousness as was imparted to it at the time of the shock. In the constantly repeated little traumata, in each expectation of contact, in each little sudden noise or light, we should—following Freud's assumption— see a tendency towards recovery, a tendency to the equalizing of

a disturbance in the distribution of tension throughout the organism. (139)

This self-healing symptom belongs to a new disorder that overlaps with anxiety hysteria and conversion hysteria but also hybridizes the two for the wear and tears of the soldier back on the narcissistic stage again. With anxiety dreams we watch the soldier's control panel go into automatic: "Here the psyche does not even wait for an external stimulus in order to react to it exaggeratedly, but creates for itself the image at which it can then become alarmed. This unpleasant symptom too, therefore, subserves the effort at self-healing" (139).

Abraham's answer to the wartime neurologists who were near missing while taking better aim at Freud's system was to go into the unconscious and sexual dimension of the ego-driven manifest experiences that the same neurologists now readily recognized—as their own, only learning from experience. Soldiers who develop war neuroses were prewar sexually labile individuals who showed little initiative or forward-march energy. Their relations with the female gender were already disturbed to varying degrees through "partial fixation of libido in the developmental stage of narcissism" (61). Their sex was a reduced affair with libido inhibited through fixation, and potency available only on condition. Concessions to their narcissism were required for social and sexual functioning. By the time of the neurotic outbreak, all the narcissistic props had been taken away: both those that were needed to make it through peacetime—the one and only wife or the regular visits to prostitutes—and then even the follow-up attempts to remake or refasten the peace props for wartime functioning through the cultivation of comradeship.

Abraham witnessed physically injured soldiers demonstrate how libido with no outside place to go applies just about anywhere, anyhow for release through self-love:

> At the outbreak of war my attention was drawn to this euphoria of the severely injured by a particular incident. On a ward in a general military hospital I had to treat four soldiers who had all suffered a severe injury to the right eye by splinters from the same grenade. . . . On the day they each received an artificial eye, a strange scene took place. The men exuberantly skipped about, danced, and laughed, just like children working themselves up into a frenzy of joy. There is no doubt that this, too, was a regression to narcissism, albeit of a restricted type. These patients repressed their awareness that by their injuries they had suffered some degree of impairment, particularly in the eyes of the female

> sex. What they had to forgo in love from outside, they replaced
> by self-love. The injured part of the body gained a significance as
> an erotogenic zone, which it had not previously possessed. (64)

Under the less physical but more material conditions of pension neurosis, narcissistic supplies are sent to the fixed fronts of an internal war.

> The fact that the neurotic feels within him the change which his
> libido has undergone is usually entirely overlooked. He is overcome by the feeling of an immense loss, and in this he is justified, in that he has actually lost his ability to transfer his libido,
> and thereby an important foundation for his self-confidence. Before the war an injured man told me that he had agreed with his
> insurance company on a certain sum by way of compensation.
> Hardly had this agreement been reached, when the thought occurred to him that this sum did not nearly cover his real loss.
> From then on the sum which, in his opinion, he should have demanded mounted rapidly until it became astronomical. (65)

Excessive greed joins phantom limbs and all the other psychic aberrations of the war zone in self-love, which "is only possible in cases where the injured person had previously shown an inclination to react narcissistically to an external blow to his integrity" (65). In this pileup of self-esteem casualties, only "psychoanalysis may fill the existing gap by providing a cure which is enduring in its effects. Psychoanalysis more than any other method of observation enables us to look deeply into the structure of the war neuroses; it may also gain therapeutic supremacy in this sphere" (67).

In Ferenczi's repeated references to war neurosis for comparison's sake in a spread of publications on widely varying disorders, one point is always being driven to the home front: actual wounds can bind the excess narcissism that, when on the loose as in war neurosis, produces disabling symptoms. This illuminates the importance of narcissism conceived as the libido pool of applicants for what otherwise seems a diversity of psychic disturbances. Injuring patients (through electroshock treatments, for example) is not, however, recommended, if only because the results produced are short attention span only. The turnover between the electrified call to attention and relapse, the impulse to skip the war and just have desertion, turns on the metabolism of narcissism without intervening in it. Plus, as Abraham emphasized with regard to disposition, wounding that can double as condition for payment inevitably opens up the bindings of narcissism and lets it all flow out into endless pension neurosis.

By 1921, in his "Contribution to the Tic-Discussion," Ferenczi relocated the detonation effect of shell shock up and down the psychopathology continuum within the breaching and opening of those fixed fronts that the crowding of narcissism with individuals or couples (as in Abraham's analysis) had required for its census. "The analogy between tics and traumatic neurosis situates this species of neurosis between the narcissistic and the transference neuroses. This double positioning is a well-known characteristic of the war neuroses" (92–93).

Abraham's sex focus follows the slip and slide of the homosexual component inside wartime psychic disturbances from the impotence-related symptoms of neurotic soldiers all the way to psychotic delusions. In fact, what Abraham tracks one by one with the neurotics is so much clearer in psychotic cases. Delusions of same-sex persecution, for example, bare their truth: they manifest sexual content (or incomplete containment) of homosexuality.

Before the 1918 conference proceeded, Victor Tausk in 1916 had performed exploratory work on the war psychology of symptoms in the flight service down the double line between neurosis and psychosis. He discovered at the front a new brand of psychosis that mixed melancholia and paranoia in equal measure, rather than, as clinicians had tended to set the relationship between the two narcissistic disorders, as top diagnosis to bottom one.

> I owe to the war several cases which will not obey the psychiatric system. These are the "war psychoses," inasmuch as they have broken out through the occasion of the war. It immediately concerns several cases in which a melancholia, fully developed in all its dimensions, equipped with all characteristic traits, coexisted alongside a no less well-developed paranoia. ("Diagnostische Erörterungen," 223)

Melancholia reflects the pathological metabolization of unused libido taken back from love relations in the outside world (230). Paranoia designates defense against the coming out of "unconscious homosexual-narcissistic components, as Freud showed in his Schreber biography. All the conditions for the mobilization of these components are given in military life, in particular through the close and exclusive contact with the same sex in the field" (231). Fantasies of omnipotence or, in reverse, of persecution grow out of the ego enlargement so typical of the narcissistic disposition of homosexuals. Tausk discovered here "a double pathological mechanism of metabolization of the withdrawn libido: the paranoid and the melancholic" (232). The melancholic is the widow of his own heterosexual libido; the pathological application of the withdrawn heterosexual libido explains in large part melancholic symptomatology (233). The heightening of the homosexual-narcissistic component in the same-sex milieu takes with it the removal of heterosexual libido. One part is rereleased as hovering libido-excess applied toward melancholic symptoms. The heterosexuality at stake here was given narcissistically or even homosexually. The withdrawal of homosexually articulated heterosexuality cannot lead to renewal: melancholia is a breakdown of narcissism accompanied by a supplemental paranoia directed against the homosexuality of the institutional frame.

In his follow-up piece on deserters, Tausk views actual desertion as a primitive interpretation of the inner flight into illness. Psychosis crowds the horizon from which these soldiers just desert:

> The profound yearning depression which precedes many of these desertions on account of homesickness, gives me to believe that desertion is often undertaken only as unconscious flight from a threatening mental illness, an "isolation psychosis." The flight from loneliness back home, where one is never lonely, is perhaps the rescue from the threatening madness. ("Zur Psychologie des Deserteurs," 194)

Closer to the front in more neurotic articulations of sexual flightiness, Tausk diagnoses a homosexual meaning in the fear of sexual impotence that underlies many cases of desertion: "Fear of the new or of beginning is a typical displacement of sexual impotence anxiety onto nonsexual activities and objects" (192). There are thus cases of desertion triggered by the appointment of a new commandant or by a new assignment. "To what extent unconscious homosexual inclinations also determine this neurosis, perhaps were even the decisive cause of the fear of impotence, I do not want to explicate further" (192).

A transference in the transmission of Freud's inside view of war neurosis causes the followers to identify or personalize narcissism as homosexuality and couple war-wounded narcissism with the emergency of homosexual impositions in the psychosexual makeup of soldiers with symptoms. There is no precedent setting in Freud for this apparently necessary cohabitation (and please hear the "parent" in the adverb sliding down the seeming of association). If the reductionism seems to gain momentum outside the Central Powers station of analysis, then the application process, in equal measure, grew in fervor the longer the distance the transference had to go to make its offering. The gift of the equation corresponds to and provokes the crisis of insecurizing in theory that skews schedules and splits anxiety. But the world war only spread the win of the combination of resistance features that had aired and erred in the prewar discourse of the primal sons and rebels, Adler and Jung. The first step toward emancipation from the father, in primal time and terms, is always the communion with homosexuality before the sons come in for the kill.

Cry Me

We shall surely have a new and larger psychology of war. The older literature on it is already more or less obsolete from almost every point of view.... More in point are the revisionary conceptions of Freud.

—G. STANLEY HALL, "PRACTICAL RELATIONS BETWEEN PSYCHOLOGY AND THE WAR"

During the war, Ernest Jones had to practice his loyalty to Freud in relative isolation (all the analytic relatives were on the other side of the war). Jones found himself attending all sorts of eclectic contexts of psychotherapy where those interested in Freud had to gather together with Jung and Adler followers, for example. During his isolation, however, Jones found a fellow Freud supporter in W. H. R. Rivers. Rivers was a stutterer whose original condition had been treated and studied by his own father. His sisters were survivors of childhood who exhibited all the symptoms of traumatic neurosis. In childhood they were the favorites of Father's prestigious colleague Professor Dodgson. Father encouraged the contact high his career might be getting and sent his daughters right through the looking glass. An inheritance of torture stammered through Rivers's welcoming reception of analysis, which openly influenced how he treated shell shock victims (who were often also afflicted with stammering).

Rivers's "The Repression of War Experience" documents (right down to the discussion following the original presentation) the level of analytic understanding or integration that could be mobilized for the Entente in World War I. Rivers understands repression to include both the radical forgetting of memories of war that the war neuroses symptomatize and a general circumstance of social conditioning (which switches to fast-forward in wartime):

> The most important feature of the present war in its relation to the production of neurosis is that the training in repression normally spread over years has had to be carried out in short spaces of time, while those thus incompletely trained have had to face strains such as have never previously been known in the history of mankind. (2)

But repression isn't restricted to socializing; it has a life of its own that "does not cease when some shock or strain has removed the soldier from the scene of warfare, but it may take an active part in the maintenance of the neurosis" (2). While the patients are thus run by repression on low maintenance, the treatment approaches include remembering, communication, and cathartic repetition of the missing memory as well as "re-education" (14).

In the question-and-answer period, Jones points out that the resistance displayed by the patient and his medical advisers is the real manifestation of the repressive tendency:

> I wish to point out that, although the phenomenon of repression is more easily observed in relation to what may be called external experiences, desires, thoughts, etc., that arise from within, and, indeed, it needs the calamitous happening of this great war to make the former very manifest at all. It is all the more important, therefore, that the latter group should not be overlooked. . . . It is also these previously repressed impulses in the personality that lend the obviously dynamic character to the war traumata, and cause the memory of them to haunt the mind. (18)

The Jungians in attendance want to switch tracks from repression to "regression in Jung's sense" (19) so that, like a regression, they can turn to Jung. Rivers may be a beginner in Freudian analysis, but he's no Jungian: he points out the mistake in regarding repression and regression as contradictory or mutually exclusive (or the latter as a Jung exclusive). He gratefully acknowledges the Freudian fine-tunings (for example, the connection Jones put through between repression and resistance):

> I am glad that several speakers have called attention to the bearing of my results on the more fundamental part of Freud's theory of neurosis, a part which, in the heat engendered by the discussion of other aspects, has attracted little notice in this country. (20)

The publication of the 1918 Budapest conference papers one year into peacetime allowed for recontextualization of Ernest Jones's isolated report on the other side of the world conflict. It was the side, as covered live by McDougall and Trotter, that jumped the gun, which Freud would correct in slo mo in 1922 (in *Group Psychology and the Analysis of the Ego*). Jones starts out by introducing the mascot of his loyal reading of war neurosis: a young woman who could not get her sexual nature together with her ego ideal, could only encounter their noncongruence with more repression into the unconscious. Forced upon marrying to give up her distance from sex (which had given her psychic balance), she soon developed a neurosis. "In a similar way with war neurosis, when the old relationship between the ego ideal and the repressed impulses has been disturbed, the incapacity can assert itself to produce a new one under the new conditions, and the expression for the repressed impulse can be found in the form of some neurotic symptom" (Jones, "Die Kriegsneurosen," 71).

Two causes of war neurosis are joined in the course of fitting in with the war effort and in outbreaks of anxiety. So, yes, it's a question of willpower; but only where there's an unconscious will is there a way for neurotic symptom formation to follow (72). Jones awards MacCurdy a citation for recognizing the sexual etiology of neurosis in peacetime, but then he draws the line when it comes to wartime conditionings, although he claims not to have joined the resistance. Although the sex drive is the strongest challenger of the ego ideal when we rest in peace, in war the conflict arises between self-preservation and ego ideal, a conflict that's big enough to produce neurosis. But, Jones asks, how are two fully conscious dispositions or relations to reality (or two ego tendencies) going to manufacture a neurosis, which always rolls down the unconscious line of production? (77). Anxiety is the answer. All neurotic symptoms defend against the development of anxiety. Unlike the nervous anxiety of peace neurosis, which originates in object libido, the anxiety that develops in the danger zones of warfare goes with ego libido. War trauma never leaves the narcissism sector. But as we now know (in 1919), self-love is the bigger libidinal "reservoir" that exceeds object love. Thus another comparison that "presses" on Jones is the one "with the protoplasmatic emanations into the pseudopods of amoebae, especially since the reciprocal relationship of the little pseudo feet to the body resembles the relationship of object love to self love" (80). Just as the organism can only stand a certain measure of object-libidinal pleasure without getting damaged, so, as the study of psychotics has shown, it goes also with ego libido. But on the psychotic side, between the flare-up of an excess of ego libido and the onset of symptom formation, there is always also an outburst of nervous anxiety, which cannot be reduced, as in the Anglo consensus, to fear of death or a wish to die to escape the horrors of life. "Our unconscious thinking translates the concept of death into a language it can understand: either denigration of the most important vital activity— a typical form of which is castration—or as a state of Nirvana, in which the ego can live on freed from the disturbances of the outside world" (81–82). Whereas chronic types of war neurotics, in whom long-standing disturbances were marshaled by war trauma, need to take to the couch for the long haul, most war neurotics can be healed quickly, as long as the procedure used has been "psychoanalytically trained" (82).

During the war, in keeping with the Allied propaganda fix on fixing war through war, Jones contemplated "whether the science of psychology

can ever show us how to abolish war" ("War and Individual Psychology,"
55). But what if "history comprises an alternation of wars and recupera-
tions," a "feature of periodicity" that has rhythm and staying power? (61).
To ground such histrionics of current events, Jones refers to an opposition
that's sparked in the corridor wars between "social psychology" and "individual psychology" (the latter genre not to be confused with Adler's name
brand). This opposition really follows a first come, first served application
policy. What happens if social psychology is in first place? "This might even
more strongly be urged in the case of modern war, which is essentially the
affair of whole societies, and in which the social phenomenon of imitation,
contagion, crowd psychology, and mass suggestion play an important part"
(62). But social psychology must already be based on individual psychology,
if only to the extent of acquiring "knowledge and control of the distorting
influences" that might interfere with the researcher's own judgment (63).
Thus there's more experimental control in individual format. What's more,
because man is always social, individual psychology is the way to go.

Jones sets up sublimation (here as in his companion piece, "War and
Sublimation") as the psychic mechanism turning up the contrast between
the individual and the social. Sublimation functions as a conscience-injec-
tion system in the conversion of unconscious impulses into social values,
and then it functions again, or is still running, when it breaks down (65).
There comes a point when the repression of conflict or opposition gives
way to sideline activities that in fact provide the institutional frame for all
the oppositions: "Sublimation takes place automatically when repression is
carried up to a certain point, the repressed impulses finding another outlet" (72). Notwithstanding Jones's lament ("how imperfect is the sublimat-
ing mechanism" [64]), when sublimation falls apart, it still converts the
same energy now into asocial and antisocial values. That's how war and
sublimation enter into free association. "War furnishes perhaps the most
potent stimulus to human activity in all its aspects, good and bad, that has
yet been discovered. It is a miniature of life in general at its sharpest pitch
of intensity" (75).

The issue of priority, which the corridor conflicts must raise up against
the mechanism that keeps on controlling (even or especially during sublimation breakdown) the outcome of the opposition between brands and
bands of psychologists always in terms of one internal relation, enjoys a
comeback with the reasserted externality of conflict in the world war: "A
cynical observer might almost say that the chief conflict in the war is over
the question of who began it. On every side it is agreed that to have caused
the war is a disgrace, the blame for which must at all costs be imputed to

the enemy" (66). The peace of the action that the warring sides are seeing or not seeing gets relocated by Jones within the precarious hold each individual couple has on social conscience in spite—in excess—of the nonoppositions or substitutions open to it. "Seen from this angle," and by this Anglo analyst, "peace may be compared with the institution of monogamy, which society accepts in theory, but never in practice" (66). The couple that stays together with the raising and erasing of denial preys on figures of jealousy or projection. The couple goes to war or adopts other forms of opposition along the one easy way available for its admission of the double other. "Whoever undertakes a psychoanalysis of men deciding to enlist in wartime will be astonished at the complexity and strength of the unavowed motives darkly impelling him and reinforcing his altruism, from the fascinating attraction of horrors to the homosexual desire to be in close relation with masses of men" (71). Jones keeps it in the other's court and courting: "The Germans have a proverb *Der Hass sieht scharf,* which means that hate enables one to uncover the motives of an enemy to which the latter is blind" (67). The bottom line to be toed in warfare is the willingness to fight, which some call patriotism, and which has psychological origins "in feelings about the self, the mother, and the father respectively. The last-mentioned is probably the least important of the three.... More significant is the relation towards the mother.... Most important of all is the source in self-love and self-interest" (68–69). As Jones's couple of reservations were already holding back through metonymy and absence, conflict between attachment to the only one (who is off-limits) and the controlling interest taken in the other of the couple always escalates into what it is, itself, narcissism style: the mother of all wars.

In "War and Sublimation" Jones introduces into his war speculations a number of adjustments and provisos that will extend into the postscript era. This time the neuroses of war are calculated in their deduction from the summary of accounts and their activities. Sublimation is refigured in terms of narcissism: "It refers much more to the peculiar and less differentiated form of sexuality known as infantile sexuality than to the familiar adult type" (82). And that's only the sex part: "The other set, which may be called the impulses belonging to the ego, including the aggressive ones, are equally in need of modification for social purposes" (82). But even when the ego does this set, the narcissistic sex charge is back: "A characteristic process whereby these egoistic impulses become modified is through their becoming invested with erotic feeling" (83). Jones frames the two sets (and at the same time describes a series of alternations unsettling the couple of sets) in the simulcast mode of trauma that keeps the two world-war contexts, like the main body of his speculation and its postscripts, separate and connected. "A curious circumstance, however—one that cannot be illustrated by any analogy from the physical world—is that the impulses continue to exist side by side in both their original and in their altered form" (83). The concluding postscript rereleases war neurosis as though the return of world warfare were nothing else:

> On re-reading this more than thirty-year-old essay I perceive that insufficient distinction is drawn in it between murdering and killing.... Murder is always connected with a sense of guilt either consciously or unconsciously, because the forbidden crime is ultimately related to the primal criminal wish to murder a parent. Pure killing, on the other hand, may be a part of reality, e.g. in self-defence, with no such reference. Naturally in warfare both acts may be committed, being one reason why it affects differently the mental integrity of different people. (87)

Ernest Jones begins his 1940 "The Psychology of Quislingism" with two propositions: "The two decisive factors on which the outcome of the present war apparently depends are aircraft production and civilian morale" (276). Quislingism, the combo of collaboration and treason named after the Norwegian Nazi sympathizer, is the "chief and most important part of the whole" of the psychological factor of civilian morale (276). In fact, Jones's guess, as good as the next, is that it constitutes what Hitler referred to as his "secret weapon" (in contrast to, or combo with, the "miracle weapon" that belongs to the factor of aircraft production Jones headlined but then dropped from his analysis of the morale issue). It's probably a secret to Hitler, but it's certainly, and even more so, a secret to the victims. But then, by proposition number three, it's about face: "The key to the understanding of Quislingism and the other phenomena connected with it is that they are all based on a peculiar inability to face, or even to recognize, an enemy" (277). Jones's topic is "complicated by an extensive aura of attendant phenomena," which, hitherto overlooked, nevertheless represent stages in the development of Quislingism, all of which "indicate either denial or else approval of the aggressiveness of the enemy" (277). Thus what characterizes the stages of this development is the "curious connection between these two attitudes of denying and approving" (277). But after exemplifying the stages or degrees of fully developed Quislingism, climaxing in the instance of the man in the street "who says, 'We could do with a bit of Hitler here'" (278), Jones admits that even at this end, "the transition from this type to the fully fledged Quisling is not an easy one" (278).

Father helps Jones out: "Every analyst has had ample evidence of the identification of the enemy in question with certain aspects of the formidable Father imago. The torture dreams about Hitler, and the still more revealing ones of friendly intimacy with him, are apt to occur in contexts that render this interpretation inevitable" (279). Thus it is the irresistibility of this Father imago that gets denied or admired. This would seem to head off those at the controls of psychological warfare at one more impasse: if the enemy's powers are decried, one tendency is fostered, if the enemy's threat is exaggerated, the second one, the one associated with Quislingism, gets promoted to the front of the headlines. But fortunately Jones can get us out of this corner "by paying heed to the matter of tempo" (280). In other words, the two tendencies are really the same. They come down to the "attempt, often by devious and desperate devices, to convert the imago of the evil Father into that of a good one" (280). We know this sounds like the therapeutically correct direction, but the direction taken "depends on the way in which it is carried out" (280). In Quislingism a "profound self-deception takes place":

> A belief is established in the power, in the inevitable success, and therefore in a sense in the goodness, of the internal evil objects and impulses, and this belief is then applied to the external enemy himself. The important step in this process is indicated by the word "therefore."

The starting point remains "the fear of the dangerous Father or of one's own dangerous impulses towards him. If one is unable to face this situation, then there remain only two alternatives: to submit to him, or to ally oneself with the dangerous forces through the mechanisms of acceptance and identification" (281). The alternatives in turn represent, respectively, the passive and the active homosexual types. "Both are *exquisitely homosexual solutions*" (281). Thus Hitler's excessive "wanting" was interpreted by certain of Jones's patients in terms of restitution, as Hitler's "wanting back" what had been taken from Germany. "The analytical point is that primary aggressive wanting was so repressed as to be inconceivable, though its existence was, after all, implied in the idea of the Father demanding back the penis of which he had been robbed" (282). This, the more passive and sexual type, submits on the basis of a "secret hostility that cannot be accepted" (282). In this type we already find the "faint beginnings of a positive admiration":

> I am speaking of the type in which the idea of aggressivity is denied and the hope entertained that it should be possible to appease the enemy by making suitable concessions. The admira-

tion may be somewhat masochistic and accompanied by the hope of obtaining a kind of protective security through coming to terms with the enemy. . . . The most complete forms of identification, however, occur where the homosexual trends are of a more active kind. With such persons tyrannical tendencies are already present which render an identification easy. One imagines this to be so with the well-known Fascist leaders in the various countries. It is possible, however, that when the alliance is complete even the most active of these types is forced to regress to the deeper level of passive homosexuality. Mussolini will probably yet follow the path of Seyss-Inquart, Heinlein, and Major Quisling himself. (282)

While the admiring identification is thus explained, the element of treason in Quislingism is not in this family way illuminated. Its secret "lies in some unsatisfactory attitude towards the Mother. Treachery, by allying oneself with the conquering enemy, would seem to be an attempt sadistically to overcome the incest taboo by raping the Mother instead of loving her. Perhaps this is why it is generally regarded as the most outrageous and unnatural of crimes, since it combines disloyalty to both parents" (283).

Jones's conclusion brings down the house Laius already brought down once upon a time before Oedipus: "The people who are most subject to the wiles of Nazi propaganda are those who have neither securely established their own manhood and independence of the Father nor have been able to combine the instincts of sexuality and love in their attitude towards the Mother or other women. This is the psychological position of the homosexual" (283).

Alfred Hitchcock's 1944 contribution to the war effort, *Lifeboat*, explored how a thinking boat of survivors of the torpedo sinking of their ship bound for Britain comes to submit to the Nazi German captain of the U-boat that went down too in the duel and who joins them as their own POW. There is only one Brit on board, but not for long. She had been sent to the States to recover from a bad case of shell shock. She was returning with her newborn on the ship that went down. Crash! Her baby is dead and is given sea burial. First chance she gets, she jumps in after him. But the man who rescued them said he struggled with her all the time, also to stop her from drowning the baby. Miss Great Britain is a too-far-goner in the full history of the war. For the rest, it's Americans, who start out upbeat and fresh, and one German, who has a plan and a secret stash of supplies. Two seamen from the wrong side of the tracks hate the Nazi on board as much as they hate their own rich, the factory owner and the journalist in mink and good-luck diamond bracelet. This double trajectory allows for the displacement at one remove of consummation of illicit submissions. In other words, the dynamic played out between one tough seaman and the glamorous journalist also plays between the lines in the unadulterated affair of passionate hatred the man is having with the German.

The ups and downs of leadership on board notwithstanding, there are throughout two shipshape figures of authority, the journalist and the Nazi German captain. They alone, just for starters, can communicate in German. The journalist is the only one in the lifeboat at the start of the film. She's all-aboard with her pileup of possessions, running her camera to newsreel in the best footage of her career. She's joined first by one rough seaman straight from the boiler room, but out of there and in the can when the torpedo struck, catching him with his pants down. In time he'll take his shirt off, too. The largest love tattoo on his chest is dedicated to "B.M." Kovacs is his name, he's working-class Chicago but Czech all the same, and he takes an instant disliking to the journalist's camera-held rapport with survival. Unconsciously on purpose he knocks the camera overboard, and its irreplaceable images go down with the torpedoed ship. In the course of the film, the journalist will also lose, again in an accident involving her rough trade-in, her typewriter. Two devices of filmmaking, from the story to the screen, are the journalist's to lose. The German keeps safe compass, energy pills, and a flask of water. But it is with a knife that he signs in as the father of all conflicts on board *Lifeboat*. A German-American who changed his name from Schmidt to Smith needs to cut off his leg to spite his death. The German, who is invested in changing Smith back to Schmidt, again just like a father, discloses that in civilian life he was a surgeon. The surgeon role belongs to the primal scene of father and son. The surgeon cuts into the body of father or son up to the turning point where he exchanges murder for healing. A father's double blessing of wounding and surviving puts the German in the ready position to receive submissions. But first he must seize the leader position in the crisis moment, the storm that threatens to break the group. For the first time revealing that he speaks English, the German takes the rudder and shouts out "Don't think about yourselves, think about the boat!" After their bare survival of the storm, the basic lifeline of water supplies has been cut off, the Americans in effect surrender to the German. He knows where his supply ship is, and now it's their only chance for survival. The German row, row, rows the boat, unstoppably singing German love songs on the way to the Fatherland's ship. At the other end of *Lifeboat*, the journalist and Kovacs are an item. But when it's discovered that their captain has been keeping his secret water supply to himself, while they have all been dying for a drink, not one of them shrinks from administering mob justice. Depression sinks in following the insurrection, and the journalist comments: "When we killed our German, we killed our motor." When they got to know the German in murder and merger, and symbolically at least to gnaw on him too, the dead father became a maternal body of nurture, an object of loss and mourning. When they killed their German, they killed their mother. But then the commentary runs her motor again, and the journalist rallies the others to disprove that they hadn't let the Nazi, who rowed for them, do their thinking for them, too. But then, when a U.S. ship approaches anyway, she's putting on makeup and playing her part in the couplifying happy ending of the group's survival. The murder of the father is rewritten through a rerun: a second German, this one young, wounded, vulnerable, attractive, seeks survival with the American group after the German supply ship toward which they let the German do the rowing is sunk by the Allies. Not all are simply thrilled about having another German on board. But after the gun he pulls is knocked out of emission, the decision is to abide by the conventions of war. The German asks, "Aren't you going to kill me?" And a spokesman for the group consensus now can ask in turn, "What do you do with people like that?" This time the question, still rhetorical, implies a diagnosis of the German military's suicidal you-or-me focus on survival, which gets the group, the U.S. versus them, out from under the corpse of the father figure.

Signal Degeneration

In 1948 Robert White gives a handbook summary of the all rise of neuroses to medical attention:

> Psychiatrists were schooled in the tradition of Kraepelin, trained mostly in mental hospitals, and thus knew relatively little about the neuroses and about the theories growing up around them. When the First World War broke out, the medical services of all countries were forced to recognize the widespread occurrence of neurotic breakdown under the stress of combat. Neuroses were found to be very common among military personnel. (47–48)

> It was clear that *war neuroses did not differ fundamentally from the neuroses of civil life*. Because of their relatively rapid development and simpler character they greatly hastened the understanding of neurosis in general. (49)

White follows Freud closely up to the point of worldwide consensus: "But certainly nothing was gained by trying to reason that the repressed motives were in every case of an infantile sexual character" (49). The soldier's conflict lies in hiding between sense of duty and fear of death. But then it became clear "that something was missing in the problem of neurosis" (50). Conflicts, conflicts everywhere, but not everyone needs a shrink. "It was necessary to find a specific point of difference between normal conflicts satisfactorily solved and neurotic conflicts solved only in the uneconomical and painful fashion of crippling symptom formation" (50). At this point Freud's focus was riveted by the ego, diversified by notions of ego-instinct and defense. The new view: "Neurosis is not merely an attempt to solve conflicts among motives, conscious or unconscious. It is the outcome of an attempt to avoid anxiety" (50). White thus sees Freud benefit at one remove (he only had his civilian patients to reconsider) from the inescapable conclusion others had drawn from the war neuroses: the central powers of anxiety and defense. Through this new emphasis on anxiety, the possibility of unity for all the different therapy trends coming out of the treatment of neurosis was real, and coming real soon (51).

It's real white of him to give Freud credit both for contradicting himself and then for being true to himself. What's more than sex acts in infancy are the facts of Freud's influence, which, and that's a fact, come always after the fact. Before getting the double signal meaning of neurosis, there was Theodor Reik to follow as he took a step to the side to consider the adjacent area of fright, or *Schreck*. You know it's fright when your life passes before you "like a film" (Reik, 13), in other words, at the speed of thought: fright is really thought-fright *(Gedankenschreck)*. To get into this movie, it takes just a moment of being taken by surprise. "Our psychic life returns in the traumatic moment to the animistic modes of thought we had overcome" (23–24).

Anxiety preparedness is the official missing link going into Freud's reconstruction of the shock effect (25). But contemplating the continuity or staying power of unconscious anxiety, Reik does a split. Anxiety proper begins within the zone of pre-anxiety *(Vorangst)* and completes itself as end-anxiety *(Endangst)*.

> It seems really to be the case that we all have access to a more or less great degree to free floating anxiety, which can rest on our unconscious feeling of guilt, as though the anxiety about the threat in certain cases can have recourse to the anxiety of conscience, the kernel of which we know as castration anxiety. A certain part of this anxiety is freed up when a threat is approaching, and appears in the form of pre-anxiety, which is stationed before end-anxiety like a fort in front of the fortress. The pre-anxiety gives a kind of guarantee or insurance that the end-anxiety will not be too intensive, that is, against the turbulent and the ego-overwhelming emergence of those unconscious childhood anxieties. (28)

The suddenness of trauma doesn't permit development of pre-anxiety and thus doesn't protect against crossover into unconscious anxiety; the suddenness also reinforces association with the instinctual reception or interpretation of the stimulus along the lines of the old expectation of danger. Symptoms appear as cost-of-surviving increase: "Symptom formation has the purpose of making up for missing anxiety and overcoming anxiety, of transposing it, as it were, into small coins" (28). In traumatic neurosis what's being made up for or caught up with has the character of pre-anxiety. Reik thus doesn't tamper with the stimulus protection plan in Freud's theory of traumatic neurosis but rather diversifies and specializes its functioning for many purposes:

> It protects against the primal anxiety *[Urangst]*. The anxiety mechanisms form here the stimulus protection, which is broken through in traumatic neuroses. In an unspecified large number of cases of this affliction it is as though the ego intuits behind the one the threat of the other one, as though the dangerousness of the external situation were the occasion to reactivate the hidden anxiety the ego reserves for the superego. (29)

In other words: the traumatic situation produces a sudden disturbance of narcissistic libidinal investments. The ego had achieved relative independence (the independence of a relative) from the superego, which was revoked in a moment of fright. It's as though the ego were thus reminded of the superego's power (projected outward as destiny). This warning equals punishment (30). Thus the repetitive dreams of war neurotics, which are related to dreams of punishment, are on rewind or re-wound: "They would really be the wish fulfillment of the sense of guilt reacting to the foreclosed (sadistic) drive impulse" (44). A profound resonance with our unconscious guilt feelings makes for the effectiveness of fright (42). That's why an actual wound seems to push back traumatic or war neurosis. Wounding, punishment, or castration satisfies the person's guilt feeling or masochism. These people have paid their tribute: now nothing more can happen to them (43).

Reik's contribution to the Freudian reception is the *Unheimlich* maneuver he performs on it. Although they don't depend on each other, the spheres of the uncanny and of traumatic neurosis overlap (34). The traumatic effect of certain experiences comes down to their giving or making, unconsciously, an uncanny impression (37). Mechanical shake-up seems essential to traumatic neurosis; it is one of the sources of the sexual excitation that gets mixed in. The mechanical force frees up the quantum of sexual excitement that becomes traumatically effective as a result of lacking anxiety preparedness or preparation. The mechanical aspect increases the special effects of immediacy and reality attending the experience of fright (36). Is it absurd to think there's something uncanny about world-controlling technology? "It releases in unconscious psychic zones the well-known reaction to the uncanny" (38). Under the cover of advancing something new—surprise!—technology brings back something ancient.

> It's possible to characterize as surprising an expectation which has grown uncanny and which really approaches us at an unexpected point of time in hard to recognize form under changed conditions. Surprise would then be the expression of the difficulty encountered in recognizing something well-known of old that has become unconscious. (39)

Sandor Rado was telling the World War II audience like it was when Freud won the First World War:

> The war cases, incomprehensible by the current theories, forced an acceptance of concepts introduced long before by Freud, and a growing recognition of psychoanalysis as a means of exploring nervous disturbances not associated with anatomic lesions. The

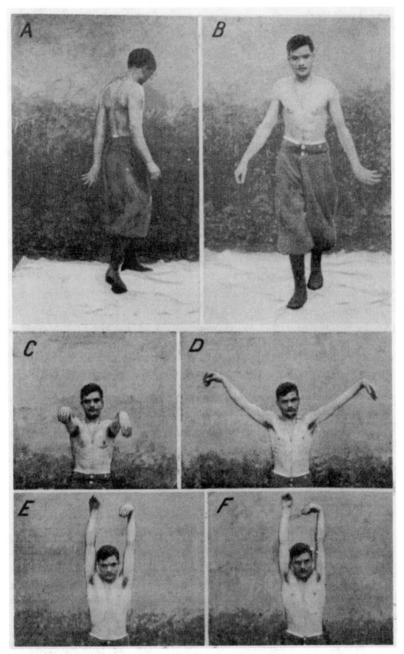

Six views of a war-neurotic soldier with symptoms of paralyzed left hand and fingers and paretic movement of the forearm. The symptoms developed five months after the soldier was wounded in combat in September 1914. The views are stills from the film documentation of this case, produced by Gaumont, and screened on 22–23 January 1916.

pattern was seen to consist of a conflict between military duty and self-preservation, with an ensuing "flight into illness," "fixation on the trauma," and a "secondary gain from illness" in terms of pension. The clinical picture was then recognized as including elements of hysteria, anxiety neurosis, phobic reactions, also a relapse to the crude forms of childish egotism, loss of sexual potency, etc. (Rado, 362)

What followed from the shift from the organic to the psychogenic point of view was a misuse of psychoanalytic terms within the greater reception area of Freud's interventions. The support this mix-up gave to the charge of simulation and malingering raised the charge or voltage of electroshock treatment and the cruelty quotient of therapy at large. The patients were misusing the terms, too, and by World War II had exhausted the lexicon of hysteria in giving proof of disability (which is, says Rado, the first unconscious idea to be inspired by anxiety on the front). Thus symptomatology withdrew from the outside (the sphere of conversion) to the inside, where psychosomatic disorders dominated every intake. Because the words had them tagged as simulators, the unconscious ideas could no longer find expression through labeling but had to go under cover in psychosis.

> The first unconscious idea inspired by anxiety is to offer glaring proof of the soldier's disability. This need gives rise to incoherent behavior fragments of symbolic value. "Look! I cannot stand, I cannot walk, I cannot use my hands, or see, or hear, or speak!" Naturally such language could be effective only as long as it remained incomprehensible to both patient and doctor and could be written down simply as enigmatic manifestations of an illness. Now that psychoanalytic knowledge has entered into common parlance, it is safe to predict that in the present war we shall see a decrease in this type of functional disturbance, and that the over-stimulated affects will instead express themselves through the internal organs, precipitating such illnesses as peptic ulcer and neurocirculatory asthenia. But these more serious interferences with physiological functions, though not hysterical in character, will serve the same purpose of bearing witness to the soldier's incapacitation. "Look! I cannot digest food; my heart is too weak to stand the strain." This psychological withdrawal of symptomology from the outside to the inside of the body, i.e., the replacement of "hysterical" by "psycho-somatic" disorders, is thus a cultural phenomenon, already observed in peacetime practice. (365–66)

Rado therefore calls in 1942 for greater unity—indeed, a "unified in-sight"—that would merge points of view as far apart as introspection ver-sus inspection over the body of the war neurotic (or psychotic). The injury a soldier receives is the essence of all emergency and always calls up "emer-gency control" (362). Once set in action, the devices of bodily pain, anxiety or rage, and (one for the intellectual side) anxious or angry apprehension elicit "riddance reflexes" and personality operations designed to forestall pain through escape from the danger zone. Nonisolated events in mental life, pain, anxiety, and rage are component parts of a highly organized func-tion that operates like an elementary reflex. But this reflex of impulses flexes in direct opposition to the soldier's sense of duty. The most efficient tech-nique for resolving the conflict is to shut down the operation of emergency control by completely ignoring the dangers, disregarding the value of one's own life, and allowing oneself thus to be transformed "into an insen-sitive technician of war": "With his self-love thus powerfully protected he can afford to lose his identity in the military unity" (364). The man who doesn't make it to disregard of danger and who therefore leaves devices of emergency control wide open to overstimulation will, unless inhibited, suc-cumb to "motor impulses of flight or mad attack" (364). Or there is, ac-cording to the principle of similar is as similar does, the hysterical desire to be overwhelmed by the situation to avoid coping with it. All these disturbed reactions are located next to an emergency exit: "Emergency control... is thus using the 'trauma' as a means of fulfilling its original purpose of remov-ing the man from danger" (365). Military problems of "self-esteem" come down to an "overactive state of emergency control," which runs on dread of exposure to further injury: "Dread of injury becomes a dread of the re-currence of that particular experience. This may be termed the traumato-phobic factor" (366). By extension, the late phase of every war-neurotic ill-ness puts "the personality under traumatophobic regime" (366). But the regime is not selective: military selection boards cannot control the incidence of war neurosis, since the predisposition is in readiness in everyone: "The decisive factor in the pathodynamics of the illness is the inhibition of 'spon-taneous' repair, that is, a shift... to... retreat, inertia and avoidance. Most, if not all, human beings contain the possibility of such a development" (161). Each therapeutic method, from administration of mild faradic jolts to the intervention of hypno-catharsis, can be "made helpful by a complete overhauling of its psychotherapeutic essentials" (367). The therapist's job is a simple one: fears must be deflated and the soldier's ego reactivated and inflated. To counter a fix on the one traumatizing event or repressed mem-ory, Rado recommends "de-sensitization of the patient to all memories of the war, whether repressed or not": "War memories must be...turned instead into a source of repeated pride and satisfaction" (367).

Owing to technical developments, Ernst Simmel had to open his 1944 reunion with war neurosis with a warning contrary to expectations of viewer discretion. See World War I, see World War II: no difference. War neurosis comprehends then as now difficulties attending changeover of peace ego into war ego. But still there is an agreement with Rado, after all, regarding the discourse and focus, if not the location, of the diagnosis tracking the internal course of violent trauma: "The last twenty-five years of psychoanalysis are particularly characterized by an increase of knowledge about the psychology of the ego. It is just during this time that under Freud's guidance we have gained knowledge about the structural and dynamic conflicts which occur within the ego itself" (Simmel, "War Neuroses," 227). Final adjustments are introduced into self-maintenance, which is the only mode for the ego to situate itself within the range of all its conflicts.

> The ego has become a battlefield itself,—because the fight for individual and national existence has been transformed into an inner struggle of the ego to "maintain itself,"—i.e. its psychological entity. (248)

What falls out by the wayside of symptom formation during the beaming up of one ego into the other one is the "transformation of real anxiety (fear of death) into neurotic anxiety" (228). On another sideline the difference between traumatic neurosis and war neurosis is at first situational: "The trauma of war...strikes the ego of a soldier, which is essentially different from the ego of a civilian. The military ego—as we may call it—has undergone a significant alteration by having been submitted to the educative process of military discipline" (229). One alteration concerns formatting. But it's one thing to hang in groups, and another to murder in packs:

> What will happen to the character of the individual when his collective character, represented by the nation, all of a sudden, by going to war, regresses to the primordial stage of pre-civilization, that of cannibalism? (230)

What will happen is that you'll be back: "We are all born little cannibals" (230). The blanket we go for is the security one: that's why, in the British experience, civilian reactions to bombings were different finally from those of shelled soldiers. Soldiers are taken out of there through flight into illness, but civilians have nowhere else to go (232). Security is the other's loss, but only a secondary gain, the use made of a symptom as a defense against an unbearable reality, is in second place: "The essence of security, which the war-neurotic-ego tends to reestablish, is security within itself, i.e. the restablishment of its narcissistic equilibrium which has broken down under the flooding of affects—particularly those of anxiety and rage" (233). Neurotic security takes out protection against psychosis. Thus the twilight zone of fainting and stupor that fills the transit state on the way to the symptom formation of the war neurosis showed Simmel the way that zones of narcissism were first unconditionally surrounding the unbalanced soldier before the choice of neurosis was upon him: "I was always inclined to consider the many incidences of disturbances of consciousness which preceded the outbreaks of war neuroses (in I might estimate 75 percent of my cases) as an attempt to regress to the unconscious condition of primordial objectless narcissim" (233). All along, the group-sizing of soldiers through military discipline was about-facing the prospect of violence on the flotation devices of regression:

> The soldier's lack of personal object love is compensated for by identification love. . . . This narcissistic-libidinal entity is reflected in the group spirit. . . . Indeed, language, which preserves the latent meaning of forgotten concepts, proves the correctness of my assumption. The term for the fighting unit which, up to this war, was the basic force of every army is the infantry. Infantry designates a group of infants. I found out about this in the dreams of my patients, and a confirmation in an etymological dictionary. (234)

"In this respect the armies of the totalitarian states are better off, since their nations have been organized on a military disciplinary basis before the war" (247). But even on the Allied side, advances in group psychology help in the current war to protect against and even counteract the danger from within.

> This is the attempt to combine with the training for blind obedience, the development of the ability to accept individual responsibility—i.e. to "take over" leadership at given moments. This is particularly possible and effective in the training of soldiers bound together in small organized units, who are assigned to specialized weapons such as tanks, planes, submarines, etc. (246–47)

Simulations

If the criminal thinks that the court will fall for such childish
simulation, even for a second believe him should he try to
play the asylum inmate, then he's very much mistaken. He's
completely sane—to the extent that's even possible for a
German!

—HANNS HEINZ EWERS, *VAMPIR*

The 1921 fourth volume of the compendium *Handbook of Medical Experiences
during the World War, 1914–18,* which was devoted to "Mental and Nervous
Illnesses," documents the wartime changeover of resistance to psychoanalysis that Ferenczi and others had already noted and tagged with the indi-
gestion charge of plagiarism or forced reading. Karl Bonhoeffer, who refers
to Ferenczi's "self-deception" in thinking that only the war had shown hysterical criteria to be important, since he himself, after all, had argued as
much in 1911 (*Handbuch,* 29), opens with the surprise of his wartime: fright
alone couldn't be doing the hystericizing if the wounded and the prisoners
of war were regularly observed getting off symptom free (7). One cannot
overlook the suggestibility factor that rises with mass affect and mass psyche (8). If one didn't want to send psychopaths to the front, it was in order
to avoid "introduction of psychic-infectious material into the mass mood"
(10). As the war dragged on, protective selective measures were dropped.
Panic put in a mass appearance, often in the form of shared hallucinations.
There is no unified, recognizable, specific war psychosis. War has ruled out
the likelihood of that genre. Instead multi-influences and causes of disturbance are in evidence in cases of (for example) psychopathic types in the
military. But many years of primitive group life with increase of tobacco and
alcohol consumption just the same had to bring forth a certain psychopathological type (25). Those around twenty years old had adolescent short attention and endurance spans that, however, got them out of the danger
zone soon enough. Those forty-five years and older were harder to reinte-
grate after duty also owing to such nonspecific factors as arteriosclerosis.
The conflict was between self-preservation and idealist organization of the
personality; the long duration of hardships led to a victory of drive over
idea. The result: "increase of defense reactions, of flight into illness" (30).
Even though their cases were likely to present themselves, after all was
dead and done, only under military conditions, the intellectually deficient
types and the psychopathically constituted, because they were able-bodied

to work or serve, weren't always found standing to be counted during the war-versus-peace mental-illness census (31). Psychopathy was in fact up (two to three times) in the wartime German stock.

Otto Binswanger now has eyes to see: "Such an abundance of male hysteria has never before been presented to us" (*Handbuch*, 45). Mainly young girls had these symptoms in peacetime (48). Robust males took over where the young women left off (63), their audio portion reduced to "childish talk in infinitive or telegrammatic style alongside undisturbed expression in writing" (65). In the war zone, in other words, physical harm only prepares the way for what's decisive: psychic transformation (47). "In peacetime we learned in the first place about hysterical pain of constitutional hysteria; with the progress of experiences of traumatic hysteria knowledge of the acquired states of this type was more precisely obtainable" (55). "Hysterical pain greatly surpasses genuine pain in its massiveness" (55). "The great simulator [*Simulatrix*] hysteria copies all forms of trembling, both organically determined (for example through multiple sclerosis) and functional" (52). "The most easily recognizable cases are those where a whole army of hysterical symptoms is present all at once or after the fact" (65).

> Here the flight into illness for specific purposes, in order to awake compassion, to attract attention is most clearly recognizable. It is noteworthy that in particular among the massively trembling one can find so many individuals who had developed or perfected their symptomatic trembling first in the hospital through psychic infection or imitation. (54)

"Acute hysterization" was broken down and parceled out under such labels as "fright psychoneuroses of the front" or "front hysteria" (in contrast to "hospital hysteria") (46). The labeling was only trying to keep up with the internal psychic process displaced out of orbit, balance, control:

> This dynamic displacement leads to a kind of splitting or dissection of the personality and thus of the unicity of our acts of consciousness. Discrete overvalued components gain an excessive influence on the total psychic happening, and indeed both on the intrapsychic and the psychic-somatic processes: and inversely undervalued components are removed from the uniform, unified flow of psychic events and in this way lose their corporeal projections. (46)

The number of these diverse psychological casualties piled up along front lines "with uncanny velocity" (48). But containment could be achieved and measured "through rational treatment" (51).

Robert Gaupp wants to know what preparations must have been under way for a person's psyche to be in harm's way just because a fright was
taken by surprise and under massive attack ("for example as a rule during
earthquakes or a surprise air attack"). How about alcohol, nicotine abuse,
anxious anticipation with side effects or conscious reception of regular events
like bombings from the air and detonations (*Handbuch*, 68)?

Psychiatry just cannot swear to the clinical self-sufficiency of consequences of fright. "Above all its clinical evaluation depends on the concep-
tual demarcation of 'neurasthenia' and 'hysteria'" (69). In addition, from
1917 on ("when far inferior substitute material *[Ersatz]* was sent to the front"),
"exaggeration and conscious simulation" became influential. Soldiers claimed
their diagnosis ("nerve shock" for example) by name. "Gas poisoning had
'become fashionable'" (71). These were the types who suddenly recovered
with the outbreak of the revolution, which they actively supported and
even led. "Political radicalism ('either completely right or completely left,
everything else is boring'—as a neurotic who was completely untalented
politically once confided in me) is in large measure nothing other than a
neurasthenic symptom" (100).

Gaupp surveys the field of disturbance genres, their ethnic yokings
and topological displacement. Colleague Cimbal proposed differentiating
"skirmish psychoses of static or positional warfare" from all the other fright
psychoses (77). What's so psychotic includes flightlike running away from
conflict, blind attacking in solo direct assaults on the enemy, or aimlessly
running back and forth. Then there's delirious clowning around, baby talking, a state that "impresses one as a total perversion of the expectable ex-
pressive movements of anxious affect into their direct opposite. It is as
though the excess of depressive affect-tension suddenly turned around into
its negative because the bow, as it were, was too taut" (79). On the ethnic
aside: "Poles and Jews sickened more easily than did the Germans; soldiers
from the Rheinland more frequently than those from Pommerania; soldiers
more frequently than the officers" (70). Even though fewer officers were
hysterical, however, they held their own in the neurasthenic category (89).
But there are actual measurements to be applied, too: war neuroses increased
the closer one was to home and the further away from the front line.

The big question remains for Gaupp: how does the fright effect, which
is normal, turn into illness? "The whole hysteria problem resurfaces here
and the battle of opinions on this matter has not yet settled down" (72). Besides, many were already psychopaths, even or especially the young volunteers at the start of the war. More successful than any therapy was the
guarantee of return to civilian life:

Deutschland: Freitragbares Sauerstoff=Schutzgerät in Kombination mit Filtergerät

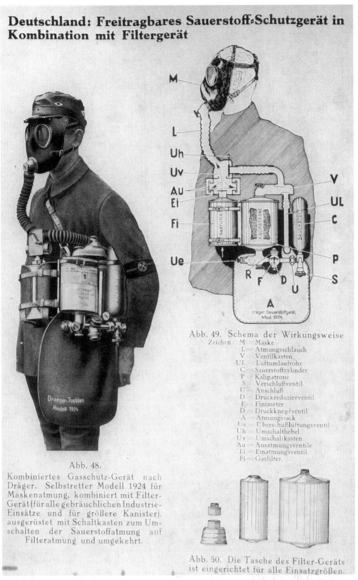

Abb. 48.
Kombiniertes Gasschutz-Gerät nach
Dräger. Selbstretter Modell 1924 für
Maskenatmung, kombiniert mit Filter-
Gerät (für alle gebräuchlichen Industrie-
Einsätze und für größere Kanister),
ausgerüstet mit Schaltkasten zum Um-
schalten der Sauerstoffatmung auf
Filteratmung und umgekehrt.

Abb. 49. Schema der Wirkungsweise
Zeichen: M — Maske
L — Atmungsschlauch
V — Ventilkasten
UL — Luftumlaufrohr
C — Sauerstoffzylinder
P — Kalipatrone
S — Verschlußventil
U — Anschluß
D — Druckreduzierventil
F — Finimeter
D — Druckknopfventil
A — Atmungssack
Ue — Überschußlüftungsventil
Uh — Umschalthebel
Uv — Umschaltkasten
Au — Ausatmungsventile
Ei — Einatmungsventil
Fi — Gasfilter.

**Abb. 50. Die Tasche des Filter-Geräts
ist eingerichtet für alle Einsatzgrößen.**

Documentation of a German brand of portable oxygen tank and protective filter designed in 1924 for future gas warfare. Exhibit 19 from the appendix of illustrations included in Rudolf Hanslian, *Der Chemische Krieg,* 1927. Reprinted by permission of Koehler-Mittler.

England: Freitragbare Sauerstoff=Schutzgeräte

Abb. 63. Englisches Sauerstoff-
Atmungsgerät Fleuss-Davis „Proto",
im Kriege gebraucht.

Abb. 64. Schema der
Wirkungsweise des
„Proto"-Gerätes.

An English model of protective armor designed for gas warfare and used during World War I. Exhibit 26 in the appendix to *Der Chemische Krieg.* Reprinted by permission of Koehler-Mittler.

Thus developed the weakening of the will to war and recovery into flight into illness, in other words the transformation of primary fright symptoms into hysterical images of the well-known and particularly obtrusive and obstinate type which Bonhoeffer and I often described, indeed emphasized from the start. (73)

Prognosis is often good. But those who remain symptomatic are "typically hysterical on the basis of a certain psychopathic inferiority" (82). Frequently the wish for pension took over where the anxiety about returning to the front had left off with the peace. Fright neurosis became pension neurosis. Under current (1920) conditions (unemployment etc.) Gaupp supposes those same old neuroses will be on the rise again. There were methods around during the war that tried to cure fright with more fright: one colleague, Much was his name, "built upon this experience his method of healing functionally voice-disturbed soldiers (creation of a scream of fear through introduction of a bullet in the larynx which produces an acute stenosis)" (84).

Just the same, psychotherapy (generally conceived) was the best way to go. Kauffmann's electro method was successful, too, but only in short circuit: the cures were not long lasting (84). Other "rapid therapies" such as hypnosis worked only on specific symptoms (98). Use of drugs to promote rest only became the habits that wore the men down. The conditions of cure often installed the disease: "One often won the impression that what was at first a purely neurasthenic illness picture had been 'hystericized' during the long hospital treatment" (99). The battle was on between states of war neurosis and insurance assessments: "Symptom pictures, which have completely different meanings in the momentary cross section in clinical, prognostic, and insurance-legal terms can appear the same" (87). Air attacks (89, 93) and the monotonous, primitive life in the trenches provided situationals for neurotic reactions. Excessive disciplining of longtime soldiers by very young new officers contributed to neuroticization. Gaupp thus joins Simmel and Freud in singling out excessive discipline as psychological grounds for the loss represented one by one as war neurosis and, en masse, as defeat in psychological warfare. Simmel cited the stress on Jews in the army when under the jurisdiction of anti-Semitic officers. Gaupp assumes that Jews are weaklings but also recounts an exercise in reading where members of a German troop were saved by a Russian Jew who recognized their Red Cross affiliation (79). And then Gaupp recognizes the bad side effects induced or inducted when young anti-Polish officers berated older Polish-German soldiers (101).

A certain Lust explains the symptoms of "barbed wire illness," which prisoners of war tend to contract by way of "excessive masturbation and pronounced abuse of tobacco" (92). "Homosexual inclinations emerged even on occasion in otherwise heterosexual men" (93). Max Nonne, who would have none of it when it came to psychoanalysis prewar, had gone eclectic: better than none is more than one. Looking back at the formative war years, Nonne documents his surprise back then at the large number of psychological casualties, his frustration over the steady rate or state of failure, and then, in league with psychoanalysis, though under the cover of synonyms supplied by Kraepelin, Cimbal, Gaupp, and Stransky, the welcome advent of certain mastery over the psy war condition: "The kernel of the Freudian

view of the affect that is stuck inside the subconscious thus came to be recognized, but defrocked of the uninhibited exaggeration and onesidedness
of the sexual factor" (103). When Nonne lists the neurologists and psychiatrists who played best supporting roles to progress, he simply includes
Freud (and one of the converts to psychoanalysis-based and compatible
eclecticism, Fritz Mohr). "Psychoanalysis is completely justified theoretically
and practically in the treatment of military neurotics. Mohr says rightly
that in accessible form, without application of daring interpretative arts
analysis is nothing else at bottom than the attempt to supply the sick person with access to the impulses of his psychic life which have remained or
become unconscious and thus to make him able to free himself eventually
from their influence insofar as pathological symptoms have arisen as a result" (112–13). For the more severe psychoneuroses (depression, obsession,
phobia), psychoanalysis is essential. Mohr and Sinn have pointed out what
Nonne can only confirm, "that only psychoanalysis is able to reintroduce
order into 'the whole person.' Whoever works with psychoanalysis needs a
great deal of time, patience, and in addition a large degree of psychological
and dialectical savvy; only then can one correctly grasp the central point of
the neurosis" (*Handbuch*, 113).

In 1915 Nonne promoted his own use of hypnosis as mainstay of suggestion therapy in place of the faradic current, which he considered overkill:
the current event isn't anything; it's the commands that are given that do
the work. "Since with neuroses every therapy is effective only through the
more or less hidden kernel of suggestion, one simply cannot do without
the suggestively effective moment of therapy conducted by the physician
himself" (113). Any charge will do: Nonne always had his patients strip
down completely to heighten feelings of dependence and helplessness (109–
110). But he says no to Binswanger's isolation therapy: not only is it grue-
some, but it also requires too many single rooms (113).

> All methods are on their own equally valuable.... That is why it
> is important that the doctor is not pledged to one method only
> but rather that he is in a position to approach the neurosis which
> is rich in malignity by different ways. Also the change in method
> signifies a recuperation for the physician, who through monoto-
> nous repetition would be exhausted by the hundreds of inter-
> changeable cases. (106)

Nonne quotes Kretschmer's flashback, which falls between resistance
and more resistance: "The whole scene has something so typical about it
for the war therapist that he still in memory begins to get bored" (108). But

to summarize the bottom line of this mobilization of approaches is still to lip-synch the statements of psychoanalysis: "getting the neurotic to prefer the flight into health to the flight into illness" (106). The intrapsychic view of conflict is the winner:

> Whoever does not have the conviction of the purely psychic ba-
> sis of all war neuroses should not attempt to treat them; whoso-
> ever is called to treat them must resolutely take up the position
> of their purely psychic origin and can do that with that much
> less worry as this position is always and again fortified by the
> successes of the treatment. (105)

The embrace of eclecticism is how Nonne self-medicates for the counter-transference his patients must survive. But then he improvises his way into the group-therapeutic bond that finally lets him hold onto intrapsychic view mastery and push back the countertransference effects from the therapeutic relationship.

The suggestiveness Nonne practiced—"an atmosphere somewhere between the tone of the barracks and the mood of Lourdes" (107)—group-psychologized all the individual cases that he drew out and quartered as ongoing transferences seeking support groups. For the physician for the first time entering this field, "the first and most important task is to produce a clan of healed patients and to maintain such a clan within a continuous tradition" (106). The group, the command center of suggestion therapy, also responds to direction: "In order to hold onto the cases cinematographically, I placed 6–8 patients next to one another on the podium and was able to place them all with one command word into the wished-for state of hypnosis" (110). One by one the suggestion or command turns on techno-syntonic implants: "It is interesting that one can make someone once healed through hypnosis still relapse through suggestion during a renewed hypnosis, and indeed the ill person becomes *reversible* with photographic faithfulness. One can speak here of engrams in the brain, which can again be reproduced by the therapist at will" (113–14). For the preservation of the species on an upbeat of the evolutionary scale, therapy must give quick rehab to the neurotics and then send them back ASAP into the selection shredder.

> The war carried out Darwinian selection in a reverse sense with
> greatest success: the best were sacrificed, those physically and
> mentally inferior were carefully conserved rather than using this
> as the occasion for having a fundamental catharsis which would
> have transfigured also through the halo of heroic death the para-
> sites feeding on the strength of the people. (112)

The military way of life, which extends to the industrial complex of war, folds measures for disease prevention and healing into its disciplinary structures of maintenance. Don't give them a pension but send them, if not to the front, then into munitions factories. Otherwise those given to neurosis will find their own antiproductive way to keep off the streets:

> It was very interesting to gather experience about the behavior of the neurotics during and after the revolution. . . . I believe that the revolution represents an endurance testing of the view of neurosis as a disease of defense and protest and of the value of the active therapeutic intervention, of the compulsive breaking through of the pathologically inverted direction of the will. (116)

The breakthrough can occur only "through a psychic operation, which can only succeed if the will of the physician is the stronger one and is experienced and recognized by the patient as such. When this conviction has gone into the blood also of the nonmedical authorities and when no ideological evaluation, but only the will to what is practically correct rules, then we will have the antitoxin to the neurosis plague" (118).

Gustav Aschaffenberg considers constitutional psychopathy or, rather, all its contaminants. He calls on colleague Stransky, who clarifies that psychopathic soldiers suffer from "partial cowardice" (*Handbuch,* 125) and run on "pseudo energy" (145). If homosexuality isn't inborn, the question remains, for example, to what extent a psychopathic foundation is necessary to this development (122). But given the lack of women, even heterosexuals must yield to their homo components or comrades (151). Aschaffenberg counsels that a one-night drunken rough-trade exchange between straights is not as bad as long-term nonsexual but homoerotic contacts. But even though Aschaffenberg allows that the inevitable involvement of homosexuals in the war didn't pose any special problems, he still toes the line where the acquired and inborn views of homosexuality overlap: "And indeed with all homosexuals you find more or less pronounced, mostly however quite strongly evident, a general psychopathic constitution" (152). Psychopathy enters into any case where "it would be wrong to speak of cowardice" (125): depression, suicide, self-destructive assault in battle, exploitation of being wounded, desertion. Obsessionals did fine at the front (as Freud also noted in a letter to Abraham at the start of the war), better, in fact, than during peacetime. The only real problems arose during training. But there was one obsessional thought in particular that caused much suffering: inability to urinate in the company of others, which made the one so afflicted keep on the lookout for roundabout ways to accomplish it solo, a preoccu-

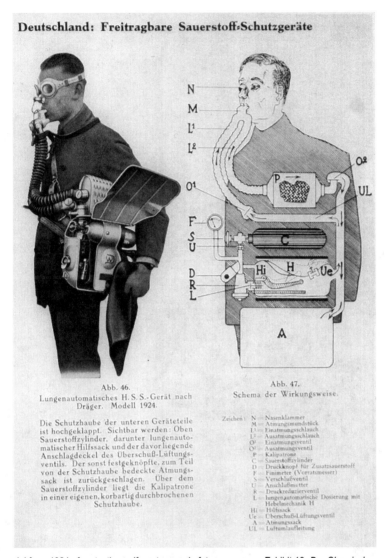

Deutschland: Freitragbare Sauerstoff-Schutzgeräte

Abb. 46.
Lungenautomatisches H. S. S.-Gerät nach
Dräger. Modell 1924.

Die Schutzhaube der unteren Geräteteile
ist hochgeklappt. Sichtbar werden: Oben
Sauerstoffzylinder, darunter lungenauto-
matischer Hilfssack und der davor liegende
Anschlagdeckel des Überschuß-Lüftungs-
ventils. Der sonst festgeknöpfte, zum Teil
von der Schutzhaube bedeckte Atmungssack ist zurückgeschlagen. Über dem
Sauerstoffzylinder liegt die Kalipatrone
in einer eigenen, korbartig durchbrochenen
Schutzhaube.

Abb. 47.
Schema der Wirkungsweise.

Zeichen: N — Nasenklammer
M — Atmungsmundstück
L¹ — Einatmungsschlauch
L² — Ausatmungsschlauch
O¹ — Einatmungsventil
O² — Ausatmungsventil
P — Kalipatrone
C — Sauerstoffzylinder
D — Druckknopf für Zusatzsauerstoff
F — Finimeter (Vorratsmesser)
S — Verschlußventil
U — Anschlußmutter
R — Druckreduzierventil
L — lungenautomatische Dosierung mit
Hebelmechanik H
Hi — Hilfssack
Ue — Überschuß-Lüftungsventil
A — Atmungssack
UL — Luftumlaufleitung

A model from 1924 of protective uniform to wear in future gas wars. Exhibit 18, *Der Chemische Krieg*. Reprinted by permission of Koehler-Mittler.

pation that could only increase his and his side's exposure to enemy fire and attack (128). This proves "that the power of the obsessional thought is greater than the fear of wounding and death" (129). Other symptoms allowed for the kind of displacement that still kept them in the service. Soldiers suffering from severe agoraphobia, for example, could be transferred to pilot duty, which solved everything: "The same sick soldiers who broke down trembling and shaking when crossing an open space felt great in the skies"

Frankreich: Freitragbare Sauerstoff-Schutzgeräte

Abb. 61. Französisches Sauerstoff-
Atmungsgerät Tissot,
im Kriege gebraucht.

Abb. 62. Schema der
Wirkungsweise des
„Tissot"-Gerätes.

A French model of protective apparatus, used in World War I, designed to protect the soldier against gas poisoning. Exhibit 25, *Der Chemische Krieg*. Reprinted by permission of Koehler-Mittler.

(129). Other psychopathic tendencies are a danger to morale: pathological lying, rumormongering, religious proselytizing. Hysterical lying fueled anti-German propaganda: "Between the pathological drive to lie and conscious deception there are no sharp borders" (149).

Ewald Stier focuses on the insurance subtext to nervous or alleged illness that is the claims category covering half of all pension recipients, "if you include those who are in reality functionally nervously disturbed, to whom, under other rubrics like heart neurosis, chronic intestinal cattarh, rheumatism, and the like, pensions are being paid today" (*Handbuch*, 171). As he contemplates the peace that is upon them, Stier reflects that all these unselected types admitted under the pressure of total war who were physically, nervously, or characterologically unsuited to the task survived the war because they fell ill often, even before making it to the front. "The great mass of those belonging to this group suffers not from accident or war neurosis but rather from a pension neurosis, that is, they suffer from their pension" (191).

According to Konrad Alt's contribution, the field of epilepsy research has diversified and doubled since the 1880s owing largely to the heightened powers of observation and assessment required by the new culture of insurance. The specialists were indeed prepared for "a sharp increase of hysterical conditions and attacks" with the outbreak of world war (*Handbuch*, 157), but epileptic seizures, which also jerked up to an all-time high, took everyone by surprise. But they were largely simulated, doubly so: for if one pointed out to the patient that the epilepsy diagnosis was out of the question and that it could only be some hysterical condition, the specifically epileptic symptoms disappeared (161). The symptoms were mail ordered from catalogs of the techno-occult: "I observed that at the time when Gustav Meyrink's *Golem*—published in March 1915—was read a great deal in the hospitals there was quite a wide-spread profusion of simulation of epileptic attacks with foam at the mouth; Meyrink's directions on how to simulate an epileptic attack (p. 405) are far from crudely presented" (162).

1915

At one point in *The Golem*, the narrator's new cell mate is really a messenger from the outside who has staged his way into prison to hand over a letter and give "instruction in epilepsy":

> "First you make a lot of saliva"; he blew up his cheeks and moved them back and forth, like someone who's washing out his mouth—"Then you foam at the mouth, like this.... Afterwards you turn your thumbs inside your fists—After that roll out your eyes"—he crossed his eyes horribly—"and then—and this part's a little difficult—you give out a half cry. See, like this: Bö—Bö—Bö,—and at the same time fall down."—He dropped full-length to the ground so that the building shook, and remarked when he got up again: "That's the natural epilepsy, the way Dr. Hulbert taught us in the battalion." (Meyrink, 282)

There's a lot of "how to" in this fantastic detection novel. The rights of the mentally disturbed to have their capital punishment waived are stressed. One of the narrator's fellow prisoners is a deranged somnambulistic medium through whom it's possible to obtain long-distance messages: "I recalled having read somewhere that in order to get sleepers to respond you shouldn't put questions to the ear but rather direct them at the network of nerves in the pit of the stomach" (301). How to live in the primal zones (and war zones) of doubling and still end up benefiting from our inevitable interest in the double, which Freud described in the essay "On 'the Uncanny'" as amounting to the ego's life "insurance" policy.

Set in a kind of prehistory (in the meantime the Jewish ghetto has made way for modern construction in an assimilationist context), the Golem crime story rolls out the occult for that projective atmosphere that *The Student of Prague* cultivated in Jewish cemeteries. Tarot, we are informed, is derived from Torah. And all the local traditions go back to the cult of Osiris and its symbol of the Hermaphrodite. The novel also goes deeply in and out of the "unconscious" and the "subconscious" for its sources and resources. It's precisely because Meyrink cannot give us the cinematic double that he opens up another, unconscious space of possibilities and combinations. The Golem is soon recognized to be a group hallucination, a kind of "psychic epidemic" that on occasion "races like lightning through the city of the Jews" (Meyrink, 54). But the Blitz includes the Jews in a larger measure or mass. The narrator speculates about a "psychic explosion that would whip our dream consciousness into the light of day in order to . . . produce a ghost" that would reveal "the symbol of the group psyche [*Massenseele*]" (54–55). Every psyche is a group of one. As the somnambulistic medium instructs the narrator: "Your psyche is put together out of many 'egos'— just like an ant state is made out of many ants; they carry over the psychic remainder of many thousand ancestors. . . . The existence of the instincts proves the presence of the ancestors in body and psyche" (312).

The occult and supernatural focus of this prehistorical, hallucinatory realm makes a couple of matches with media-technological and science-fictive forces (an alien people from another planet is even evoked or contacted at one point). The symbol that carries the book furthest from the occult to the futural is that of the Hermaphrodite, affirmed not as ultimate goal of development but as the new beginning without end (217–18). The affirmation comes after the same character attributes Jewish overattachment to the children to "an instinctive fear" on the part of the Jewish "race," "that one could die out and not fulfill a mission, which we have forgotten, but which lives on in us darkly" (214). The other dark live-in is the racial contaminant. Meyrink's narrator wonders why, in a prison full of insects, physical inspection was still required for determining whether *he* was infested. Did the authorities worry that "there could result a miscegenation of alien insect races"? (272).

Norbert Wiener picks up another transmission in *God and Golem, Inc.*, the combination of letters that turn on the Golem, which turns on three points in common with cybernetics: "One of these concerns machines which learn; one concerns machines which reproduce themselves; and one, the coordination of machine and man" (11). After admitting the likelihood of Darwin's scenario of selection as transmitter of phylogenetic learning or "learning in the history of the race" (27), Wiener goes on to give the cybernetic alternative to reproduction:

> Thus the machine may generate the message, and the message may generate another machine. This is an idea with which I have toyed before—that it is conceptually possible for a human being to be sent over a telegraph line. . . . At present, and perhaps for the whole existence of the human race, the idea is impracticable, but it is not on that account inconceivable. (36)

When toying with the idea during World War II, Wiener was engaged in research for the U.S. military, which he led in the direction of cybernetics, a catchall concept for mechanization of communication, control, and statistics. The techno-hub of this coordination effort would be the numerical computer, a binary machine using electronic tubes only and running on automatic for the duration of the computing operation. Such a computer could serve as control panel for vaster electromechanical amalgams that carried out complex human functions—like tracking enemy aircraft with antiaircraft artillery. In the uncanny prehistory of "Golem Incorporated," the cyborg was two-faced at once: both public enemy number one (the Axis pilot) and our best friend (the Allied antiaircraft gunner).

The cipher-programmed Golem participates in the future of what can be conceived but also erased. Their common conception and possible destruction make the Golem the emanation of the ghetto: just as removal of a label, a cipher, stops him dead in his tracks, so the ghetto population, we read in Meyrink's novel, could be erased with the removal from their brain of one tiny concept, one extraneous striving, or even perhaps a pointless habit (33). A techno-relation is coming down this line that goes beyond the doublings of cinema, the focus of Paul Wegener's 1920 postwar remake of *The Golem*. The movie is captive to the doubling that the film medium alone can capture. The film performs the links and limits of Jewish assimilation that are given the lie in a transgression, in image and name, that doubles as last-ditch defense granted the Jewish people in crisis, but which is given in time to turn against the Jews. The cinematic doubling goes the way of the feminine, the Christian, the childlike, the goyim. The nothing that the Jews get in the double bargain is represented as the condemned site of male-to-male writerly transmisssions inside economies or households doubly bereft of Mother (who has gone uncommemorated). The movie asks to put to rest what is already at rest.

In Meyrink's novel, the Golem is borne up out of the spirits or doubles of trauma and trauma treatment. As unconscious automaton, the Golem extends or reflects back the narrator's own traumatized condition of amnesia. It turns out that the narrator was treated by hypnosis not to readmit the traumatic memory but to seal it off by putting in its place the fake recollection of the walled-in past. The repressed memory is a dupe that bears a trace memory of the repression. The installation by the treating psychiatrist of a fantasy or false memory to aid a suicidally depressed patient was, according to Rudolph Binion's reconstruction and recalculation of Hitler's case of war neurosis, the probable source of that vision of Germany calling on Hitler in person to come to her rescue, which did swing the patient's mood around, but also marked a beginning of delusional formations of the total necessity for final solution. Between the doubling Freud saw going down in war neurotics (which Meyrink's novel, like the Rye and Ewers collaboration *The Student of Prague*, telepathically picks up on) and the dou-

Deutschland: Freitragbare Sauerstoff-Schutzgeräte

Abb. 57. „Audos Mr. 2" — Zweistundengerät der
Hanseatischen Apparatebaugesellschaft Modell
1925 mit Optolix-Maske.

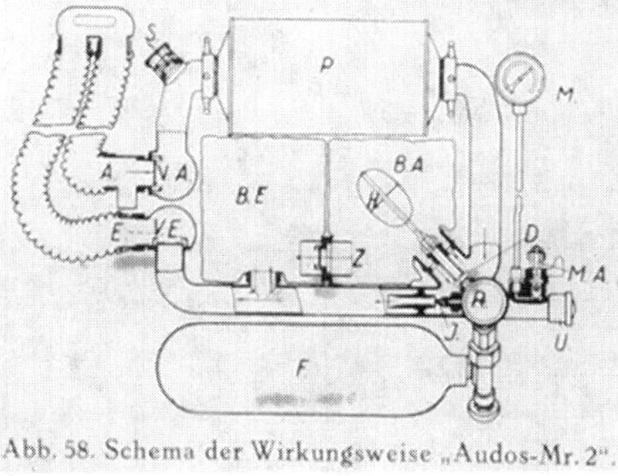

A =	Anschluß für Ausatmungsschlauch
E =	Anschluß für Einatmungsschlauch
V A =	Ausatmungsventil
V E =	Einatmungsventil
P =	Patrone
B E =	Einatmungsbeutel
B A =	Ausatmungsbeutel
H =	Hebel des Dosierungsventils
D =	Dosierungsventil
R =	Reduzierventil
J =	Injektor
U =	Umgehungsventil
M =	Manometer
F =	Sauerstoffflasche
Z =	Zwischenventil
S =	Spülventil

Abb. 58. Schema der Wirkungsweise „Audos-Mr. 2".

German model of protective apparatus for future gas warfare, 1925. Exhibit 23, *Der Chemische Krieg*. Reprinted by permission of Koehler-Mittler.

ble doubling of quick-relief hypno-treatment produces the rallying mood swings of a war economy. When the narrator experiences an upsurge of health for a change (he tends to alternate between feeling like a living corpse and suffering the crush of rejection), he senses his thoughts lining up like an army awaiting his command (90). Now that he feels like "army and

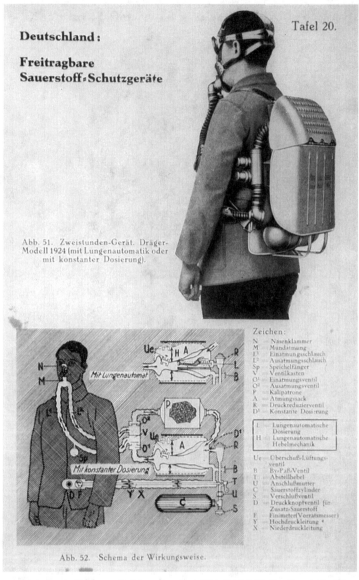

German model of protective armor for future gas wars, 1924. Exhibit 20, *Der Chemische Krieg*. Reprinted by permission of Koehler-Mittler.

king" in his own "empire," he can recognize his zombie-contained downswing as his former enslavement to a "horde of fantastic impressions and dream visions" (91).

Mediatization comes from outside as the influence of the Wegener film (and of Rye's doubling movie, too), but it is already deep inside the novel's material in the spontaneous remission of trauma through amnesia and doubling. Meyrink went straight to the front with his 1915 book; he prepared for and accompanied its release with a media blitz campaign that could only benefit, as though the made-for-the-movie novel, from the release of the first Wegener picture. But when the notion of the real double in the novel, the one that can drive you insane, is conjured up as the x-ray emanations and sensations of our own skeletons, then we have gone beyond references to the film medium (which are explicitly available, for example, in the story of the Rabbi's laterna magica performance at the court of Emperor Rudolf) to a reception of technologization as, at the same time, internalization of trauma.

Nice like Eissler

Among official accountings of psychoanalysis meets war neurosis there's the one kept by Kurt Eissler, whose *Freud as an Expert Witness* looks forward and flashes back around the 1920 trial of military-psychological crimes to which Freud was summoned as authority in the treatment of male hysterics. This represented a turning point made twice over: first, against J. Wagner-Jauregg, who was under investigation for wartime malpractice, and who now gave Freud respect at this trial time in both their careers (whereas before Freud had been Wagner-Jauregg's lowlife); and, second, against the entire neurological, psychiatric—you name it—establishment that had completely derided Freud's work on male hysteria in the 1890s. During the world war, these same resisters were proclaiming the continuum of shell shock disorder with the hysterias of peacetime. Eissler, however (like all more recent historians of Freud's encounter with war neurosis), sees this point of victory turn against Freud and psychoanalysis. Eissler doesn't look between or behind lines for the real range and staying power of an influence. What the neuropsychiatric group tries to take back after the war is irrevocably there. It is especially hard to recognize the contours of Freud's model in all its pervasiveness throughout the departments of treatment of nervous disorder when the static on the line to the Nazi era of psychotherapy and psychoanalysis is on a direct line to one of the late arrivals of Freud's victory. Here is a sampling of Eissleresque misrepresentations or part-objectifications:

> But whoever deceives must somewhere know the truth, and without noticing it, Kretschmer himself gave a decisive place to the unconscious, a concept against which he wrote a passionate polemic in the following year (1919), stressing his respect for Freud at several points....
>
> Kretschmer's doctrine, stripped of its modern entanglement of concepts, is nothing more nor less than a resurrection of the old doctrine of wish-fulfillment fantasy *[Begehrungsvorstellung]* and weakness of will. The two belong together. Mohr... called it a disastrous error "that the curability of neuroses is shown as a result of good or bad will." He was quite right.... The war had demonstrated the wide distribution of neuroses and had also proved the existence of the underworld, which Kretschmer denied in his publication on the unconscious.... The war had shown that repressed material could seize possession of the ego at any

time. It would have been the right moment to open up the access
of German psychiatry to the influence of Freud. But Kretschmer's
papers finally put a stop to this possibility of development.

Kretschmer's doctrine had a profound influence on German
psychiatry. This happened against a trend which proved not to
be strong enough. (341–43)

But in 1944 Kretschmer could still be found on advisory committees of dis-
sertations devoted to *Daseins*-analytic explorations of psychosis in the context of war. His front man, Klaus Conrad, whose research will qualify for
full coverage further down these pages, maintained a virtual school of psychiatric thought inside Nazi Germany, organized around the same intrapsychic model that had forced entry into all the adjacent departments of treatment when psychoanalysis won the First World War. Mohr (more about
him, too, later), whose loyalty to psychoanalytic psychotherapy during
World War I Eissler recognizes up front with approval, was still in 1944
praising both psychoanalysis and Nazi Germany for providing the contexts and conditions for the intrapsychic cure of homosexuality, of an orientation now viewed, bottom line, as the reserve force behind all war-neurotic symptom formation. Discontinuities exceed themselves in this mode
of uncanny continuity.

Eissler catches Freud slipping one century off the date of the Budapest
meeting to which the military sent official delegates who then brought back
the news that sealed the deal for Freud's science. But according to Eissler,
this slip in the retelling of the therapy competition for top position as shell
shock's treatment of choice reflects a nostalgia and dis-appointment with
destiny (rather than, for example, the outright impatience of someone who
already holds the lead).

> Freud's repressed thought may easily have been that if this deci-
> sion had been taken earlier, the superiority of psychotherapy
> based on psychoanalytic insight would have been proved, and
> the intrinsic truth of psychoanalysis convincingly demonstrated
> to the whole world. (389)

When Eissler rightly corrects such figures of the German neuropsychiatric establishment as Karl Bonhoeffer, he focuses only on their prewar
records. After the war, Bonhoeffer told off Ferenczi's telling on his come-
around to psychoanalytic insights during wartime with know-it-all reference
to his own 1911 article on hysteria. After consulting the piece, Eissler points
out that Bonhoeffer's preemptive reading of the hysterical type advanced a

so-called will to illness as the cure-all explanation that did not admit "an unconscious wish, but an act of will for which the hysteric is responsible. The step from disturbed activity of the will to malingering was a scarcely perceptible one. In the end hysteria was actually put on an equal footing with malingering" (253–54). But Eissler's understanding of influence is on an equal footing with conscious willpower and intention; it was an unconscious influence that Ferenczi diagnosed at the end of the war in the discourse of the resisters, one that denial races to cover and confirm.

When summoned as expert witness in 1920 at the trial of psychiatrists, with Wagner-Jauregg at the front of the line, charged with the maltreatment of war neurotics during the lost war, Freud's science, according to Eissler, was "not yet integrated into academic psychiatry" but "was still a foreign body in Central Europe" (21). Here's Eissler's quick composite sketch of Freud's interest in trauma and traumatic neurosis: "As early as in the meeting of the Vienna Society on February 20, 1908, Freud outlined the basic structure of traumatic neurosis, which took a prominent place in the explanation of war neuroses in *Beyond the Pleasure Principle* (1920)" (354). Something's missing there.

But Freud *was* on a roll, thanks to the drumroll the military gave him at the Budapest meeting in 1918. One year later Freud was advanced to full professor. At the 1920 trial he was already able to agree with those representatives of the psychiatric establishment he had grown so accustomed to disagreeing with, but whose own work in the meantime (since the wartime) was now fundamentally influenced by psychoanalysis. Freud is asked to summarize differences of second opinion between him and Wagner-Jauregg:

> There is no opposition between us in our conception of these conditions; in this we are in complete agreement. I would only venture the opinion that he draws the boundaries of simulation a little too broad. With regard to many of these cases, I would have seen fewer malingerers and more neuroses, but this is not a difference of principle. I know, as he does, that all these neuroses are a flight from the conditions of war into illness. This term originated with me, and medical science has accepted it. The concept of purposefulness was first applied to neuroses of peacetime. Every neurosis has a purpose; it is directed toward certain persons and would disappear at once on a South Sea island or in a similar situation, for there would no longer be a reason for it. I am happy to be able to affirm that complete agreement exists between us about the understanding of neuroses,

and I can only underscore the evidence *Hofrat* Wagner has presented. It is very curious that such neuroses do not occur during captivity. There are two reasons for this. First, the motive of extricating oneself from danger does not exist, and second, the neuroses would do no good: one would not thereby escape from captivity. Thus the motivation is missing. All these neurotics are, in our estimation, fugitives from war. The number of those who feigned illness should be small. (58–59)

But Freud's colleague for a day, Wagner-Jauregg, interrupts with the evidence of "Confessions!" Freud continues:

I do not want to argue about that. The majority of these conditions arose by [force of] strong unconscious intentions; among these, the intent to restore personal independence has been forgotten to be mentioned. For many educated people, it was dreadful to have to submit to military treatment, and bad treatment by their superiors had an influence on many in our army and that of Germany. In our attempts to heal neurosis by psychoanalytic methods, we have found that rage against superiors was often the principal motive of the illness; many cases which did not originate at the front but in hospitals behind the front line provided this elucidation. (59–60)

Once it has been established that Kauders, the ex-soldier pressing charges, had suffered a wound or shock or some stimulus that didn't at first stray from the somatic range, Freud still holds onto the pearl of his wisdom:

But that is nonessential. The injury was only the grain of sand; a neurosis later developed from the small injury, and at the time he was at the Wagner Clinic, he was evidently neurotic. That this was taken as malingering did him an injustice. He stood under the influence of this injustice that the patient felt and that affected him in a particularly exciting way. All neurotics are malingerers; they simulate without knowing it, and this is their sickness. We have to keep in mind that there is a big difference between conscious mental refusal and unconscious refusal. The conscious and the unconscious are always conjoined in an individual, however, and if I confront a neurotic who claims and believes that he is organically ill with a statement that he is not, he will be offended, because it is partially true. People are offended only when something is to the point. So it irritates neurotics to be informed that we do not believe they have an organic illness.

I have the impression that here we have one of those numerous cases in which a neurotic has been intensely irritated by being told that he is a malingerer and is not sick at all. Thereafter, he developed hostility against the physician and a misconception of the latter's intentions. (61–62)

Unstoppable

Down the record of the hearing, Freud can't stop himself: he shoots his life's load of watching his work, which was what's new in treatment, danger-zoned out of the running. Now he can tell the true story:

> This we experience over and over again. When new methods are used, the patients mistrust them and say that they are terrible. . . .
> When I started my treatment, it was said that it made people crazy, that they got into all sorts of states. Colleagues took pains to spread these ideas, also only because it was something new. (66)

But then Wagner-Jauregg's reflex kicks back in. He is of the opinion that psychoanalysis has run out of time, especially in any war run by untranslatable commands:

> Concerning psychoanalysis, I would like to state that this type of treatment often takes God knows how long, and that is why this method is not usable in war. The circumstance of foreign language has been admitted by Professor Freud. (66–67)

Three could join the skirmish right here around the question of the pure applicability of Freud's science, given its peacetime rep or rap for taking all the time in the word. Freud admits that for wartime the analytic recipe stirred in new ingredients and plenty of shortening:

> CHAIRMAN: According to Professor Freud, treatment needs individualization.
> PROFESSOR FREUD: It has been carried out even in war.
> PROFESSOR WAGNER: But only in singular cases.
> PROFESSOR FREUD: In large numbers. But it was shortened by hypnosis. It took extraordinary pains, but it would have been worthwhile in especially difficult cases.
> CHAIRMAN: These are questions for the future. Science will decide which opinion is correct. (67)

Although Eissler sets aside for World War II a newer appreciation of how qualified the seriously ill can be for success in the military at war (256), even already back in the First World War, the rewiring of the nervously ill to a war effort that's otherwise a natural for them could well have been just the goal for Freud's short-term reorganization of the analytic agenda. Whereas E. Raimann, also on the record for the second day of the hearing, reads the eclecticization of the psychoanalytic war work as proof that these other procedures allegedly mixed in with analysis under the supervising analysts were the only items on the field of the big test (29), Freud (and the military in 1918) read the back of the collection *Psychoanalysis of the War Neuroses* differently. Eissler's commentary, in mourning after what repeated the near miss of Freud's total victory at the end of the war, cuts the second day in court as demo of total loss: "The second day of the hearing brought complete victory for Wagner-Jauregg and a crushing defeat for psycho-analysis" (103). But he is at least as mistaken on that score as his recollec-tion of World War II developments in treatment is dead wrong: "As far as I know, there was scarcely any talk of electrotherapy during the Second World War" (113). When the book gets thrown at something, Eissler assumes that the chapter too is closed. By the fourth operation on the appendix, Eissler could have been giving a more balanced account if it weren't for his general tendency not to find influence in what has already fallen between the acts:

> But the war had altered the attitude of the psychiatrists to the neurosis. They had at last realized that the traumatic neuroses were a form of psychic illness, which many of them had previ-ously denied, in accordance with the scientific materialism of the nineteenth century, which would not recognize the autonomy of the human mind, or, perhaps, was not capable of recognizing it. (384)

As Freud testified in earshot of old-time resisters who already counted, without their knowing it, among the many deserters who had recently crossed over to the side of psychoanalysis, the difference of opinion that re-mains, even within the new eclecticized context of cooperation, concerns the dosage of conscious difference between where neurosis takes over and malingering leaves off. According to Eissler, Freud's dynamic point of view saw through the recent history of shell shock therapy to the larger setting of the treating physician's own double duty bind:

> In order to come to grips with the illness, it had to be de-nied by the physician. A method which compelled the malin-gerer to give up his simulation must also—it was said—dispel the neurosis. . . .
> If the neurotic was treated as a malingerer, the physician fi-nally fell into the trap set for the patient and began to forget that the neurotic was actually not a malingerer. (385)

Instead of following the slide into a continuum with psychopathology, ma-lingering took a run on willpower for a wider range where it became interchangeable with "hysteria." Eissler tracks this World War I development all the way to the giveaway refusals of restitution by the post–World War II West German government to hysterics:

> But the step from disturbed activity of the will to malingering was a scarcely perceptible one. In the end, hysteria was actually put on equal footing with malingering, for up to the most recent past—I believe even at the present day—the diagnosis of hysteria is grounds for disqualification in the German courts for restitution for injuries suffered in the course of persecution for racial or political reasons. It can be seen from this that German psychiatry is still suffering from "war damage" caused by the First World War. (254)

Wagner-Jauregg based his sense of degree of malingering on the contradictions in a soldier's statement. Yes, "*contra-diction*" signifies resistance, "speaking against" an other, an authority. But do neurotics or psychotics not evidence contradictoriness in the manifest of their crashed attempts at flight? Eissler sees what's so negative about the soldiers as doubly so, as positively protective:

> The malingerer, like the neurotic, is dominated by his unconscious—by a compulsion which, like the neurotic symptom, serves to protect against very deep unconscious anxieties. (275)

Citing Hamlet as the classic case of the so-called malingerer who "shams a disease from which he really suffers," Eissler sees malingering or simulation caught up in an unreliable sense of two-timing, or what Jacques Lacan refers to in his essay on *Hamlet* as the arrival always at the hour of the other:

> It is the symptom of a very complicated disturbance of the total personality; to get to the bottom of this disturbance is no easy matter. The malingerer is obliged by the nature of his disturbance to take his sickness, so to speak, into his own hands and to arrange and apparently voluntarily produce what the natural course of the disturbance does not bring about. (Eissler, 273)

Good Machine

The analytic tradition gives Otto Fenichel credit for summarizing and synthesizing the theories of traumatic and war neurosis that followed Freud's lead. By Fenichel's 1945 accounting, the model for the breakdown is still machinic, but less endopsychic and more egoic:

> The traumatic neuroses offer a unique opportunity to study the fact that the ego is an apparatus developed for the purpose of overcoming past traumata and for avoiding future traumata; traumatic neuroses represent an insufficiency of this basic function of the ego. (*The Psychoanalytic Theory of Neurosis*, 128)

In Fenichel's account of traumatic neurosis, which puts more of an emphasis on the ego than a stress, the splitting overlooks (without surveying) that, in Freud's thought, doubling split off war neurosis from prewar traumatic neuroses. Fenichel sees instead the continuous functioning of one basic ego model of psychic life. Where low maintenance or good mileage is the goal and frame, agreement with the 1945 consensus that psychosis has been on the rise can't be far behind:

> In World War II there are reported many more schizophrenic or schizoid episodes of short duration that ended spontaneously than in World War I. If reality becomes unbearable, the patient breaks with reality. But enough preconscious attention remains to re-establish the contact with reality as soon as it becomes bearable again. It may be that the recent prevalence of psychotic mechanisms in traumatic neuroses corresponds to the prevalence of "character disorders" among the psychoneuroses. (126)

Fenichel agrees with Kardiner, however, that where the psychotic combination inside traumatic neurosis is not spontaneous, lasting defects are etched into the personality: "The resulting picture is that of a very restricted personality living a simple life on a low level, comparable to certain psychotics or to personalities that have overcome a psychosis with scars in their ego.... Probably this unfavorable development is due to constitutional or psychoneurotic complications of a narcissistic nature" (128).

Fenichel's survey is certainly fit to tie up these loose ends around the loose canon of psychosis. But the centerpiece of the brief war-neurosis coverage, Freud's own account, is radically revised, updated, and colorized for the 1945 ego model. As the tampering with the transference guarantees, Fenichel's review of the analytic assessments of war neurosis cannot but make them up as it goes along, that is, make up for the inconsistencies he's having with Freud's scheduling of concepts-in-progress. Fenichel does not see that Freud's brief skirmish with war neurosis, however introductory and extraneous it may seem on top of the collection of the works to be reread, makes its foray into undiscovered territory that would afterward be claimed for the science that followed. But the primal-scene status of the introduction cannot be admitted by the Fenichel synthesis or summary. Instead, a refinement was introduced into an existing body of knowledge, according to Fenichel's translation of the key terms he quotes and glosses. That Freud's surprise distinction between peace ego and war ego serves as his first design on the split-level ego lair of ego and superego *is* a primal. Fenichel prefers to put war-neurotic doubling in its place, and missing prefixes in Freud's mouth, so that the point to be made is precise, believable, and syntonic with the institution or history of progressive diagnoses of traumatic neurosis.

> In his discussion of war neuroses, Freud called attention to a fact that complicates the role played by the superego in traumatic neuroses ... the intrapsychic representative of fate may consist not only of the genuine superego, which has been acquired in childhood, but also be made up of later and more superficial identifications with various other authorities. Such superficial and passing identifications may sometimes be very influential and come into conflict with the genuine superego. Freud spoke of these formations as "parasitic doubles of the superego," which for certain periods may usurp the power of the superego.... Freud stated that war conditions may create a "war superego" of this kind, which not only permits the expression of impulses otherwise forbidden but even makes demands that are tempting to the ego because its genuine superego never permitted such impulses to be brought into action. According to Freud, one finds in many war neuroses that a "peace ego" rises in defense against a "war superego." (125)

According to this fantasy about Freud's research, the father looked forward to where he arrived last at an eclectic but reunified joint research project that the sons were conducting only to make his nonintrusive but wise and ego-fortifying point. A transferential crisis of this order in the transmission of Freud's own thought can only reflect claims of disownership. Eric Witt-kower and J. P. Spillane set up the same recycling has-been in order to style with the more-Freudian-than-Freud kind of attitude. The reference goes to the "(peace and war super-ego of Freud)" ("Survey," 2).

Invitation to the Vampire

The collectivization and institutionalization of the spell, on the other hand, have made the transference more and more indirect and precarious so that the aspect of performance, the "phony-ness" of enthusiastic identification and of all the traditional dynamics of group psychology, have been tremendously increased.

—T. W. ADORNO, "FREUDIAN THEORY AND THE PATTERN OF FASCIST PROPAGANDA"

It can be argued that General Patton's allusions to divine intention and presumed reincarnation—"I have seen this battlefield before at an earlier time"—were most likely used as a successful method to protect his cryptologic sources.

—DON E. GORDON, *ELECTRONIC WARFARE*

Politics is a form of social therapy for potential suicides.

—HAROLD D. LASSWELL, "THE PSYCHOLOGY OF HITLERISM"

Projecting an East-West axis onto the automatism of change let roll in Eastern Europe, Robert M. Gates had seen the future. It was a primal that made it into the headlines: "CIA Nominee Says Mysteries Upstage Secrets." Gates urged the Senate Intelligence Committee members to face two problems out there, one solvable, the other one unresolvable. But the big problem was that the number of unresolvables was growing "geometrically" while the number of solvables was declining at the same rapid rate. "Secrets are things that are ultimately knowable, stealable—you can find them out, they exist, you can target them, you can go after them.... Mysteries are those things where nobody knows what the answer is" (*Los Angeles Times*, 23 September 1991).

War, diplomacy, and espionage have been on one continuum with the triadic organization of command, control, and communication—which is to say they've run on secrets (which is why they were running on empty). Psychological warfare or propaganda, or in other words mass psychology, has, beginning with Germany's defeat in World War I, been working double time to release or contain mysteries. Freud's *Group Psychology and the Analysis of the Ego* appeared at a time when psychological warfare (which *is*

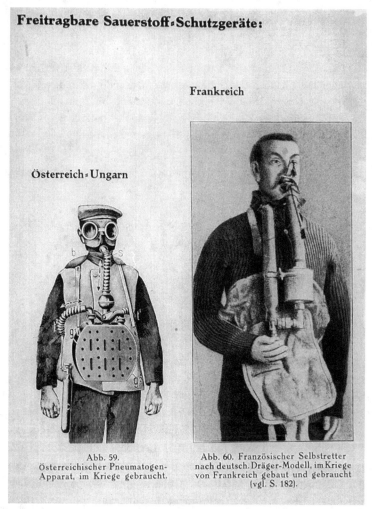

Freitragbare Sauerstoff≈Schutzgeräte:

Frankreich

Österreich≈Ungarn

Abb. 59.
Österreichischer Pneumatogen-
Apparat, im Kriege gebraucht.

Abb. 60. Französischer Selbstretter
nach deutsch. Dräger-Modell, im Kriege
von Frankreich gebaut und gebraucht
(vgl. S. 182).

Two models of gas-war equipment worn during World War I by Austrian Hungarian soldiers (left) and French soldiers (right). Exhibit 24, *Der Chemische Krieg*. Reprinted by permission of Koehler-Mittler.

mass psychology) was already on a roll (the book was a direct hit world-wide with military psychologists).

The prehistory of this convergence of theory and practice can be synchronized with two popular vampire phantasms or fictions that double featured traumatic origins in espionage. In *Varney the Vampyre,* the series or serialization of Varney's vampiric being begins when his undercover work helping Royalists out of Cromwell's England is discovered by the other side and turned around to include both sides of a double agency: henceforth he must turn in to Cromwell's police the clients who paid for safe

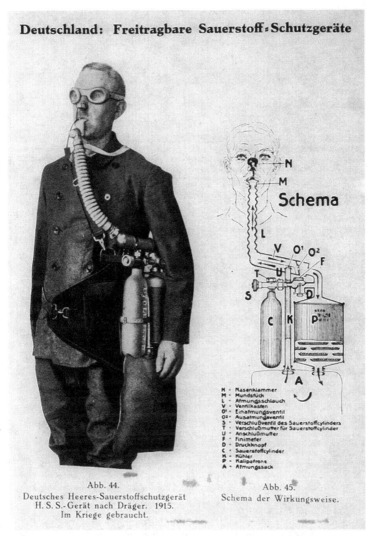

German gas warfare armor used in World War I. Exhibit 17, *Der Chemische Krieg*. Reprinted by permission of Koehler-Mittler.

exit. After the interview with the regicide Cromwell, which, in intraview, exchanges the role of secret agent man for the other one of double agent, Varney returns home and, as though there were some connection, murders his twelve-year-old son. "I was so angry at the moment, that heedless of what I did, . . . I with my clenched fist struck him to the earth" (Prest, 856).

With the murder of his son, of the father inside himself, Varney turns, in a flash, into a vampire who must feed on a child's blood bond with mother and, under cover of the vampirism even the vampire puts on to

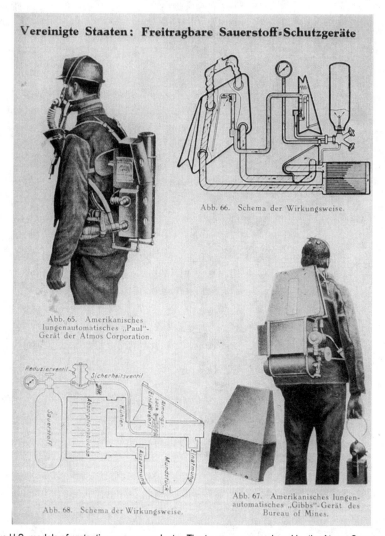

Vereinigte Staaten: Freitragbare Sauerstoff-Schutzgeräte

Abb. 66. Schema der Wirkungsweise.

Abb. 65. Amerikanisches lungenautomatisches „Paul"-Gerät der Atmos Corporation.

Abb. 68. Schema der Wirkungsweise.

Abb. 67. Amerikanisches lungen-automatisches „Gibbs"-Gerät des Bureau of Mines.

Two U.S. models of protective gas-war gadgetry. The top one was produced by the Atmos Corporation and bore the nickname "Paul"; the one on the bottom was developed by the Bureau of Mines. It is not stated whether these were used in World War I. Exhibit 27, *Der Chemische Krieg*. Reprinted by permission of Koehler-Mittler.

conceal designs on other systems of circulation, must go for the gold locked up with other family secrets. In the guise of occult mystery, the open secret of his vampirism, Varney recovers secret capital along the same dotted line that leads to other secrets symptomatizing the family under the attack of his overt operations. In the opening story that gets syndicated throughout the eight-hundred-plus pages of the vampire's repeated attempts, ultimately, to put himself out, it's the Bannersworth family secret of the father's suicide, downed with the secret capital father took with him, that fills the family pack.

Reading the ingredients of this identification from the back of its projection, Varney puts on his vampirization of the Bannersworth family in order to cut to the crypt and make off with the capital. But the psychic fit was too perfect, too autoanalytic: the secret identifications and transferences to which the mystery-covered attack required access are at the same time externalized and resolved. Condemned to be a vampire and to pretend to be a vampire, that is, to target secrets under the cover or banner of occult mystery, Varney can't get out of the no-win spin of being a symptom in a self-cleaning psychic apparatus.

The connection that lies in the future remains behind in *Varney the Vampyre* as the waste product of occult mystery, which the vampire cannot control or integrate within his intelligence service. Everyone agrees, in the wake of the vampire's flight, that mob violence has been released through the belief in, or rumor of, the vampire's existence. The vampire is the target or mascot of a destructive and autodestructive crowd psychology that belief in his vampirism has at the same time produced. The backfire of occult belief that creates an out-of-control crowd was documented (in simulcast with *Varney the Vampyre*) in treatises on superstition-induced panic in group format. By the time of Gustave Le Bon's crowd psychology, this mob violence could be brought under the control of a hypnosis-based theory of unconscious teleguidance. This prehistory of modern mass psychology at the same time covers, within a complex shared by vampirism and espionage, the origins of psychological warfare.

Stoker's *Dracula* and Le Bon's *The Crowd* were contemporaries who made the same group. In Stoker's group portrait, the collective spirit or psychology of the vampire hunters emerges to counter and contain the long-distance and undercover work that's a natural for the vampire. The hunters turn to, on, and into the mediatic outlets of a gadget love that comes complete with a group bond. It's a group formation that revs up across an East-West trajectory that was first projected by Arminus Vambery, who was Stoker's informant and instructor when it came to occult phenomena. Vambery's knowledge of Eastern folklore, customs, and occult beliefs came life size. He was a scholar-adventurer who traveled the East (Lawrence of Arabia style) under the cover of native outfits. Based on his on-location study of the national psychologies of Asia and Eastern Europe, Vambery published countless newspaper articles in support of what he liked to refer to as "England's mission in the East" (Vambery, 370).

It was my quality as an eye-witness which brought me into the
arena of political contest. The explanations I have to give refer,
therefore, rather to the motives which have prompted me to
adopt a certain line of policy. (358)

At the time, it went without saying that he was spy for Britain. Whether
scholarship, journalism, or espionage, Vambery's contribution was, in the
first place, to the psychologization of foreign policy and military intervention.

In the background of Stoker's novel lies another psychological interventionism that goes by the fictive name Van Helsing, the cited name Charcot, and the missing name—Freud. Freudian readings of *Dracula* are admitted by the one fundamental law that, beginning with Stoker, vampirism
must observe: the vampire can penetrate a household or economy by invitation only. In other words: dread covers for desire. But this invitation is at
the same time under the vampire's remote control. It's unconscious. But it's
also an inside job. When Freud diagnosed the vampire phantasm in *Totem
and Taboo,* he issued the invitation to the vampire from within that alternation between identification and projection on which the work of mourning
runs. The other's death creates a disturbance that comes at you with the
force of the occult. But on the inside, it's a case of secret death wishes running for the cover of a projection that brings back the dead. Projection—
both the kind missiles travel and the same kind that packs death wishes inside the vampire's attack—requires that inside the target area one would
strike long range, one must also already have "intelligence," that is, knowledge of the other.

The total thought control of all-out information gathering, which puts
up a defense of secrecy while going for the secrets of the enemy, keeps no
secret from the group members on the inside, on the same side. This intelligence of the other coextensive with Stoker's novel creates what the vampire hunters call at the end a "mass of typewriting" that contains neither
secrets nor proofs. It's a psychology or a style. This "Dracula Style," as it
came to be known, a style of information gathering and sheer citation, resur-
faced in Stoker's writing one last time in *The Lady of the Shroud,* his other
vampire novel. But this one's even less about the occult phantasm of vampirism than it is, up front, about hostage-taking, covert operations, psychological warfare, and espionage. Its "I Spy" dimension folds out as the rescue (through undercover British assistance) of an Eastern European country
from Turkish takeover; but it also folds in at least twice over to characterize
unconscious jealousy of the other and the lengths or wavelengths an uncle
goes to in order to locate and then shadow his heir. Here's uncle to nephew:

You were of so adventurous a nature that even my own widely-spread machinery of acquiring information—what I may call my private "intelligence department"—was inadequate. My machinery was fairly adequate for the East—in great part, at all events. But you went North and South, and West also, and, in addition, you essayed realms where commerce and purely real affairs have no foothold—worlds of thought, of spiritual import, of psychic phenomena—speaking generally, of mysteries. As now and again I was baffled in my inquiries, I had to enlarge my mechanism, and to this end started—not in my own name, of course—some new magazines devoted to certain branches of inquiry and adventure.... By means of *The Journal of Adventure, The Magazine of Mystery, Occultism, Balloon and Aeroplane, The Submarine,* ... *The Ghost World,* ... I was often kept informed when I should otherwise have been ignorant of your whereabouts and designs. (35)

The heir to, and target of, his uncle's spying meets the Lady of the Shroud on location Back East. She's his mystery woman. And in a heartbeat he's totally in love. But he can't be sure (it's a desperately familiar indecision and division) whether she's a vampire or a real woman—or what. The one reason he's pretty convinced she's vampiric: "She had to be helped into my room—in strict accordance with what one sceptical critic of occultism has called 'the Vampire etiquette'" (76). The mystery woman's visitations must be kept a secret from his Aunt Janet, who shares the castle with him. Aunt Janet's so-called second sight has, just the same, already picked up her nephew's nonrelation (the one called love) with the vampire. It's a covert operation folded into their household, their one-on-one. The nephew comments on Aunt Janet's mobilization of second sight: "It is like a sort of dual existence to her; for she is her dear old self all the time, and yet some other person with a sort of intellectual kit of telescope and notebook, which are eternally used on me" (98). But the nephew doesn't know what he's thinking about when thoughts of his Lady inspire him to see love and war as separate and unmixable. Because it's love that shows him the way to assist the locals in their war preparations. When he's with his Lady, words can't express it: instead they communicate nonverbally through a kind of seeing-eye language, the "satisfying language" of love. It's an unambiguous, unambivalent code. And it's what's needed at the heart of war readiness:

We must have some method of communication. In this country where are neither roads nor railways nor telegraphs, we must

> establish a signalling system of some sort. That I can begin at
> once. I can make a code, or adapt one that I have used elsewhere
> already. I shall rig up a semaphore on the top of the Castle which
> can be seen from an enormous distance around.... And then,
> should need come, I may be able to show the mountaineers that
> I am fit to live in their hearts. (100)

A long-distance communications system modeled after the look of
love must group-psychologize the one-on-one format of personal communication and run on open secrets. As was the case with the vampire hunters,
so with the Eastern Europeans defending themselves against the incursions
of the Turkish Bureau of Spies, there can be no secrecy, no couplification, at
the level of command, control, communications:

> Where there are neither telegraphs, railways, nor roads, any ef-
> fective form of communication must—can only be purely per-
> sonal. And so, if they wish to keep any secret amongst them-
> selves, they must preserve the secret of that code. I should have
> dearly liked to learn their new code . . . but as I want to be a help-
> ful friend to them . . . I had to school myself to patience.
>
> This attitude so far won their confidence that before we
> parted at our last meeting, after most solemn vows of faith and
> secrecy, they took me into the secret. (112)

While secrets and codes form a unilateral defense against the other, the
mystery of the Lady's vampiric existence was staged for psychological
warfare purposes. When it was announced that the Lady, who is in fact the
local ruler's daughter and heiress, had suddenly died (it turned out she
was only in a coma or trance), the populace was urged to keep her death a
secret from the outside world; even her father was not informed, since he
was on an undercover assignment of foreign diplomacy that could not be
interrupted to give him this message. That's why the news of her return to
life would have shifted the so-called mental balance of the populace from
the externality of the secret to the projective outlets of mystery. Psychological warfare intervenes, then, to protect the internal conditions of war readiness through a controlled release of projection. This is how the PR bosses
explain it: the people "might not be willing to accept the fact of her being
alive" and "might even imagine that there was on foot some deep, dark
plot which was, or might be, a menace, now or hereafter, to their independence" (152). The occult mystery of a vampiric lady of the shroud was
projected to keep the people undivided and unambivalent. "The priest-
hood undertook . . . to further a ghostly belief amongst the mountaineers

which would tend to prevent a too close or too persistent observation. The Vampire legend was spread as a protection against partial discovery by any mischance" (153).

But in the make-believe in-between zone of seeing and being asked not to see, the Lady helps him see through her and thus rescue them both from the unresolved transference, the identification, that was a feature of the original avuncular testament that got him there in the first place. In the prehistory of the espionage that, beginning at home, would extend to Eastern Europe, a communication from nephew to uncle had already hit the top of the charts, scoring the unambivalence that all along guided the intelligence department as "sacred duty" (34). This is the uncle's response, as though there were a connection, to the nephew's message that puts them on the line given through the post: "It was like your mother coming back from the dead" (33). The content and cause of the "Lady of the Shroud" strategy or subterfuge bring us back to Spy Master's dead mother, where the logic of their connection has been stored. Back East with his Lady, he can't help himself: he has to break for station identification. "There is not one of us but has wished at some time to bring back the dead" (97). It's on this return or comeback that their counteroffensive was finally mounted. The nephew watches his at once high speed and absolutely still warship (made in Britain) "steal in like a ghost" (147).

The telecommunications system and group psychology plugging along into the language of love had to have been, all along, transmitting the broadcasts of an encrypted loss or pathogenic identification. When the Turkish spies are routed, all systems are go: a big one is scored for unambivalence over the dead body of the enemy, the unidentified—or unidentified with—other. The Turks are defeated "as a child wipes a lesson from its slate" (170). That the end is in sights is signaled from on high with the rescue of the father ruler by aeroplane. This preemptive flying and bombing mission, which represents the first air attack in history or, in any event, in literature, takes future war to the skies, the final frontier that World War I, according to Freud, had to be fought over once the first crossing of the other's airspace destabilized the borderlines.

1905/1909

Throughout the period of war hysteria there was a disposition
to confuse the propagandist (on the opposite side) with the spy.
The propagandist is the antithesis of the spy. The spy attempts
to abstract from your mind something that is useful to his
employers. The propagandist tries to put something into your
mind that is not yet there.

—GEORGE SYLVESTER VIERECK, *SPREADING GERMS OF HATE*

Like a Fifth Column hiding in subterranean cellars until the
hour to strike arrives, the depressed states do not emerge into
the scene of the war neuroses until comparatively late in the
course of the individual case. Once in ascendance, however,
they dominate the clinical picture, taking precedence over the
symptoms both of anxiety and of conversion.

—ROY GRINKER AND JOHN SPIEGEL, *WAR NEUROSES IN NORTH AFRICA:
THE TUNISIAN CAMPAIGN (JANUARY–MAY 1943)*

A future war will call at least equally large numbers of men into
action. The tremendous endurance, bodily and mental, required
for the days of fighting over increasingly large areas and the
mysterious and widely destructive effects of modern artillery
fire will test men as they have never been tested before. We can
surely count then on a larger percentage of mental diseases,
requiring our attention in future war.

—R. L. RICHARDS, "MENTAL AND NERVOUS DISEASES IN THE
RUSSO-JAPANESE WAR"

The Russo-Japanese War was one of those head starts, like the U.S. Civil
War and the Boer War, that physicians were given to prepare for World War I.
Cases of battle stress with resulting psychiatric breakdown were diagnosed
and treated in the Russian army. The attending physicians looked out for
the secondary gain, the flight into illness, and what they referred to as the
"evacuation syndrome"—all of which led their treatment (you saw it first
with the Russians) to cultivate relations of proximity to battle out of principle and in practice. This hands-on head start fell between the disconnec-
tions between Russian psychiatry and psychology, which by Soviet times
could look back on no common origin or history and, at best, when contact

was established, total conflict. The split between psychiatric interest in brain physiology and psychological interest in character strengths and weaknesses that mixed in the mode of ambivalence in the German World War I discourse of the medical establishment was kept separate, split off, throughout its Eastern delegation (the Russian specialists were all, traditionally, trained or made in Germany). Under Stalin both psychological tendencies, psychoanalysis and psychological testing, were outlawed. Psychiatry was left to go ahead with its organic basis.

But between 1900 and 1917, and then again in the twenties, psychology had absorbed, much as in the West, Freudian influences. While most went the way of the Stalin-time purges, a few pockets of the influence were still hanging in there: even a director of the Bekhterev Institute could be analysis compatible in his method of treatment as long as the password was in order (he called his approach "psychogenic analysis"). Interest in psychology (in the medley of approaches suspended between testing and analysis) was brought back in the sixties under advisement of the military. In 1967 the military made a course in psychology a requirement in all its schools. Soon it was mandatory part of the curriculum at the Political Academy. If only for psychological-warfare purposes, it was not uninteresting to know under what assumptions the Western military complex was running (in California you can read the horoscope forecast not because you believe in it but because the other you're trying to influence does). The new show of military support for psychology turned on channels of human engineering research targeted at military equipment design. Motivation and resistance to stress and trauma now concerned the military looking forward to the nuclear war environment. Armies tend to plan for the last war. Soviet short-term therapy reached World War II levels of a trailing-behind mix of conditioning, administration of feedback mechanisms (including hypnosis), and drug treatment. In the 1980s the eclectic range for neurosis therapy added biofeedback, massage, group therapy, sensitivity sessions, counseling, dance therapy. But during World War II the Soviets had no policy of psychiatric or psychological selection or treatment. Basically the Soviet military took the fodder approach to combating the Germans (who were already nervous about the limitedness of their own resources). Even if there were loads of psychiatric casualties, they were loaded back into the fodder front: the Soviets were thus more successful in containing the eventual manpower loss that results from war neurosis. The Soviet Union got more out of its men than any other nation at war ever did. Military units were kept running and fighting down to 30 percent left (when 30 percent were gone, the U.S. military brought its units back into the safety zone). Only in military aviation psychology was a high level of research maintained throughout this period. The period that the air force has always put to military-psychological resistance kept the influence of science, no, literature, no, psychoanalysis always on the society-wide airwaves.

Between *Dracula* and *The Lady of the Shroud*, as between *The Interpretation of Dreams* and the case study of Dora, the decoding of secrets emerges as a too limited line of communication and defense. When Freud started casing Dora, he hoped to apply and demonstrate "how an art, which would otherwise be useless, can be turned to account for the discovery of the hidden and repressed parts of mental life" (*SE* 7:114). But Freud also discovered a thing called transference, and it was not so much a symptom; it was a mystery, one that, if left unresolved, set a half-life to the analytic decoding of secrets (or symptoms).

> Transference is the one thing the presence of which has to be detected almost without assistance and with only slightest clues to go upon, while at the same time the risk of making arbitrary inferences has to be avoided. Nevertheless, transference cannot be evaded, since use is made of it in setting up all the obstacles that make the material inaccessible to treatment, and since it is only after the transference has been resolved that a patient arrives at a sense of conviction of the validity of the connections which have been constructed during the analysis. (*SE*, 7:116–17)

What Freud picks up from his teen patient is that, in its unresolved state, transference is the beam of unambivalence keeping the patient in the undivided state of catastrophe preparedness. The adolescent or perpetually adolescent group sends out its information-gathering service to shadow the couple (both the parental one and the futural one). Dora, who's in the ready position for the one-on-one, is surprise attacked by the covert operations of the other woman or man, the matricentric outlet of group psychology. Her only system of defense—her own continuum of communication, control, command—is unresolved transference. Unresolved transferences or identifications make the ego's crowd, the internal and eternal one of ghosts. And it's that crowded feeling that Dora, unprotected by intelligence of the other, goes for.

Dora checks in with Freud's agency already locked onto the transferential beam of spy loyalty. At the time, Freud thought secrets alone were his concern. But Dora had come to his praxis to share the fantasy—the mystery—of unresolved transference, of unambivalent I Spy loyalty. And just as a spy can become a double agent but can never leave or betray spy systems to the outside, so a patient, as Dora taught Freud, cannot get out and betray analysis on the outside but can only check in with another transference, in fact with another analyst. According to histories of Freud's most famous patients, the analysand never leaves the intelligence service of psychoanalysis but, at the limit, can even make a career out of a double agency that is at the same time loyalty to the system.

Like, You Know, I Don't Know

In no other war in history have "words" been so important as
in the world conflict of 1914–1918. Along with the development
of airplanes, tanks, poison gases, and other marvels of military
technique, a propaganda system for purposes of warfare was
then set up which for scientific perfection rivaled the military
system.

—GEORGE G. BRUNTZ, *ALLIED PROPAGANDA AND THE COLLAPSE OF
THE GERMAN EMPIRE IN 1918*

What made the psychological warfare of World War II peculiar
was the fact that our enemies fought one kind of war ("warfare
psychologically waged," or total war) and we fought them
back with another. Theoretically, it is possible to argue that we
had no business succeeding.
    But we did succeed.

—PAUL M. A. LINEBARGER, *PSYCHOLOGICAL WARFARE*

Invitation to and intelligence of the other are not military (or vampiric) externals and exclusives. Metapsychological fact of life in the mass lane: You
only know what the other thinks you know. This twist (and warning shout)
is so true of all information gathered at, and filling up to, the group-psychological or total war level. Thus the plainest text around—a true emergency shortcut—is Ladislas Farago's 1941 Survey and Bibliography *German Psychological Warfare*, which the U.S. Committee for National Morale
commissioned and issued as the manual and warning label to the second
coming of world war. Without index or alphabetical order throughout the
bibliography but only under each topic by topic, the reader is still forced to
follow the "HOW TO READ THIS BOOK" inserted between table of contents
and text: "It is suggested that the Survey be read in its continuity." It's a
catch-up course in one reading. One year later, Farago gave the sense of urgency another shot with his follow-up compilation of German sources, *The
Axis Grand Strategy*. In that introduction too, he touched on the still open
(and shut) secret of Nazi total psychological coverage:

> The Germans indulge themselves in open discussion of what other
> people consider deep military and diplomatic secrets. This frank-
> ness has worked to their advantage, because the rest of the
> world has hesitated to believe what the Nazis did not hesitate to
> reveal. (vii)

First sentence of the 1941 survey: "One of the truly important features of the present war is the Germans' skillful use of psychology in revitalizing military strategy and tactics to fit the changed requirements of Total War" (1). The guide points out the German military's self-assessment of its defeat in World War I as all blindness and hindsight about the lack of psychological military training back then. A certain "Weniger describes how the last war—as all former wars—revealed that purely military campaigns were in reality sequences of psychological phenomena" (47). These phenomena, which add up to group psychology, must be sent up to the front to fortify the German side and beyond to undermine enemy morale society-wide in the forum of psychological warfare: "Total war inevitably made man himself (his attitudes and sentiments), rather than arms and supplies, the focal point for determining ultimate victory or defeat" (47). Group psychology is always modeled on the shocks and shots of catastrophe preparedness it contains: "Specific national characteristics are analyzed through the study of a nation's reactions to cultural phenomena, natural catastrophes, economic and political depressions" (53).

The military effort to understand or follow group psychology was in the service of targeting the "resistance" of the enemy nation at the group rate (49). Total war is psychological warfare. The air force, first sent on reconnaissance missions to reduce all that one did not see to sheer visibility, was assigned (as a follow-up) air raids that were shows of terror directed for and against the captive audience of civilians, whose resolve had to be totaled. On the other side, the hysterical visibility and superficiality of Nazi air raid precautions reflected the Nazis' purely psychological concern or culture industry: civilians were to be put in the ready position of preparedness, that group effort that gives internal and eternal shelter. Bombardment would in fact total their resolve. "Before this war, the Germans conducted large-scale experiments of artificial panics among soldiers, civilians, and school children. The lessons derived from these experiments were utilized in making German troops as panic-proof as possible, and in generating panic among the enemy" (44).

Nazi research in psychological warfare (and thus in group psychology) is acknowledged in 1941 as being in advance of what we were packing into our military complex. As was the case with Nazi aerospace experimentation, Nazi military psychology scored results that American research took over during and after the war. On the Nazi side of World War II, at once a "war of nerves" and a "war of movement" according to the survey, all psychological approaches were tried out. "To obtain a systematic and balanced study of complex practical problems, the Germans have indeed adopted some of the methodology of physiological psychology, psycho-analysis, experimental psychology, social psychology, genetic psychology, and cultural anthropology" (52). At the same time that the Frankfurt school hit the streets and began group-psychological exploration of the culture industry, Nazi psychological observers or "psychological spies" were sent abroad to observe the foreign mass-media culture and bring back for use in psychological warfare a so-called "symptomatic mass picture" (55).

The survey part (three) devoted to "German Psychological Warfare" opens with a Nazi quote:

> In the past people migrated from place to place; today ideas migrate from people to people. We are in the midst of an ideological upheaval of unprecedented magnitude. (45)

The survey decodes to plainer text: "The Nazi revolution is taking place at a time when war itself is going through its own social and technological revolution. This process started in the last war which marked the final break with all traditional conceptions and techniques of warfare, ushering in a new era of 'revolutionary wars'" (45). The plainest text around is the bibliography: The German military was the first to read Le Bon. And Freud. In the compilation of Nazi reading lists, we find two annotated Freud entries: *Mass Psychology and the Analysis of the Ego* and *Contemporary Thoughts on War and Death*. The former is glossed as "the raw material upon which the Nazis base a major part of their psychological offensives"; the latter is said to be "still widely read and anonymously quoted among German army psychologists" (109, 95). It's as though the induction of psychoanalysis and psychotherapy into the U.S. military followed the trend the Nazis set.

In Fritz Lang's *Ministry of Fear*, the best-selling book written by a noted psychiatrist and psy warrior (and Nazi spy) officially billed as adviser to the British war effort is entitled, by now so ambiguously, *The Psychoanalysis of Nazism*.

Spiritual Child

Viktor Frankl, a survivor of Nazi German enslavement and mass murder in concentration camps, had his memoirs to thank for his formulation of the "third Viennese school of psychotherapy," logotherapy, which (according to the 1964 cover of *Man's Search for Meaning*) was developed during his persecution both as and in addition to "the crystallization of his theories as a result of those hellish experiences." *Man's Search for Meaning* at the same time belongs to a Holocaust genre documenting the practice of psychoanalysis and psychodynamic therapy among inmates in the death camps. Frankl: "The tender beginnings of a psychotherapy or psychohygiene were, when they were possible at all in the camp, either individual or collective in nature. The individual psychotherapeutic attempts were often a kind of 'life-saving procedure.' These efforts were usually concerned with the prevention of suicides" (125). Is the evidence of eclectic, supportive psychotherapy in the camps a leftover from an earlier era, or is it also the home-grown representation of what lies outside imprisonment, like the cabaret "improvised from time to time" that Frankl attended as inmate (64–65) or the spiritualistic séance he also witnessed in camp (which demonstrated in his view the presence of the "spirit" of the "subconscious mind") (55–56)? The care with which Frankl avoids direct contact with the names of psychoanalysis while agreeing with their basic meaning could be a case in pointing to the overlap between his eclecticism and that of the "new" German standards of therapy (standards that in turn predate the Nazi order). In discussing the level to which a prisoner's inner life was thinking, Frankl cites his "colleagues in camp who were trained in psychoanalysis," who "often spoke of a 'regression' in the camp inmate" (44). Down the pages "sublimation" will be modified as "so-called" (177). General therapeutic phrases like "subconscious mind," "defensive mechanism" (98), "inferiority complex" (99), and "delusions of grandeur" (100) make it into Frankl's discourse without about-facing the distance between what's new or now and what's just one-sided, outdated, Freud identified.

Although Frankl is proud to point out that he never served as psychiatrist in camp but remained an ordinary prisoner (10), outside his medical affiliation, playing it as it lay, he served as psychotherapist to his Capo chief, who just couldn't stop confiding in him. That is how Frankl remained under Capo protection (41). In his suicide-prevention work with fellow inmates, Frankl discovered the single most successful intervention was to point out a future goal, which comes complete, once in focus, with the free gift of inner strength (115). This practice was perfected as what he reached for to help himself:

> I forced my thoughts to turn to another subject. Suddenly I saw myself standing on the platform of a well-lit, warm and pleasant lecture room. In front of me sat an attentive audience on comfortable upholstered seats. I was giving a lecture on the psychology of the concentration camp! All that oppressed me at that moment became objective, seen and described from the remote viewpoint of science. By this method I succeeded somehow in rising above the situation, above the sufferings of the moment, and I observed them as if they were already of the past. Both I and my troubles became the object of an interesting psychoscientific study undertaken by myself. (116–17)

At a low point in block morale, the warden, "a wise man," addressed the group: he acknowledged all their suffering but diagnosed all recent deaths as resulting from giving up hope. Then he gave up the floor to Frankl, who, for his first number, pointed out that it could be a lot worse. Then he spoke about the future. But he also gave the past a part to play in his encouraging words: "Not only our experiences, but all we have done, whatever great thoughts we may have had, and all we have suffered, all this is not lost, though it is past; we have brought it into being. Having been is also a kind of being, and perhaps the surest kind" (131). Can he count the many ways in which we are able to give life meaning? But you can count on this: they had already given, and it was their "sacrifice." "The purpose of my words was to find a full meaning in our life, then and there, in that hut and in that practically hopeless situation. I saw that my efforts had been successful. When the electric bulb flared up again, I saw the miserable figures of my friends limping toward me to thank me with tears in their eyes" (133).

After the war Frankl finds a quick way out of defining his logotherapy in response to an American doctor's question: "Can you tell me in one sentence what is meant by logotherapy? . . . At least, what is the difference between psychoanalysis and logotherapy?" (152). The comparison stopover gives him a way:

> Logotherapy, in comparison with psychoanalysis, is a method less retrospective and less introspective. Logotherapy focuses rather on the future, that is to say, on the assignments and meanings to be fulfilled by the patient in his future. At the same time,

logotherapy defocuses all the vicious-circle formations and feedback mechanisms that play such a great role in the development
of neuroses. Thus the typical self-centeredness of the neurotic is
broken up instead of being continually fostered and reinforced.
(152–53)

That's why the third Viennese school of psychotherapy addresses the will
to meaning to triangulate the dynamic duo, Freud's pleasure principle (or
will to pleasure) and Adler's will to power (154). Logotherapy specializes
in analyzing the "existential frustrations" that can give rise to "noögenic
neurosis," which rises above mere "psychogenic neurosis" (159): the latter
reflects the push and pull of conflicts between drives; the former emerges
from conflicts between various values (160). Easier said, then undone: "Logotherapy... is an analytical process. To this extent, logotherapy resembles
psychoanalysis"—with the difference, again, that "it does not restrict its
activity to *instinctual* facts within the individual's unconscious, but also
cares for *spiritual* realities such as the potential meaning of his existence to
be fulfilled, as well as his *will* to meaning" (163). Even in the tightest spot
imaginable, you alone can come out deciding for one side versus another.
"In the concentration camps, for example, in this living laboratory and on
this testing ground, we watched and witnessed some of our comrades be-
have like swine while others behaved like saints. Man has both potentiali-
ties within himself; which one is actualized depends on decisions but not
on conditions" (213). These are transference-free zones of responsibility in
reporting.

When Frankl arrived at Auschwitz, loss struck first when his manuscript
was confiscated right on the spot he was in. It was the first version of the
book in which Frankl would introduce logotherapy after the war. He in fact
owed his survival not only to the future-oriented tenets of logotherapy—
not only to the invention and testing of these new therapeutic standards—
but also, and most immediately, to the work he undertook of reconstructing
his "spiritual child," the book that predated his arrival at camp but which,
upon arrival, he also had to survive:

Certainly, my deep concern to write this manuscript anew helped
me to survive the rigors of the camp. For instance, when I fell ill
with typhus fever I jotted down on little scraps of paper many
notes intended to enable me to rewrite the manuscript, should I
live to the day of liberation. I am sure that this reconstruction of
my lost manuscript... assisted me in overcoming the danger of
collapse. (165)

The "essence" of logotherapy—indeed of "existence"—comes down to the "paradoxical intention" that one live this time as though it were already the second time around. The "categorical imperative of logotherapy" demands that we live as if living already for the second time and as if we had acted the first time as wrongly as we are about to act now. Thus the person addressed is invited "to imagine first that the present is past and, second, that the past may yet be changed and amended" (173). This is a roundabout way of including and concealing what was in Frankl's case the reconstructive work of preserving and reversing loss. "I should say having been is the surest kind of being" (191). Is that another way of saying that one never had anything to lose? A measure of containment is Frankl's sizing up of pain, on the basis of his camp experience, as a concentrate that upon activation can expand only always so far, and at its limits comes in one size fits all:

> Yet it is possible to practice the art of living even in a concentration camp, although suffering is omnipresent. To draw an analogy: a man's suffering is similar to the behavior of gas. If a certain quantity of gas is pumped into an empty chamber, it will fill the chamber completely and evenly, no matter how big the chamber. Thus suffering completely fills the human soul and conscious mind, no matter whether the suffering is great or little. Therefore the "size" of human suffering is absolutely relative. (69–70)

In other words, words Frankl finds only for the manuscript, his "spiritual child," human suffering fills the self—but in relation to the other, in particular the relative, it is at the same time absolute. One fact of camp life that Frankl doesn't address is the duress of impeded, minimized, or suppressed mourning upon—their own doom notwithstanding—the survivors of so many dead.

The "existential vacuum" that's packed, according to Frankl, inside our collective twentieth-century neurosis must therefore also predate not only the postwar era but even the onset of Frankl's ambiguously formative camp experiences, including his in-camp therapeutic interventions and the ongoing reconstruction of his lost work. Only the names (may) have been changed to project the nascent status of his logotherapy. "Feedback mechanisms," for instance, would appear specific to the post-WWII lexicon of psychotherapy en vogue. "Having shown the beneficial impact of meaning orientation" (in other words, logotherapy as Frankl applied it to the concentration camp setting), "I shall now turn to the detrimental influence of that feeling of which so many patients complain today, namely, the feeling of the total and ultimate meaninglessness of their lives. They lack the awareness of a meaning worth living for. They are haunted by the experience of their inner emptiness, a void within themselves" (167). Only distress busts the boredom that monopolizes the bored. Like Adler and Jung before him (Jung goes unnamed because Frankl is qualifying for the Viennese finals of psychotherapy and because his logotherapy reads like an Adlerian version of Jung), Frankl adds his will to the triad formed with Freud in the context of contest: "Sometimes the frustrated will to meaning is vicariously compensated for by a will to power.... In other cases, the place of frustrated will to meaning is taken by the will to pleasure" (170). The other two therapies and theories are secondary to Frankl's will and, if made primary just the same, are symptomatic of the frustration of Frankl's will.

While interred in Dachau and Buchenwald from 1938 to 1945, Ernst Federn, son of Paul Federn, the colleague Freud chose to sit in, as referee or witness, when Felix Boehm visited Vienna to discuss the future of psychoanalysis in Nazi Germany, performed the duties of an improv analyst based on the exposure or hearsay associated with his time spent in the inner circles of psychoanalytic culture. He is entitled to describe himself as a "psychoanalyst by birth" (Federn, 4). He trained as psychoanalyst after the war in the United States. Back then, in Nazi Germany, Federn's clients belonged, as was the case with those Frankl granted or rather counted as audience, among the better-positioned camp inmates.

Federn met Bruno Bettelheim and Dr. Brief during his camp internment; the latter, the only one out of three already fully trained as analyst at the time, did not survive. Bettelheim, who was released after one year, turned his in-camp observations into an article Federn goes ahead and cosigns:

> Bettelheim and I had noticed the degree to which the mechanisms of defence that Sandor Ferenczi and Anna Freud have described as identification with the aggressor could be observed amongst the camp inmates. Who made this observation first I cannot tell today, but it was a significant one. What Anna Freud had described of children and what every nursery-school teacher can confirm can also be found among adults and most clearly when they are in a regressed state of mind. In other words Bettelheim, myself and later Brief found confirmation of two important psychoanalytic findings: Under severe mental strain man regresses and develops infantile mechanisms of defence.... Historically speaking, Bettelheim reported our observations in a paper that made

him well known. How much his experiences at camp influenced his later work with mentally ill children he has shown in his many books. (5)

Dr. Brief served as Federn's "supervisor." One Jewish prisoner newly arrived from Amsterdam was accused by the "block elder" of having stolen a piece of bread. "During the following night this man urinated between the two beds, one of which he occupied. There was a great upset over this occurrence and renewed threats to kill this unfortunate man. I had observed that he had urinated between the two beds and not in the bed itself. It was, I thought, not a case of enuresis, but one of symptomatic action. I had also noticed that the Dutch word that he had used meant the same as washing away, or cleansing. I offered to treat this case and to solve it" (5). Once permission was granted, Federn told his client that he did not believe in his guilt and would intervene on his behalf with the block elder. Then he interpreted the man's urinating as signifying the wish to cleanse himself of all charges. "His wrongdoing stopped. Dr. Brief did not think that it was my interpretation that accomplished this, but the fact that I had taken away his anxiety by promising to help him. However that may have been, my reputation as a psychoanalyst was established" (6).

One anecdote, however, extends the genre view of in-camp psychotherapy, before push comes to ovens, to overlap with one edge that pulls up and opens wide inside German society on the outside, although perhaps as preserved in the camps from another time zone:

There were many such occasions for me to use my psychoanalytic knowledge. Once my hands were badly frozen. That was in November 1938. I was excused from work, and my hands were completely wrapped up, and I went to the clinic. There it was arranged that the Jewish physicians were not the physicians, but the assistants, and non-Jewish handymen performed the operations. . . . So there were two Viennese Jewish physicians, very prominent, one was Dr. Kriss and the second was a certain Dr. Verö. Kriss was down in the hospital, Verö up in the Jewish clinic, and the "surgeon" was named Denhardt, a big, very good looking guy from the Rheinland, a miner or a carpenter. He was an excellent surgeon. So I come to the clinic, and they remove my bandages, my hands were completely gangrene. While I sit there, Verö asks Denhardt: "Do you know who this is? He's the son of a famous man, the psychoananalyst Paul Federn." Denhardt then turns to me and asks: "Do you also know something about psychoanalysis? Can you explain the Oedipus Complex to

me?" Thereupon I sat down with my hands, which at that time
didn't hurt yet, and explained the Oedipus Complex to him. In
response he said, you did that very nicely, now let's operate. . . .
That saved my life back then. (Plänker, 158)

The false surgeon, a fellow prisoner but a Gentile, who had been an inmate
since 1933 (Federn, 6), and the false analyst congratulate each other on their
correct understanding of the Oedipus complex, still the common lingo for
Austrian and German Jews and at least one German Gentile at the Dachau
concentration camp in 1939.

Bettelheim's famous 1943 essay on his internment in Nazi Germany
makes out the figure of miner or carpenter turned surgeon to be the main
subject of the concentration camp, which he views essentially as lab space
for the production line of model Nazi German citizens. While each individual prisoner is broken down, the rest of the population is thus terrorized by
the prospect of these prisoners as hostages for their own good behavior. In
addition, the camp setting provided the Gestapo with a "training ground"
and an "experimental laboratory" in which new and improved methods
for controlling whole populations inside and out could be studied. The
Gestapo also learned firsthand the minimum in food, hygiene, and medical
attention required to keep a population barely alive but still able to perform hard labor under the aegis of negative reinforcement only. For his
1943 paper, however, Bettelheim chose to focus on one aspect of the psychological significance of the camps, one more upbeat and functional than
the murderous racially determined meaning or purpose, namely on *"the
concentration camp as a means of producing changes in the prisoners which will
make them more useful subjects* of the Nazi state" (419). When Bettelheim
touches on the clinic setting where physicians worked as nurses and car-
penters served as surgeons, he does not explain the role change in reference to racial law but ascribes it, rather, to the psychological view held by
the Gestapo that a prisoner allowed to exercise his true profession was not
really being punished.

Keeping it third personal, Bettelheim subsumes his study of his camp
experience, and in this he resembles the inventor and reconstructor of logotherapy, under whatever it took him to survive: "The study of these behaviors was a mechanism developed by him ad hoc in order that he might
have at least some intellectual interests and in this way be better equipped
to endure life in the camp. His observing and collecting of data should rather
be considered as a particular type of defense developed in such an extreme
situation. It was individually developed, not enforced by the Gestapo, and

based on this particular prisoner's background, training, and interests. It was developed to protect this individual against a disintegration of his personality" (420–21). He was thus the first subject of this investigation once he realized that two souls, alas, crossed his heart: "But soon he realized that what happened to him, for instance, the split in his person into one who observes and one to whom things happen, could no longer be called normal, but was a typical psychopathological phenomenon" (421). The first phase of his research assuaged his anxiety about going mad: "If I did not change any more than all other normal persons, then what happened in me and to me was a process of adaptation and not the setting in of insanity" (421). Dissociation or splitting was just the beginning. The final phase of adaptation issues in identification with the aggressor, acceptance of the Nazi judgment, even when called down upon everyone just like you. *"It seems that what happens in an extreme fashion to the prisoners who spend several years in the concentration camp happens in less exaggerated form to the inhabitants of the big concentration camp called greater Germany"* (452). Who knew that the Gestapo was seeking in and through the camps to "produce changes in the personality of the prisoners" (424)?

Bettelheim recognized two participants in his psychological research project, a certain Dr. Alfred Fischer, who in the meantime had escaped to England, where he was on duty in a military hospital, and another one who remained nameless in 1943 since still at Buchenwald (423 n. 9). They were the only two Bettelheim could find "who were trained and interested enough to participate in his investigation." Their support was appreciated, especially since "they seemed less interested in the problem than the author" (423). Unlike Frankl, Bettelheim didn't have the opportunity to construct or reconstruct his thoughts on paper. "The only way to overcome this difficulty was to make every effort to remember what happened. . . . He tried to concentrate on the characteristic and otherwise outstanding phenomena, repeated his findings again and again to himself—time was abundant and had to be killed anyway—made a habit when at work to go over all the material he could remember so as to impress it better in his memory" (422).

Bettelheim breaks down the research population into new and old prisoners. "It has been mentioned that the main concern of the new prisoners seemed to be to remain intact as a personality and to return to the outer world the same persons who had left it; all their emotional efforts were directed towards this goal. Old prisoners seemed mainly concerned with the problem of how to live as well as possible within the camp. Once they had reached this attitude, everything that happened to them, even the worst atrocity, was 'real' to them. No longer was there a split between one to whom things happened and the one who observed them. Once this stage was reached of taking everything that happened in the camp as 'real,' there was every indication that the prisoners who had reached it were afraid of returning to the outer world" (437). Whom was he protecting?

One example of identification with the aggressor packs a silent exchange between Bettelheim's camp experience and Federn's: "Practically all prisoners who had spent a long time in the camp took over the Gestapo's attitude toward the so-called unfit prisoners. . . . Bad behavior in the labor gang endangered the whole group. So a newcomer who did not stand up well under the strain tended to become a liability for the other prisoners. Moreover, weaklings were those most apt to turn traitors" (448). According to Federn, he first met Bettelheim over the issue of not fitting in:

> At the time of Bettelheim's stay there [at Buchenwald], from September 1938 to April 1939, life was very bad indeed, but it was possible to survive, even for a person as unsuited to the practicalities of life as Bettelheim. He owes his survival to the chance of finding work in the stock-mending shop, where he could live in relative safety. He could also take advantage of the fact that he wore thick glasses; for reasons I could never find out, the SS guards showed some respect for these.
>
> I met Bettelheim on the occasion of an activity consisting in throwing bricks for a distance of about two feet from one another, in a kind of human chain. . . . Bettelheim dropped every piece I had thrown to him. This was dangerous, because . . . a guard might notice and give a beating. I made a remark about this, to which Bettelheim answered: "Is that your brick?" . . . We shook hands and remained friends from that hour. (4)

We Won!

The Nazis were paranoids: real good at interrogating the other's unconscious but at the same time totally unable to get into their own from both
sides now. The not-seeing that is Nazism could not admit the seeing-through,
the seeing through to the end in sight: that is, the resolution of the transference. That's why the Nazis could never completely exclude Freud's science,
but in no time insisted that the first or training therapy could not be with a
psychoanalyst. During the war, son of Göring (the son, that is, of the politi-
cian's cousin, the Adlerian in charge, right down to the end of the war, of
the Nazi society in which all the therapies that had originally split off from
Freud's science were reunited) wanted to be analyzed. That's right, son of
Göring or Göring's nephew was into psychoanalysis. So to get around Nazi
law, Göring argued that his son was already pretrained with a nonanalytic
therapist and therapy: the analysis could proceed under cover of its being
in second or secondary place.

By the Gulf War, U.S. lines of defense would seem to have found a military mass psychology to plug into. One step in this direction had been
taken during World War II when free copies of Stoker's *Dracula* were distributed to the GIs. After the bomb, panic posters that focused on the side
effects of spreading rumors made the rounds. Even at the 1984 L.A.
Olympics, "rumor centers" were still being set up to contain the contagion.
That takes U.S. psychological warfare up to *Varney the Vampyre*, but pre–Le
Bon, and definitely pre-Freud. But the Gulf War was state of the art group
psychology.

But even as TV did come full circuit in the Middle East media war, the
legacy of a segregation "was there," too: the splitting that disconnected
the allies and enemies on both sides (the allies and enemies who were fighting World War II) from antiwar activists who were resisting the Vietnam
War. In the midst of an eternal rerun of phantasms, the Patriot system raised
the first real-time challenge to Nazi control of the airwaves. Thus was flexed
the ultimate attainment of the state of the art (or art of the state) in what the
Germans were the first to call psychological warfare. But the Nazis already
lost, right? But they only lost because they didn't know when to stop winning. That's a danger that goes with the unresolved transference. The control of the airwaves (that is, of psychological warfare and group psychology) had remained, up to the Gulf War, unconsciously on the eternally and
internally winning side of Nazi loss.

Front page of *Weekly World News* during the Persian Gulf War, 1990.

As the first twelve American casualties threatened to preempt U.S. war readiness by switching on the newsreel technology of Vietnam's funereal commemorations, the media war flipped to the sitcom: the war dead had been shot by their own side. The channel switch to "friendly fire" instantly unblocked the metabolism threatening to shut down as grief stuck. The war effort was so efficient (that is, friendly) that not only were enemies killed but even some of one's own had to go. According to Freud's genealogy of modern group psychology, all that's fair, including love and war, gets replaced by friendship and suicide, the set responses that fit onto another set—the TV set.

If television came full circuit in the Gulf War, in which the TV coverage *was* the total war, with friend and foe alike getting with the same program, even this video portion, which gave us the point of view, instant by instant, at the end of the missiles, was still stuck on Nazi Germany's mobilization of the same bonds and bombs of live transmission. Back in primal time, TV was used to monitor weapons experiments, indeed, to exercise remote control over the bombs and rockets themselves, and to extend its live coverage, via a network of public "television rooms," throughout the Nazi inside view of the war effort.

The inner state of the U.S. military's growing rapport with psychological warfare was outlined in Nazi psychologist Schoenemann's 1939 endopsychic portrait of the United States. Following out lines of thought Freud and William Bullitt were the first to throw out, Schoenemann too concludes:

> The "innate pacifism of the American people often assumes the attitude of messianism. . . . War is identical with militarism which Americans abhor, but a war for peace, a war to end war, is not only permissible but even necessary. . . . The democratic ideology is the core of that crusading mood which led to American intervention under President Wilson. Under President Roosevelt, it again represents a danger of the first magnitude, threatening our security and our future." (Farago, 55)

But it takes one to know one. Mass psychology begins, in prehistory, with the internalization of conflict as nonviolence or pure violence brought to us by the Christian mass. But there are two tracks on the preprogram. Internalization can go suicidal, but it can also race psychosis to the autoanalytic prospect of a therapeutic closure. It's a question of the transference.

One last takeoff is scheduled down these pages inside the Farago beachhead (where the Nazis knew just what we thought they knew, and then we knew it, and told ourselves so). For now we follow Farago's reading list out of our real-time travels and into some of the references and through their references into the next, less structured phase of entry into the military-group-psychological complex of total war. A 1920 Freudian military-psychological essay "On Premonitions of Death in the Field and Their Effect" ("Über Todesahnungen im Felde und ihre Wirkung") gets included by Farago in this 1941 reconstruction of the reading assignments that keep on going into Nazi German psychological warfare. E. Schiche focuses on intimations of death that play a covert role in numerous superstitions that circulate among soldiers on a down mood swing. Opening up the covert more completely, Schiche relies on Freud's *The Psychopathology of Everyday*

Life to find the death wishes operating within the superstitious advance previews of fatality. So often comrades of a fallen soldier appear shattered by their total recollection that the deceased had only just recently expressed his sense that he was next. "As dead man he was the mute witness for the surefire realization of the premonition, and his death had for the others a paralyzing effect that went beyond natural mourning and had to open up psychic access, by allegedly offering proof for the general correctness of all intimations of dying, to this or some related superstition" (175). It's a belief that cannot but spread by suggestion, by the "possibility of transference," since spontaneous transmission is assisted by the tight quarters of military life. The too silent soldier is often in the sealed lip service of the superstition that the communication of premonitions guarantees their fulfillment (176). More deeply down this sliding scale, a soldier's open declaration that he knows his number's up recommends "taking into serious consideration the possibility of conscious or unconscious suicidal thoughts; but the conscious intention to commit suicide cannot be proved, and even the subconscious intention could be uncovered only with the rigorous application of the psychoanalytic method" (177).

When Freud turned to group psychology, it was already part of a military complex that psychoanalysis had accessed first case by case in the treatment of war neurotics during and right after the First World War. The publicized success of the psychoanalytic intervention in war neurosis, which guaranteed the Freudian system's first admissions of influence on psychiatry, kept on going, even under the Nazis (indeed were under Göring's— Hermann's too—special protection). There are more than just a few Nazi connections between war neurosis and psychological warfare that can be given in place of countless others. These first two examples have been selected only for their immediate remove from any official transmission or tradition. Their grassroots resistance to psychoanalysis is the very measure of the ongoing influence of psychoanalysis in the outer reaches of the military complex. Only Farago could see, and now we can too, that the question of the influence of psychoanalysis in the Nazi era or in our own time is not answered, not by a long warning shot, with the interrogation of the usual suspects.

In "Psychology of Combat and Military Leadership: The Soldierly Attitude toward Anxiety," Mierke pulls up short before the greater-psychoanalytic route through early childhood and declares that "the roots of neurotic anxiety can be followed back usually into early youth or to a severely terrifying experience" (2). Predisposition is always already there: inferiority feelings and so on. Once there's been that detonation of a shocking

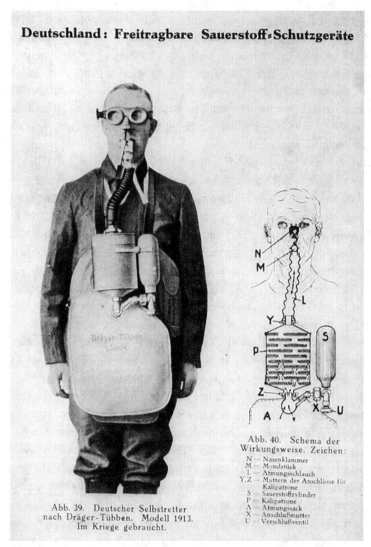

Deutschland: Freitragbare Sauerstoff=Schutzgeräte

Abb. 39. Deutscher Selbstretter
nach Dräger-Tübben. Modell 1913.
Im Kriege gebraucht.

Abb. 40. Schema der
Wirkungsweise. Zeichen:

N — Nasenklammer
M — Mundstück
L — Atmungsschlauch
Y,Z — Muttern der Anschlüsse für
        Kalipatrone
S — Sauerstoffzylinder
P — Kalipatrone
A — Atmungssack
X — Anschlußmutter
U — Verschlußventil

German model of gas-warfare protective devices developed in 1913 and used in World War I.
Exhibit 15, *Der Chemische Krieg*. Reprinted by permission of Koehler-Mittler.

experience, "remains" and "traces" stay put and recycle or regenerate the anxiety: "The system of reference has undergone a displacement; no longer threat from the outside, but rather from within is feared" (3). "Psychoanalysis and Individual Psychology attempted to go deeper into the essence of these disorders but slipped on the way upon bizarre and extreme notions (traumatic repetition of the act of birth, relations with libido)" (5). "The displacement of the relation of tension into anomaly, which can prepare the

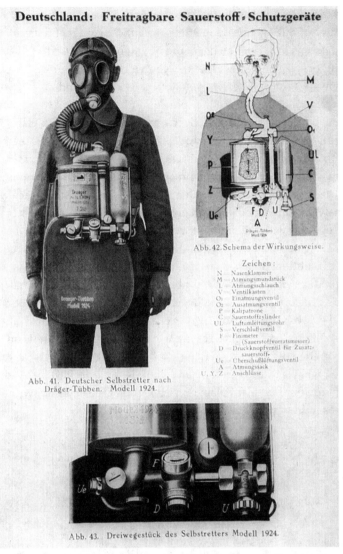

German model of gas-warfare armor, 1924. The German term for these portable protective machines is *Selbstretter,* "self-rescuer," as in do it yourself, be autonomous and automatic in your survival, but also as in every man for himself. Exhibit 16, *Der Chemische Krieg.* Reprinted by permission of Koehler-Mittler.

way for breakdown, is experienced as anxiety" (6). Whatever deepens the tension or apprehension belongs to the "breaching factors" that give away the dotted line to breakdown (7). There's even such a thing as "anxiety about anxiety," and it's such a panic (9). After his lineup of anxiety "dispositions" like the figures in a morality play, Mierke reads the code of anxiety:

anxiety prepares, warns, defends; sometimes it's a warning light on the fuel gauge of our energies, sometimes a cautionary signal pointing to oncoming danger (18–19). The only cure he can offer, however, is to develop community spirit and tough it out. If you've got those neurotic shock fragments inside your psyche, and you do, just watch out and protect yourself but keep on marching. One either prevails or breaks down. Neurosis is just another ingredient in anyone's development or makeup. To claim that it alone already excuses you from duty is a put-on. Just remember the models of self-sacrificing mother love or of the comrade loyalty among men.

Paul Würfler throws out the prospect of "pilot neuroses" coming soon but warns against the current military-psychological trend to break down and analyze neurosis down to many different neurotic genres that match and accessorize with the different weapons and machines (124). We need to set our insights on neurosis at large and not get sidetracked by all these specific conditions if what we really want is "healing." There is always some predisposition (perhaps in all of us) to neurosis, which means the neurotic's history is not of the degeneration persuasion, nor is it coming down the psycho-path, but always reflects specific experiences in earlier phases of life—"in the first place in early childhood" (125). In the one (anyone) so predisposed, neurosis is a matter of "taking it to heart," as the saying goes; what is thus taken too hard wounds self-esteem (125). And when making up your treatment plan, don't forget that the neurotic symptom always has meaning (126–27).

> Certainly the neurotic has lived inauthentically and is fighting with a false front, but it doesn't mean that one should disdain him but one should rather restore him if possible and redirect him. . . .
>
> May this presentation succeed in keeping us from overlooking the neurotic in what's human, and in making us understand him better and treat him more effectively. (128)

Gustav Störring, whose name reflects and refracts the "disturbance" he's after, compares "The Differences between the Psychopathological Experiences in the World War and in the Current War and Its Causes." So far in this war there are very few tremblers; in fact, this time around there are by and large no severe hysterical reactions (27). The blitz-war was egosyntonic and, with the rapid "I" movement it facilitated, could already be seen as therapeutic (27). The get-tough attitude has kept soldier in front line but has, admittedly, given a slight rise to the suicide curve (27). The extended apparatus, the military unit, is self-cleaning, running on death drive, over and out. On the lighter side, patients are no longer told that their affliction "isn't organic"; that was mistake number one, the big one, in the Great War. Störring underlines the time frame and the date before signing off: it's been the two first years of the war, two years of reversal of the unmournable loss of the Great War. (Two years is the model time frame of mourning.) He is thus at the same turning point that Farago addresses in 1941: "As things stand today, however, the Germans have staked rich claims on the use of psychology in Total War" (Farago, 1). However: "Germany has no exclusive lease on the psychological amplification of strategy and tactics" (1). Störring just hopes the winning streak will continue. The two-year mourning period didn't take.

The Hitler Principle

Poppelreuter was ready with his treatise *Hitler, the Political Psychologist* right in time for 1933: a first version, a series of lectures prepared in 1932 already, had been prohibited by the administration because it was felt their delivery would invite all kinds of volatility in from the streets into the corridors of the university. Now Poppelreuter is free to point out that Hitler's political psychology, which comes complete with the course manual *Mein Kampf*, has the proof to show of a successful "scientific experiment" (6). The only precedents to be found for *Mein Kampf*: Le Bon's crowd psychology and more recent developments in the psycho-techniques of winning and influencing (7). That Hitler's psychology has a biological focus means that it is not fixated on consciousness but rather addresses the psychic side or inside of all the great interdependencies of life, all of which are organically grown (9). Hitler found, ready-made, two theories: one, conflict is the father of all things; two, mutual understanding, tolerance, is the goal (9–10). Hitler accepts both facts of life and, rather than worry about their proper timing and placing, simply sends the *Volk* totally to the foreground and thus resolves a widening impasse by calling for *"conflict with all that threatens the* Volk *totality, peace for all those who are for the* Volk *totality!"* (10). Now that's a surefire imperative. But the actual working of the crowd relies on a displacement upward of ambivalence from the individual to the group. Because once Hitler united the two competing views of the masses in one double vision, a sense of when and where the one or the other crowd characteristic predominates was furthermore required: "The masses are good on the one hand, valuable, smart, etc., on the other hand however they are inferior, stupid, etc." (10). Hitler relies implicitly on crowd capacity for getting into ideals (that intersection of in-group mutual identifications that Freud called ego ideal). What Hitler needed was a new ideal, one that would fit the psychological situation of the masses. So on the third day he synthesized "National" and "Socialist" to cut us a totally new ideal (11). Hitler recognized that Marxism had only borrowed a popular notion of justice for all; Hitler had equal borrower's rights to recall it at any time (12–13).

The foundation of the ideal's makeup is the "relatively low niveau of the masses" (14). For starters, he didn't get hot and bothered about the nonmassified members of society. It must have been hard on Hitler, who's so smart and educated, to adapt his mode of communication to what's filled up to the level of mass communion. With "iron discipline he forced himself to remain primitive" (15).

Group psychology isn't really like child psychology, because in the latter case we're dealing with a tabula rasa of sorts, whereas in the later case we have whole billboards of already advertised beliefs that must first be countered and contained. Hitler knew that he would have to wipe the state or slate clean right up to the group level. Propaganda became Hitler's internal, psychic administration of the masses. To this end there was no dimension that he left unpsychologized as yet another portion of Nazi self-reflexivity and performativity. Hitler was one of the first to give the lost world war and the peace that was handed down psychological interpretations: on their side as the consequence of excellent enemy propaganda, on his side as the result of "poor applications of advertising within our own *Volk*" (18). Hitler's conclusions: propaganda is not objective or scientific but a weapon of war. The Entente did the right thing. Why couldn't the Germans counter in kind? "Did the German people engage in war in order at some future point in history to find praise for their decent way of losing wars?" No, Germany waged war to protect the *Volk*, not to end up with it on the face. "It was the damned duty and responsibility of the leadership at least to make use of the same weapons the enemy was employing without any scruples" (19). A certain Swedish writer apologizes today for his own involvement in the spread of atrocity stories about the Huns; he considers the episode tantamount to "war psychosis" (20). But Poppelreuter dismisses the diagnosis and notes instead that the gentleman had succumbed, like so many others, to very effective propaganda.

Rather than undervalue the enemy, as had been the attitude in World War I, it's important to mobilize the people around a dead or alive struggle. The Germans in World War I were convinced that the old order of government had lost the worldwide confidence vote. Nothing more. The Germans fell hard for the Fourteen Points (21).

Hitler didn't make the academic mistake of considering the masses and their leaders only in isolation as separate psychological categories: Hitler sees for miles that there's group psychology only because there is leader psychology (and vice versa). Psychology's loss is Hitler's slogan:

the masses need and want the leader
the leader needs and wants the masses! (23)

Dishonest manipulation of the masses for their margin of profit was the Jewish undertaking. But the Jews aren't even as smart as some anti-Semites think they are: they didn't see that this kind of puppet governing, ventriloquization, and corporation can't last long at all, neither by natural nor by psychological law (24–25). But when the masses are given permission to recognize their leader as leader and can increase their own value with their standing request to be taken to or by him, then, as Hitler says (as does Le Bon before him), the masses are woman, leader is man.

> (The scientific explanation that with this love affair we are addressing the process of so-called "identification," through which the one person forms a new psychic-biological unity with another person, with a group or with masses of people, can be mentioned here in passing for the professional psychologists.) (26)

Poppelreuter stresses that Hitler succeeded psychologically against all the odds against him in the press and radio. The stress relieves the burden of losing the Entente's press forward of media-coordinated propaganda. By relying exclusively on what the Germans had so fatefully neglected, Hitler wins the war, the loss, back within an internal representation of the former setting of struggle and losses. But he goes one step further or deeper into the inside of propaganda's psychology in a self-reflexive mode: he creates, on the first day, psychological warfare (which is one up on the old propaganda).

> One could, even though of course this would be one-sided, characterize Hitler's victorious struggle against his enemies as the triumphant fight of psychology against unpsychology. (33)

There was call for psychic healing in Germany. National Socialism heard that call and returned it with political interest.

The pre-Nazi epoch was the era of neurosis, Johannes Hobohm declares, and now, since 1933, the *Volk*-illness of psychoneurosis is being overcome, healed, once and for all. Millions were in danger of catching this affliction against which only few indeed were resistant. Neurosis spread without immunity. Because Nazi biological views are in complete support of the unity of body and psyche, psychotherapy has become the treatment of choice, the norm of socialization. It's therapy time for Hitler and Germany.

Without a higher love of ideal or community belonging, one starts up the avoidance that "leads with psychological necessity to neurosis. Unconsciously the egoic-anxious person flees into illness. The contradiction between reality and one's life arrangements *[Lebensarrangements]* then leads to the physically and psychically cramped and rigid style" (42). Hobohm lists four good signs of nationwide healing: rising interest in sports, the restructuring of the social insurance system, the rise in birth rates, and the overcoming of class differences (43). The whole of the German *Volk*, which, once upon a time, had been so sick inside, has now been signed up for treatment "according to a vastly-formatted psychotherapeutic plan of heal-ing [Heilplan]" (43). Propaganda-suggestiveness, the other large-scale *appli-cation* of the therapeutic method, just doesn't pack the same power to change a person as does the therapy conducted closer to the net or rather gross of human interest. This power of psychotherapy has been proved by the trans-forming, deep work demonstrated by "psychoanalysis" (43). More impor-tant, then, than the speaker blast of influence by suggestion is that every German today experience, in session, the changeover.

Elastic Anschluß

We even see increasing understanding of human behavior exploited by the Nazis to undermine us by psychological warfare.

—TALCOTT PARSONS, "RACIAL AND RELIGIOUS DIFFERENCES AS FACTORS IN GROUP TENSIONS"

The importance of the problem of national character at the present time is obvious. If we wish to wage psychological warfare, we must know something about the character of our enemies. For instance, how they react to bombing and casualties.

—ERICH FROMM, "ON THE PROBLEMS OF GERMAN CHARACTEROLOGY"

No one knows German psychology better than the Nazi leaders. What they have succeeded in doing with these sixty-five million people they have done scientifically.

—GEORGE BOAS, "HUMAN RELATIONS IN MILITARY GOVERNMENT"

More than one group of leaders will attempt to make clever use of the residue in modern man of those magical fears which psychoanalysis has made accessible to psychology.

—ERIK ERIKSON, "HITLER'S IMAGERY AND GERMAN YOUTH"

George Hartmann looks forward "Toward a Reasonable Peace," which requires of psychologists, however, that they leave the war setting and conditioning behind them. But Hartmann knows they will need their backs covered:

> We thus behold the sorry spectacle of Anglo-American and Russian psychologists, on one side, and German and Japanese practitioners, on the other, mutually canceling each others' energies as technologists. (200)

> But as soon as he begins to dabble in affairs of state (as morale-builder, propaganda analyst, psychological warfarer, and other evolving functions) there is a real danger that he will succumb to *mass* thinking, in both senses of that phrase. (200)

Reunification of psychological (or technological) approaches must spread across national boundaries no longer fortified down the divide of world war side taking. While identifying with "the drift of the modern world," which "is definitely toward greater planetary unity" (205), Hartmann's science fiction sensibility politics admitted a fairly high tolerance for the melancholic rescue operations of annexation (*Anschluß*). He puts his footnote in his mouth by following reference to Australia's role in the Boer War with a free association, the postal kind. Even more freely, Hartmann's annexation itinerary duplicates the moves made by the Göring Institute to set up shop in the chain of war commands, first in Vienna, then in Paris. "German tribalism as much as sheer economic need, was behind the understandable and wholly legitimate demand for *Anschluß* with Austria; but I recall that when I told a Nazi student abroad that I favored *Anschluß* with France also, he looked at me with amazement, saying, 'But we don't want to be Frenchmen!'" (206 n. 5). Hartmann's planetary unity plans duplicate before they subsume the Nazi goal of "Greater Germany" (as the body of annexations was called). He was so preoccupied with the survival of the species that he simply forgot about the other race before space. The periphery of greater psychoanalysis was occupied by the study of national character. Before he knew it, Hartmann was taking a research field trip along these lines when he asked the Nazi the France question.

In the afterword to Farago's *German Psychological Warfare*, Kimball Young unpacks the study of character as the prize at the bottom of the double barrel that Farago was looking down when he was overcome with the urgency of depth-psychologizing our military complexes on the spot:

> It is particularly important for our military authorities and cooperating psychologists to realize that mere intelligence-testing is inadequate in modern warfare. The Germans, despite a certain aura of mysticism in their concepts, properly recognize the central significance of "character"—that is, social, emotional, and temperamental qualities. (62)

The character the Germans show is another double feature. In the course of his own comparative study of national character (assassinations), Young points to a paradox within the complete package of German rigidity: a certain "mental elasticity" has been trained into the Germans that is reflected in endless and uninhibited research that the Nazis accelerated in sync with the war effort.

Gregor Ziemer's *Education for Death* was highlighting the elastic-fantastic building of interests that was indeed the aim of school training in Nazi Germany.

> Nor is there to exist a rigid system of lesson plans. A history class, for instance, should be so organized that it can deviate at any moment from routine and avail itself of new material provided by Nazi activity. A biology class must be integrated only to the point where the instructor can make use of new racial angles as the Party wishes them stressed. For a while Russians were enemies of the State, then became allies, then enemies again. The schools reflected this change carefully and in detail. The schedule in a geography class must be so adjusted that new parts of the globe can be discussed as they become objects of interest subsequent to new conquests.

The study of geography had been reunified out of the too many separate studies and given one double focus: race and space (158). Instruction in foreign affairs alternated between repetition of the litany of lost territories and, for future reference, thorough study of the strong and weak points in the natural defenses of neighboring foreign countries and their suitability for strategic military positions. One class "spent one semester studying synthetic foods" (160). As though there had been a purpose to book burning beyond censorship or the natural selection through exposure to the feelings of the *Volk,* there are no textbooks anywhere in Nazi German classes. They go on plenty of field trips (physical education must be promoted whenever possible). After one nature tour that included observation of an anthill, the teacher summarizes the lesson:

> "And everywhere you looked," the teacher declared, "you saw how nature employed the *Fuehrer Prinzip,* the principle of leadership.... Ants, for instance, did their assigned tasks without questioning." And, he asked his class, "which ants saw to it that the commands of the leader were carried out, and saw to it that everybody worked for the benefit of all?"
>
> "*Die Soldaten,* the soldiers," shouted the class. (66)

On his covert field trip to the Anthropological Museum in Berlin, Ziemer listens in on more summaries. In front of the glass case with stuffed Sioux Indians, the teacher recognizes the Indian as the only example of pure race in the United States.

The display of Semites living in their flat-roofed Oriental house
evoked this: If the Jews had stayed in Palestine, there would be
no trouble in the world today. (74)

Norman Meier's *Military Psychology,* which also includes extensive bibliographies for each section, documents the surefire advantage the Nazis
hold as the leaders in psychological warfare (30). "The revelations of the
morale committee made through its publication of *German Psychological
Warfare* astounded its readers by the extent to which the Nazi regime had
regimented the psychologists of Germany" (34). Meier points to German
awareness of the greater gadget love and adaptability that will be required
by the technology and organization of a mobile versus a trench war: "For
the trait so prized in mobile warfare, the German staff has introduced the
term mental elasticity. To sift out those unlikely to fit the requirements of
certain special forces, they have made use of characterology" (35). Characterology thus also addresses, in these elastic terms, a specific psycho-techno-
compatibility.

The mobility of this war aims at the speed with which the Axis must
win—or else lose out to the Allies in time. Up front this mobility goes for
the stockpiles, the oil wells, the gold. The Geopolitical Institute in Munich
serves no higher purpose than nonstop mapping out of the resource centers with dotted lines along which the German forces must take their cut.
Their ruthless attitude and their "more effective and distinctive" weapons
drive the Germans and Japanese onward on missions of cash-and-carry,
looting-tunes adventures. Aviation, which takes the biggest slice of the sky,
is especially prepped psychologically. "Its requirements are exacting, and
constant study that is still proceeding and expanding has been necessary to
enable the human element to keep within hailing distance of the mechanical developments" (109).

After all the selection has been made and done, those soldiers who
succumb to war neurosis are, according to the German art-of-the-state research, the ones (you know which ones) who experienced "excessive 'mothering'" (255). "Individuals with low energy reserves, previous emotional
disorder, or insomnia are especially prone to its onset" (279).

In his introduction to the bibliography he compiled for the June 1941
issue of *Psychological Bulletin,* "German Military Psychology," H. L. Ansbacher turns on a couple of highlights. First, the characterological approach
has the upper hand in Nazi Germany. Practically, that means even when
they're testing, the German psychologists give first consideration to the

overall personality (373). Thus selection is based on tests, yes, but they're just testing; to determine whether the candidate will pass the only real test around, the so-called blood test of battle, characterological examination has the final say (385). The other highlight hits the spot of Nazi German psychological war interests, specifically, the maintenance of morale. "Under morale, egotism and vanity, homesickness, queerness, and homosexuality are seen as endangering the *esprit de corps,* and advice is given for dealing with such cases. The positive factors are social interest and a general belief in one's own value" (375). The negativity that the research on morale does factor in is the problem of desertion, which comes down to the soldier's "readiness for capture"; "the psychological state of the soldier before his capture . . . is produced partly through enemy propaganda and consists in a reorganization of the psychological field to the effect that one sees the other point of view and feels no longer exclusively identified with one's own cause" (378).

Attention was drawn right away, beginning in 1933, to the open deck with which the Nazis were playing in preparation for hitting the decks of all-out war. After one offensive textbook on the science of defense by a certain Ewald Banse was taken out of circulation by the German government to prove the new regime's commitment to peace, an even more formidable book by Banse caught Anglo-American attention. This book too was then officially censored, but not before translation rights had been secured for the 1934 edition of *Germany Prepares for War: A Nazi Theory of "National Defense"* (the English display copy of *Raum und Volk im Weltkriege*).

> It seemed to us as publishers that the English public should be given an opportunity to judge the character of Professor Banse's teaching and to realize what ideas, fateful, perhaps, for our own security, the German youth was imbibing from its leaders. The course of events following our decision to publish an English translation of the book may be left to speak for themselves. If what is written here constitutes an indictment of a powerful nation and its leaders, it cannot be denied that the actions of that nation, both in propagating this book and in their attempts to prevent us from publishing it in an English translation, are justification for making it. (vii)

But Banse keeps his directives for future work and reference so general that one wonders if the book wasn't a Nazi plant, to divert attention from the real sophistication that was going into the German psychologization and theorization of total war. Yes, Banse recommends the psychology of

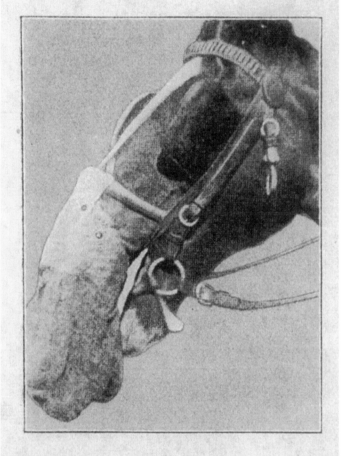

Gasschutz der Tiere:

Abb. 69.
Englische Pferdegasschutzmaske.

English protective wear for horses exposed to gas warfare. One of four images in exhibit 28,
Der Chemische Krieg. Reprinted by permission of Koehler-Mittler.

groups for assessing the selective fit between type of citizen and the soldier
type he'll prove to be in "the blood-test of battle" (52). But all we know for
sure is that he would mix for Germany a witch's brew "derived from the
earth and from the air, from industry and transport, and from the study of
national and individual psychology" (348). The book really only gives a
long line or list of credits to the Entente for psychologically faking out the

Abb. 70. Deutscher Sanitätshund mit erbeuteter russischer Hundegasschutzmaske.

"German first-aid dog with confiscated Russian gas mask for dogs." Included in exhibit 28, *Der Chemische Krieg*. Reprinted by permission of Koehler-Mittler.

Central Powers, and then proceeds, with little "how to," to do a turn-the-tide chart complete with maps of territories to be conquered next time around. In the English-language context, Banse blunders into the international scene threatening to initiate—and lose—another worldwide conflict.

Before Farago began restoring the balance between the United States and them in the fighting-words resources of the psy war, bibliographies compiled in Nazi Germany for the fortification of the German leadership in the battlefield of psychology of warfare included references to Lasswell's works. His 1927 *Propaganda Technique in the World War,* for example, made the list in the 1938 *Bibliographie der geistigen Kriegsführung,* edited by Felix Scherke and Ursula Gräfin Vitzthum (and introduced by an air force general).

Already in 1927 Harold D. Lasswell could assess, with some sense of future rebound or foreboding, the damage suit that the conquered nations had filed away, against the Entente, for psychological cruelties. If the Germans believe they were done in by enemy propaganda, that, under the psychological influence, whatever was weak or foreign in the makeup of the home front collapsed behind the lines that were still holding out, then this reflects the counteroffensive that the Central Powers issued through constant warning labeling of the poison of the "All-lies."

> They were, therefore, predisposed to attach very great importance to propaganda. . . . Patriotic Germans are anxious to understand the nature of the non-coercive weapon which was wielded so successfully to their discomfiture in war-time, and there is today a more luxurious flowering of treatises upon international propaganda (its nature, limitations and processes) in Germany than anywhere else. (*Propaganda Technique,* 3–4)

Military unity is easier to maintain for "the aggregation of disciplined men in a dehumanizing environment. The civilian lacks the automatic discipline of drill and remains in an environment in which his sentiment-life (his *human* life) continues" (11). Lasswell presupposes that the resistance to war in modern nations is so great "that every war must appear to be a war of defense against a menacing, murderous aggressor" (47). But civilian unity can be built up through repetition and amplification of a few basic ideas: enemy propaganda lies (79), they started it (55), and they snoop to conquer by "infecting wells, cattle, and food, not to speak of wounds" with the newly discovered germs (82). "The civilian mind is standardized by news and not by drills" (11). Opinion must be mobilized: "Talk must take the place of drill" (221). Because power cannot in fact teleguide unidirectionally wishes that are commands, propaganda is here to stay, for the fantasy. "It is the new dynamic of society, for power is subdivided and diffused, and more can be won by illusion than by coercion" (222).

Not So Fast

The essay everyone forgot to reread in plenty of time for World War II, all Anglo-Americans agree, is Thomas Salmon's 1917 "Recommendations for the Treatment of Mental and Nervous Diseases in the United States Army," which was based on the experiences of the British army. The essay is plumbed or full with stray references to submarine attacks that represented for those disabled to return home by sea the return of the war front. Submarine pressure thus brought treatment even of the chronic and nonrecoverable cases closer to the front. In England the outpatient population of shell-shocked soldiers created a new indigent class requiring care facilities subsidized by the War Office. What about the United States, Salmon asks, where only the rich can afford to have neuroses and treat them too? But the acceptance of neurosis worldwide in the course of the war will spread the health around.

> It is freely predicted in England that the wide prevalence of the neuroses among soldiers will direct attention to the fact that this kind of illness has been almost wholly ignored, while great advances have been made in the treatment of all others. . . . Today the enormous number of these cases among some of Europe's best fighting men is leading to a revision of the medical and popular attitude toward functional nervous diseases. (876)

Clarence Farrar, publishing his study in 1917 in the *American Journal of Insanity,* provides a service similar to Salmon's, only this time based on observations of Canadian troops. Farrar counts two classes of war neurosis that reflect their place of onset, in camp or at the front: there are the anticipatory war neuroses (neurasthenic and hypochondriacal reactions), and then there are the so-called trench neuroses. The placement of their origin triangulates the scheme: there are cumulative, convergent, and catastrophic ways for the etiology to proceed. But when it comes to the PR for a psychogenic comprehension of trench neurosis, the account is no longer orderly but direct, even uncanny: "The war has served materially in illuminating the subject of the neuroses in general and has dislodged some fairly well entrenched beliefs concerning them" (710). First the presentation loosens up, then the author loses it, over an analogy (that's really a transference) with the conflict of war neurosis:

> Just as in certain conjugal situations where affection is on the wane we sometimes observe an excessive protestation of devotion, especially in public, which betrays less of genuine inclina-

tion and more a perhaps imperfectly realized effort to compensate a perhaps equally vague consciousness of dereliction in assumed obligations; so in the victim of war neurosis there may be a corresponding strife of motives each expressing itself in its own way—on the one side patriotism, duty, the herd-instinct discussed by Trotter; on the other, the phylogenetically earlier and more immanent instinct of self-advantage. (713)

Except for some practical tips (like treatment in proximity to the front), the psychiatric reception of shell shock on the Entente side really needed to fill up with some brain drain. The analytic war influence was spread as thin over there as was Anglo-American PR psychology in the reception, over at Central Powers, of propaganda.

A compelling documentation of this third degree of influence by psychoanalysis, a rote response under questioning that left the losing streak in theory that, sometime after 1941, the Nazis could no longer convert into practice, is given in the double-duty ready-made, Charles S. Myers's *Shell Shock in France, 1914–1918*. Based on Myers's war diary back then, it waited until 1940 to appear. It appeared to be time:

> It is so long since any book has been written on so-called "shell shock" that the present volume may well serve to re-enlighten members of the general public as to its nature, and to convince them how dependent it is on a previous psychoneurotic history and inherited disposition, on inadequate examination and selection of soldiers fitted for the Front Line, and on the lack of proper discipline and *esprit de corps*; and how necessary it may be to adopt apparently harsh measures in order to diminish the undoubted "contagiousness" and the needless prolongation of the complaint. (ix)

Myers says a mouthful and bites off as much eclecticism and greater psychoanalysis as everyone else can eschew. In 1915 he was the first to publish on the relatedness to hysteria of what he was the first to designate "shell shock." But he originally opened his hysteria concession on the physical side of what he also sought to include, the literal meaning of the name he gave the war disorders:

> I attributed them, as they are now generally attributed, to mental "repression" and "dissociation," but I was inclined to lay some emphasis on the physical shock produced by the bursting of a shell as a prime cause of "dissociation." Later familiarity with the disorder, however, showed that emotional disturbance alone

Rauch= und Nebelerzeugung:

Abb. 73. Französische Infanterie greift hinter einem Rauchvorhang an
(nach F. Heigl).

"French infantry attacks from behind a curtain of smoke." Top of exhibit 29, *Der Chemische Krieg*. Reprinted by permission of Koehler-Mittler.

was a sufficient cause, and thus led to the neglect of possible factors of a physical nature. This I believed to be an error. I was at first by no means convinced that all cases of "functional disso-ciation" arose solely from mental causes. The high-frequency vi-brations caused by an exploding shell might, it seemed to me, conceivably produce an invisibly fine "molecular" commotion in the brain which, in turn, might produce dissociation. (11–12)

Above the undertow of never relinquishing the "but" of resistance, Myers respectfully submits to the authority of the "past twenty-five years," with "thanks to the work of Janet, Prince, Freud, Jung, Adler, . . . Jones and many others" (20). This interim work, already back then, refilled the prescription of Myers's own term—shell shock—with the vicissitudes of the ego shell in an internal setting. Those "high-frequency vibrations" he can't let go of come back to haunt him through the popularity of his term and its new dis-content:

There can be no doubt that, other things being equal, the frequency of "shell shock" in any unit is an index of its lack of discipline and loyalty.... It is hardly surprising, then, that the very recognition of the term "shell shock" as a disease is liable to promote its frequency. Like all emotional disorders, "shell shock" is of a highly contagious nature. (39–40)

When he hears that frequency again, push comes to move over, and Myers dissociates himself, on impact, from psychoanalysis, first because it's so sexual (no problem), then because it's too into conflict (what's left?).

Pass the Buck

The English report announced completely officially that the
Germans were dropping Cholera bacteria over enemy cities,
then in the enemy lands they poison wells. Their airplanes
killed only infants, children, and women, and their brutal
treatment of prisoners of war cried to heaven. Hands, feet,
breasts and genitals of ten-year-old girls were cut off, the
unborn infant torn out of the womb and carried around
triumphantly at the end of the bayonet: that was the highest
point of their culture!

—HANNS HEINZ EWERS, *VAMPIR*

In his 1916 monograph *Psychological Aspects of War,* Magnus Hirschfeld shows
Germany's empty hand, especially if we redeal the names in the title as
"psychological warfare." His concluding hope is that the war of the present
will make the war of the future impossible. And he cites Romain Rolland
(and thus already shows he has the spirit), who could see the European
community coming together soon out of this blood baptism (31–32). The
world war is the downside of all the other "world" events and combos the
age has been producing on fast forward: world congresses, world trade,
world language, world religion (30). War is two-faced; it's the most personal and the least personal thing around: it can be taken personally because it challenges the whole person, and it's impersonal because the attack
is not directed against you in your individuality but against the nationality
of the enemy (19). But this goes for the drive to break with the status, the
static state, and go ex-static in war euphoria. In the case of Italy's late decision to enter the war, for example, only war psychology can help Hirschfeld
understand it at all—as a case of "war psychosis" (22).

    The Sexual History of the World War, compiled by Hirschfeld in collabo-
ration with a group of physicians, scientists, and historians, sticks to his
field glasses, the voyeurism he's good at in German contexts of seeing in
order to be, oneself, not seen. Look! Look! The nurse was there. During
World War I, nurses established "a cult of the wounded whose erotic background did not remain concealed" (59). So where's the so-called sex sublimation by war, the theory that's such "a bastard-hybrid of psychoanalysis
and patriotism" (79)? Mental disturbances in the military were set off by
sexual frustrations, period:

The abnormality in the sexual conditions aggravated the general feeling of dissatisfaction almost to the point of madness and induced psychopathic mental states and depressions which were frequently erroneously attributed to fighting alone. (81)

Those who survived their imprisonment are even today, for the most part, psychic invalids as a result of the morbid stamp that those years impressed upon their sex life. (255)

There were unmistakable stop-and-go signals that wartime conditionings of sex displacement were getting to the fighting men. Tattooing engraved the consequences of sexual abstinence on the body of evidence (90). There was heavy "trade in pornographic (especially masochistic) photographs," for example. And among the French soldiers, "photographs of coitus scenes and phalli of plaster" changed from hand to hand job (86). German military psychiatry expert Dr. Gaupp is cited by Hirschfeld as being real interested in one of the captured phalli, which he put on exhibitionism at a military medicine meeting. "There were all sorts of notions concerning the possible uses of the instrument" (86). The German audience volunteered: perhaps for brutal violations of German women? Or was it just a gag, or maybe a pederast's toy?

It seemed much more likely that the object was really a talisman, only the size and weight of the object were against this explanation. Perhaps there was a sort of exhibitionism here in which a sexually perverse person would become excited at the sight of the shame and insult that women would feel when confronted with the giant phallus. It was Iwan Bloch's hunch that the purpose of the instrument could be found in a sort of fetishistic substitute reaction. In the professional circles of Germany, this question aroused considerable interest. It may be likely that this was merely an individual find which in normal times, free from war psychosis, would not have aroused any great interest or led to such intricate and fine-spun conclusions concerning French eroticism. (86)

Hirschfeld documents the big development, at least on the German side of interpretations of the phallus, of the sort of same-sex love-comradeship that Richard Wagner extolled in his *Art of the Future*. Although when it came to the involvement of homosexuals in the military, the Central Powers tended to see Redl (the Austrian official whose secret orientation gave the enemy grounds for blackmail and information access) (135), it became evident just the same that the homosexual volunteers who were out there were especially prepared, suited-up, vitalized soldiers (Hirschfeld, *Sexual History*, 139). "This surprising energy and activity on their part is really amazing when one remembers that their nervous power is generally lower than that of the normal man" (139–40). (Was that you, Hirschfeld?) Taken to the higher power of war's test, other misconceptions could only disprove themselves: "It was commonly believed that the homosexual officer did not know how to maintain the proper distance from his subordinates and that therefore his presence in the army might prove to be a source of insubordination" (144). While feminine urnings could be spotted right away in the Red Cross following Walt Whitman into pieta nursing scenes of farewell to buff arms (148), pseudohomosexuality characterized much of camp life where everyone was getting a rise out of masturbation. The local entertainment accordingly dragged out crossover prospects that increased overall tolerance for homoerotic relations. "Naturally women's roles were everywhere played by the younger officers" (254). Hirschfeld thus fills in the blank stare of unidentified (unidentified with) ecstasy in his 1916 war report with an upbeat account of prospects for homosexuality that are in the army now.

In the Family

"The masses are taking us in," he thought, "the masses are
digesting us. We're nothing but nourishment for them, nothing
else. And we don't move—we are only moved along:
peristaltically."

—HANNS HEINZ EWERS, *VAMPIR*

The 31 December 1995 issue of the *New York Times Magazine* rang out the
old with a news story entitled "Edward L. Bernays and Henry C. Rodgers:
The Fathers of P.R." There's really only one paternal lineage here: it was at
a later date that Rodgers applied PR as a local aesthetic in Hollywood. By
feeding the gossip columnists with choice releases about his clients, the
columns had no choice but to close ranks and feed the info back through
and to the mass-media public as the latest news about the stars that were
thus born. Bernays, however, was "the father of public relations" (Gabler,
28). Besides, he was Freud's nephew.

PR was the propaganda legacy Bernays picked up from his World War
I experience (on the U.S. side). His "brief stint during World War I with a
Government agency formed to propagandize America's war effort convinced
him that show-business techniques could be applied to corporate clients.
As he later wrote, 'I could create events and circumstances from which fa-
vorable publicity would stem'"(Gabler, 28). Bernays took responsibility for
the commodification of information, the introduction of pseudoevents that
boundary blended between, say, information and misinformation or actual
event and sponsored event.

Bernays wrote *Crystallizing Public Opinion* at a time when, for him at
least, the plural for the media could rhyme within the occult register with
"mediums." It was the post–World War I time for the occult sciences, the film
medium, and psychoanalysis to flourish. The witch-hunt that we thought
we had overcome returns to haunt us in the mode of uncanny confirma-
tion. "Today there is an equal number of people who believe just as firmly,
one way or the other, about spiritualism and spirits" (64). The open-headedness of consumers, who with "little knowledge about a subject almost
invariably form definite and positive judgments upon that subject" (63),
can only be topped by an occult analogy: "What they want and what they
get are fused by some mysterious alchemy. The press, the lecturer, the screen
and the public lead and are led by each other" (86).

Bernays would clarify a certain confusion in the popular mind between the "public relations counsel" and the propagandist: the former "interprets the client to the public, which he is enabled to do in part because he interprets the public to the client" (14), whereas the latter is presumably more one-way in orientation. He nominates his own position for the group mascot of mass-media society: "The headline and the cartoon bear the same relation to the newspaper that the public relations counsel's analysis of a problem bears to the problem itself" (171–72).

It's no surprise to Bernays "that the man who is outside the current of prevailing public opinion should regard the daily press as a coercive force" (71). That a newspaper slogan like "'We print all the news that's fit to print'...can exist and be accepted is for our purpose an important point" (77–78).

The theoretical portion of Bernays's PR job has the greatest charge, even though it pretends to be just a book review of E. Dean Martin's *The Behavior of Crowds.* His favorite Martin doesn't mean crowds to mean a "physical aggregation of a number of persons."

> To Mr. Martin the crowd is rather a state of mind, "the peculiar mental condition which sometimes occurs when people think and act together, either immediately where the members of the group are present and in close contact, or remotely, as when they affect one another in a certain way through the medium of an organization, a party or sect, the press, etc."...
>
> The main satisfaction, Mr. Martin thinks, which the individual derives from his group association is the satisfaction of his vanity through the creation of an enlarged self-importance. The Freudian theories upon which Mr. Martin relies very largely for his argument lead to the conclusion that what Mr. Henry Watterson has said of the suppression of news applies equally to the suppression of individual desire. (100–101)

The impossibility of complete suppression, however, determines Bernays's appreciation of the covertness or complexity of conformity. Bernays keeps his uncle inside a good object, Mr. Martin, but, for his side, prefers to lean on W. Trotter to trot out the example of resistance to technological advances as another measure of the conservativism of groups. But Trotter's words, under these conditions, begin to point in another direction.

> If we look back upon the developments of some such thing as the steam engine, we cannot fail to be struck by the extreme obviousness of each advance, and how obstinately it was refused assimilation until the machine almost invented itself. (107)

Abb. 74. Einschlag einer italienischen Nebelmine hinter öster-
reichischen Stellungen bei Vodice (Karst) im Sommer 1917
(nach F. Heigl).

"Detonation of an Italian fog mine behind Austrian lines near Vodice (Karst) in the summer of 1917."
Bottom of exhibit 29, *Der Chemische Krieg*. Reprinted by permission of Koehler-Mittler.

The PR counsel thus steps in right where it's already happening, speeds
up techno-history, which is the historical horizon of his work, so that the
momentum need no longer be left entirely to technology inventing itself.
Bernays works the double account of technology and the unconscious. It's
an account that holds a big investment in group psychology, and specifically
what Freud localized as the group-of-one. That's why Bernays won't take
any more Lippman views of PR or propaganda as reducible to censorship.

> From my point of view the precise reverse is more nearly true.
> Propaganda is a purposeful, directed effort to overcome censor-
> ship—the censorship of the group mind and the herd reaction.
> The average citizen is the world's most efficient censor. His own
> mind is the greatest barrier between him and the facts. (122)

He's Got a Group Mind to...

For the first preface to *The Group Mind* in 1920, William McDougall organizes a protest that his work was projected and in preparation for fifteen years now. But first he had to publish *Introduction to Social Psychology* (1908) to provide the necessary foundation, an acceptable account of the constitution of human nature:

> But group psychology is itself one of the fields in which such testing and verification must be sought. And I have decided to delay no longer in attempting to bring my scheme to this test. I am also impelled to venture on what may appear to be premature publication by the fact that five of the best years of my life have been wholly given up to military service and the practical problems of psycho-therapy, and by the reflection that the years of a man's life are numbered and that, even though I should delay yet another fifteen years, I might find that I had made but little progress towards securing the firm foundation I desired.
>
> It may seem to some minds astounding that I should now admit that the substance of this book was committed to writing before the Great War; for that war is supposed by some to have revolutionized all our ideas of human nature and of national life. But the war has given me little reason to add to or to change what I had written. (viii)

In the 1926 preface to the second edition, he can now agree with the "influential group of German workers" (or he sees that they agree with him). They're the ones "who expound the psychology of *Gestalt* or *Configurations*" and "strike the keynote that the whole is more than the sum or aggregate of its parts and that the life of the whole requires for its interpretation laws or principles that cannot be arrived at by the study of the parts alone. Leaders of this school have briefly indicated that they are led to insist on this truth in part by consideration of the social life of men and that their psychology will have important bearings upon social problems.... And I see no reason why the group mind should not be regarded as a *Gestalt* or configuration of a larger order" (xiv). In the main text, chapter 10, "Other Conditions of National Life," McDougall recognizes war's unifying hold over nations: "History offers no parallel to these effects of war; and it is difficult or impossible to imagine any other common purpose which could exert this binding influence in a similar degree." But there are other forms of international rivalry that have corresponding effects: "The international rivalry in aeronautics affords a contemporary illustration" (144). Another type of national organization which imposes submission and is not "the product of a natural evolution through the conflict of individual wills . . . is the kind of organization of which a modern army stands as the extreme type and which is best represented among modern nations by Germany as she was before the war" (152):

> In a State so organized there inevitably grows up an antagonism between individual rights and interests and the rights and interests of the State. It is psychologically unsound. This fact was revealed in Germany by the tremendous growth of social democracy, which was the protest against the subordination of individual welfare to that of the State. (153)

Indeed, "the existence of a nation organized in this way is a constant threat to the nations of higher type; and, as we have seen, it may compel them at any time to revert to or adopt, temporarily at least and so far as they are able, an organization of the lower and more immediately effective kind. And this threat was the justification of the nations of the Entente, when they demanded a radical change in this political organization of Germany" (154).

But this extreme type serves as model, in *Outline of Abnormal Psychology*, for McDougall's Freud-resistant, Jung-compatible view of the group-of-one as a series of microassociations that, as part of everday-time programming, is in your dreams, and in the endopsychic finale of dissociation, especially during the prime-time competition of multiple personality disorder, is on most spectacular inside view.

> I suggest, then, that in cases of multiple personality we get a glimpse of the system of reciprocal influences between many monads which constitute the life of the whole personality. In dreaming, which occurs in a state of slight general dissociation, the normal personality reveals his composite nature. (551)

> All the facts of this order point to the view that the communications between the monads are direct or immediate, that is to say unmediated or, as we may say, telepathic. (551)

> Complete integration according to this plan gives to the supreme monad control over the whole system. A close analogy obtains between such a system as I am sketching and such a social hierarchy as the Roman Church or any army in the field. (546)

These last two examples entered Freud's *Group Psychology and the Analysis of the Ego*, on second thought or as afterthought, as the contrasting types of group identification, contained in an appendix. Freud enlisted the army for the model of identification with the greater flexibility, one that still admitted a difference between love and (mutual) identification or, on the downside, between war and suicide. McDougall also skips the communion without end going down in church identification and proceeds with the army analogy only:

> The commander-in-chief of the army sits at the centre where all lines of communication converge; but the items of intelligence, the messages gathered in all parts of the field, are not transmitted directly to him; rather they are transmitted though a hierarchy of officers who select and digest all such messages into condensed reports. (546)

McDougall literalizes the analogy, at least to the extent of tuning in the animation of "multiple personalities," thereby at the same time keeping the army at metaphorical or illustrative remove. This is where McDougall's resistance to the identificatory underworld of psychoanalysis meets the Freudian "dogmatic" denial of the "reality" of the "multiple personality" (523).

By the time he has made it to this message center, he has indeed spent quite a long period of the book in training with Freud. In dissociation from the contrast in their group views, McDougall gets lost in the details of repressing and representing Freud's first system, the one McDougall jumpcut by starting with the second system, namely, with the group. The first and biggest show of resistance is put on right where Freud, in his reading of Dostoyevsky, predicted that it would always have this effect. It is from this crisis point onward that McDougall struggles to differentiate the original, unique "negative" of his thought from a fast photo lab of analysis in which even the negatives are transferences, copies, clichés, imprints designed for reproducibility.

> Surely one would need to be very strongly under the influence of Freud if one is to accept this involved and complicated derivation of homosexuality from the Oedipus complex! Surely the two factors which he, in common with all others, recognizes are sufficient, namely, the organic factor and seduction!
> But, granting a repressed homosexuality, what shall we say of the derivation from it of all Paranoia? (411)

As the motor of negative transference between men, of unacknowledged same-sex dependency or attachment, Freud's theory at this relational juncture can't be followed by McDougall. What he has to say about the connection to paranoia is projected before him, performed at one remove or removal, as the decompensation of Freud's discourse:

> The world of concepts in which Freud conducts his tours of discovery is so fluid and shifting that it lends itself to every manipulation. Every emotion, and every sentiment, is ambivalent, is both itself and its opposite, and can at a moment's notice be transmuted into something radically different; every sign and symbol and symptom can be interpreted in opposite ways. There is only one fixed point, one invariable rule, namely, that, in one way or another everything must be given a sexual significance.
>
> Even the Ego can become the other, and the other the Ego, by the mysterious process of identification; and the Ego instincts, which at the outset are set clearly apart from the sex impulses, are in the end beset and invested with libido, until they also lose their distinctiveness and become swallowed up in the vortex of sex. (413)

To identify his own position without identification, McDougall alternates between citing himself (some earlier lecture) and Jung, beginning with Jung's agreement with his points taken up against Freud over the bodies of symptomatizing soldiers.

> Jung begins by pointing out that the neuroses of the war have revived interest in the traumatic theory of the neuroses, and in the principle of Abreaction.... "This conception [*Abreaction*], apparently so clear and simple, is unfortunately—as McDougall rightly objects—like so many other equally simple and therefore delusive explanations, inadequate.... McDougall, therefore, has laid his finger on the right spot when he argues that the essential factor is the dissociation of the psyche and not the existence of a high-tension affect, and hence the essential problem in the therapy is the integration of the dissociation and not the abreaction." (460–62)

McDougall now is all aboard the Jungian negative transference. He agrees that Freud overlooks the all-important relationship to the physician with his highly sexed notions of transference. It's basically a question of rapport, as in suggestion, "the relationship to an object in the living present," "not as an object of sexual desire, but rather as an *object of human relationship*" (469). For Jung and McDougall, transference is always negative transference, an unfortunate, "slavish" subset of rapport, that should be avoided as total obstacle in the course of treatment (468).

Giftraucherzeugung:

Abb. 78. Giftrauchentwicklung aus amerikänischen Giftrauchkerzen [Toxic Smoke Candles] in der Nachkriegszeit.

The effect of American Toxic Smoke Candles. Post–World War I photograph. Bottom of exhibit 31, *Der Chemische Krieg*. Reprinted by permission of Koehler-Mittler.

McDougall's theory of dissociation comes out of his work with shell-shocked soldiers whose symptoms he observed break down into two groups according to the link or limit interposed between the dissociation and affect:

> The dissociated dispositions retain their connections with the emotional centers; while in . . . the simple paralyses, the dissociation occurs at so low a level in the nervous system that the dissociated elements are no longer able to reach or to affect the emotional centers. If this be true, then the emotional calm of the soldier suffering from a well-marked functional paralysis is due not merely, as we might be inclined to suppose, to his consciousness of possessing a disability which secures him from a return to the battle-field, but also is due to his freedom from that circular reciprocal self-maintaining activity between the dissociated disposition and the emotional center, which is the ground of most of the symptoms of those patients who suffer from dissociations of a higher level. (458)

The "dissociative barrier" must therefore be broken through. Hypnosis or suggestion is adjunct of choice in treatment aimed at "readjustment" (470). Or it could take another shock or stimulus or a complete change of setting: "For many cases of war-neurosis such a radical change was produced by the termination of the war or by honourable discharge from military service" (464).

But shock waves still resonate within the analytic conception of sublimation, which joins homosexuality and paranoia in completing the system of Freud's thoughts on "libido" (the same ones that McDougall and Jung, on second thought, placed on top of the discard pile): "There is perhaps in the Freudian conception of sublimation some tinge of the error we found to underlie the practice and theory of *Abreaction*, namely, the view that charges of *libido*, quantities of energy, become locked up in the complexes of 'the Unconscious' like so many charges of compressed air" (473).

But if he chooses to meet psychoanalysis in the war zone, it is also because it was here that psychoanalysis too set precedents (notably through Simmel's work, which Freud cosigned as psychoanalytic) for all the eclecticist compromises. But McDougall takes this to be a contradiction in all the terms of analysis, one that proves him right (rather than, for instance, showing him up as superseded). Suggestion cannot be kept out of analysis; indeed, McDougall quotes Freud's words from 1919: "Just as in the treatment of war-neuroses, hypnotic influence might be included" (428). The company McDougall keeps, he parts with.

French Frieze

The testament of the French response to World War I neuroses, *The Psychoneuroses of War,* by G. Roussy and J. Lhermitte, advocates turn-on of electric current to get to the breakthrough of mastery. It fulfills the wartime requirement of speed:

> It really depends on producing a kind of "crisis," . . . until the patient is finally "mastered." . . . The cure of a psycho-neuropath really consists of a mental contest, resulting in the victory of the physician. This, in conclusion, is the secret of psychotherapy. (168, 171)

The French couple manipulates the crisis of the epidemic because they relocate it as media event, as retrogression within the genealogy of media and madness: "The severe attack of hysteria major described so minutely by Charcot . . . had almost disappeared from medical observation . . . until its revival during the war with all its wild and extravagant characteristics" (115). While the treatment of strict isolation is given credit for the remission, it was also the flash of photography that erased while recording the arches of Charcot's hysterics—and stored the images for flashback. The psychic apparatus in this hysteria model is essentially a medium of storage of old emotions tagged by many possible souvenirs which, when there's the right commotion, get replayed. The shock of commotion seconds the emotion that's already playing back. Diachronically and synchronically, it's all about revival: "The essential element is emotion, or more often the sum-total of emotions which, acting on a constitution with congenital or acquired predisposition, creates this special disposition to revival of the terror" (114–15). The newest flowers of revival are the "Sinistroses" of war. The delirious and restless elaboration on the idea of unjust treatment places this psychopathic condition in proximity to "psychoses of demand" (137). The electric treatment, with specialized application to sensitive spots like the scrotum, doubles, then, as the sinister medium of reeducation. The French term for the treatment session goes, like a foreign body, untranslated: each time it's séance. It's the revival of the fits, the video portion that also stopped flashing when Freud put on his ears and took down what went audio.

The master's voice was heard in 1915. Le Bon released a study of the war in progress *(Enseignements Psychologiques de la guerre européenne)* that makes a rambling rise to the occasion in the nineteenth-century mode of German feuilletonists writing in Paris about the *Volk* back home. He counters all the general positive characterizations of the Germans in the neutral press. But he encounters in himself, in the French soul for which he stands, one nation or notion of philosophy which he group psychologizes at the corners until it's the German who becomes the total group member even or especially when he takes himself individually. That's why a German's such great material for adaptation to technologization: the German is entirely now-ive. He takes dictation and orders that report back to him as his own take-out orders of the techno-gadgetry he, group-of-one, just adores.

Doyle Cover

Arthur Conan Doyle, both author of the Sherlock Holmes detection stories and the leading expert in the field of Spiritualism, was strung high and fine-tuned on top of cases of melancholia. Thus he maintained a splitting economy between secrets and mystery. His artist father already composed one self-portrait with hemlock; even in the Holmes, then, there was, mysteriously, surely a hemlock of suicidal impulsivity. His greatest publicity came his way when he defended mediums who were being investigatively reported as frauds. In 1923, *The Case for Spirit Photography*, Doyle comes to the defense of individuals but also, in the first place, of the idea:

> It is possible in the presence of certain individuals, whom we call mediums, to produce effects which are super-normal and which would appear to indicate intelligences acting visibly quite independently of ourselves. (20)

The effects produced are photographic, with the undead finishing their plates. The spirits represent themselves as so-called extras in the photograph, looking just like photographs, but unlike any their nearest and dearest can recall having beheld (33–34). Sometimes they have not beamed on in completely, but we see them in transition, objects developing out of ectoplasmic bags (like the pods in *Invasion of the Body Snatchers*) (37). But always those photogenic parts that we instantly recognize are especially "animated": "The psychic faces are sometimes more animated and lifelike than the original photographs taken in life" (35). The psychic camera or apparatus takes the pictures:

> One can only suppose that it is in some way connected with the psychic process, and some have imagined a reticulated screen upon which the image is built up.... At the end of about a minute [the medium]...gave a short of shudder, and intimated that he thought a result had been obtained. (23)

The intelligences communicating to us through mediums are our unmournably dead. Here is one typical shot of recognition: "The face bore a strong resemblance to that of my elder sister, who died some thirty years ago" (24). Doyle cannot keep back the incidentals that got him in the position of champion of the impostor mediums: "It may be remarked incidentally that my own strong desire was to obtain some sign from my son who had passed away the year before" (22).

In *The History of Spiritualism,* at the safer distance of history, Doyle gives us the particulars of his son's death, the model for his search for a way back for spirits from the shoot:

Many people had never heard of Spiritualism until the period that began in 1914, when into so many homes the Angel of Death entered suddenly. The opponents of Spiritualism have found it convenient to regard this world upheaval as being the chief cause of the widening interest in psychical research. It has been said, too, by these unscrupulous opponents that the author's advocacy of the subject, as well as that of his distinguished friend, Sir Oliver Lodge, was due to the fact that each of them had a son killed in the war, the inference being that grief had lessened their critical faculties and made them believe what in more normal times they would not have believed. . . .

While it is true that Spiritualism counted its believers in millions before the war, there is no doubt that the subject was not understood by the world at large, and hardly recognized as having an existence. The war changed all that. The deaths occurring in almost every family in the land brought a sudden and concentrated interest in the life after death. People not only asked the question, "If a man die shall he live again?" but they eagerly sought to know if communication was possible with the dear ones they had lost. They sought for "the touch of a vanished hand, and the sound of a voice that is still." Not only did thousands investigate for themselves, but, as in the early history of the movement, the first opening was often made by those who had passed on. The newspaper Press was not able to resist the pressure of public opinion, and much publicity was given to stories of soldiers' return, and generally to the life after death.

In this chapter only brief reference can be made to the different ways in which the spiritual world intermingled with the various phases of the war. The conflict itself was predicted over and over again; dead soldiers showed themselves in their old homes, and also gave warnings of danger to their comrades on the battlefield; they impressed their images on the photographic plate; solitary figures and legendary hosts, not of this world, were seen in the war area; indeed, over the whole scene there was from time to time a strong atmosphere of other-world presence and activity.

If for a moment the author may strike a personal note he would say that, while his own loss had no effect upon his views, the sight of a world which was distraught with sorrow, and which

Abb. 75. Vernebelung von Ostende gegen englische Flieger-
angriffe (nach F. Heigl).

Creation of fog cover over Ostende to protect against English air attacks. Top of exhibit 30, *Der Chemische Krieg*. Reprinted by permission of Koehler-Mittler.

was eagerly asking for help and knowledge, did certainly affect his mind and cause him to understand that these psychic studies, which he had so long pursued, were of immense practical importance and could no longer be regarded as a mere intellectual hobby or fascinating pursuit of a novel research. Evidence of the presence of the dead appeared in his own household, and the relief afforded by posthumous messages taught him how great a solace it would be to a tortured world if it could share in the knowledge which had become clear to himself. (225–27)

Trot Out

An ocean of colors; there were yells: War, war against Germany!
Against the Huns, the barbarians, the murderers of children—
against the arch enemy of all humanity, the Germans.

He knew: that was England's great victory. This is where it
was won, not on the fields of Flanders or of Poland. It was at
once the end of Bismarck's inheritance, the end of Germany.
Now there was only one thing left: die with dignity.

—HANNS HEINZ EWERS, *VAMPIR*

Trotter tries to conclude—all the while at the same time updating—his
study of mass psychology in time for World War I. Because he had already
sketched out much of the outline prewar, when the herd instinct and the
types of gregariousness available to the psychological or sociological study
of the bios entered the test lab of world war, Trotter was there, measuring
his results and forecasting returns. That was in 1915. The 1919 edition, then,
supplies a final series of follow-up reservations and confirmations.

> The general purpose of this book is to suggest that, especially
> when studied in relation to other branches of biology, [the science
> of psychology] . . . is capable of becoming a guide in the actual af-
> fairs of life and of giving an understanding of the human mind
> such as may enable us in a practical and useful way to foretell
> some of the course of human behavior. The present state of pub-
> lic affairs gives an excellent chance for testing the truth of this
> suggestion, and adds to the interest of the experiment the strong
> incentive of an urgent national peril. (6)

Do foretell! The interest Trotter added in 1915 follows an endopsychic
trajectory through mass psychology's share in propaganda or psychological warfare. In other words, whatever Trotter has to say about German
psycho-sociality continues to be true even or especially if it's only the performance of the discourse's own propagandistic principles. By 1919 Trotter
really sees results:

> The result of the experiment has been decisive, and it is still a
> possibility that the progressive integration of society will ulti-
> mately yield a medium in which the utmost needs of the indi-
> vidual and of the race will be reconciled and satisfied. Had the
> more primitive social type—the migratory, aggressive society of

leadership and the pack—had this proved still the master of the less primitive socialized and integrative type, the ultimate outlook for the race would have indeed been black. This is by no means to deny that German civilization had a vigour, a respect for knowledge, and even a benignity within which comfortable life was possible. But it is to assert that it was a regression, a choice of the easy path, a surrender to the tamer platitudes of the spirit that no aggressive vigour could altogether mask. To live dangerously was supposed to be its ideal, but dread was the very atomosphere it breathed. Its armies could be thrown into hysterical convulsions by the thought of the franc-tireur, and the flesh of its leaders made to creep by such naive and transpontine machinations as its enemies ambitiously called propaganda. The minds that could make bugbears out of such material were little likely to attempt or permit the life of arduous and desperate spiritual adventure that was in the mind of the philosopher when he called on his disciples to live dangerously. (233–34)

Germany or Prussia was the original "war machine," at least according to British projections. Trotter reads the instructions to the machine as limiting its operations to the half-life of unchallenged nonstop aggression. As soon as resistance meets the one-way transference of the psychic war apparatus or economy, where infrastructure, staying power, or communion of relations should have been, we now find only moral collapse. The Germans do not war within limits: their onslaught is total, the more so the closer defeat appears. At the end of World War I, the first Blitz was one of these offense inventions the Germans shoot up the losing end of their wars; it was the fantasy, beyond more and more cutting of losses, of instant, miraculous loss reversal through sudden press forward and breakthrough.

The magnitude of the world war, Trotter advises, could be picked up along with the side effects of destabilization: Germany doubled over with ruthless scandalmongering, espionage, and deliberately cruel treatment of inferiors by their superiors (182–83), while in England "outbursts of spy mania" (149) arose with the war's onset to accompany a newfound "vitality of rumor" that was evident on all sides of the conflict. "That rumors spread readily and are tenacious of life is evidence of the sensitiveness to herd opinion which is so characteristic of the social instinct" (144). The herd instinct is at altruistic maximum when it is (as it must be) heard.

After giving the personality and presentation some grooming tips, Trotter gives Freud's contribution a prominent place in his 1915 assessment of psychology's real advances in support of the herd instinct. What Trotter recognizes in Freud's theory is a model for comprehending conflict that even at the time of war is not stuck on externals. Within a discursive relay folding mass psychology back on psychological warfare, Trotter makes an unconscious word choice: the Freudian model of conflict is endopsychic.

> It seems to be a fundamental conception of the Freudian system that the development of the mind is accompanied and conditioned by mental conflict. (72)

> True conflict, the conflict which molds and deforms, must be actually within the mind—must be endopsychic to use a term invented by Freud, though not used by him in this exact application. (81)

Endopsychic conflict belongs, in the big picture, to a scheme of development Trotter keeps referring back to evolution. Development is evolutionary, then, precisely because sudden changes can, like adjustments introduced in the past on time travel trips, alter both the direction and background of progressive time. First, with regard to personal development:

> The evolution of this [developmental] series is sensitive to interference by outside influences, and any disturbance of it either by way of anticipation or delay will have profound effects upon the ultimate character and temperament of the subject (73).

Then and again, organic evolution gets addressed:

> It is to be remarked . . . that there is strong reason to suppose that the process of organic evolution has not been and is not always infinitely slow and gradual. It is more than suspected that, perhaps as the result of slowly accumulated tendency or perhaps as the result of a sudden variation of structure or capacity, there have been periods of rapid change which might have been perceptible to direct observation. (101)

The model of conflict Freud introduces into Trotter's take on evolution holds the place of the war within Trotter's long-range reading of the developmental plan that led to and must survive the world war. "The war was the consequence of inherent defects in the evolution of civilized life" (162). Before its all-out regression into a more primitive, aggressive mode of gregariousness, Germany represented an "epoch-making" advance when "the necessity and value of conscious direction of the social unit" came to be recognized and implemented (163). Under the pressure of conflict, the Germans chose as their main socializing idea that of a lupine war society or economy based on perpetual aggression and victory. The "ultimate source of the submarine and aircraft campaigns against England" thus lies in Germany's "steady insistence upon the necessity of aggression, upon maintaining the attack at whatever cost of life" (188). This choice by the Germans of, and regression to, a premature type of gregariousness had, in "the differentiation of themselves from other European peoples," "biological significance" (170). Trotter notes with amazement the barbarism of German invective against England. Trotter keeps it one-sided, even though he will later admit the existence of Allied propaganda, which he minimizes as in every sense a slight, but to which the Germans once again characteristically overreacted. What's the matter, Hun? And when it comes to German self-assertions of patriotism and other meglo states, Trotter goes colonial and sees, as he says later about the prospect of German victory, "black": "It shows itself at times as . . . outbursts of idolatry, not of the pallid, metaphorical, modern type, but the full-blooded African kind, with all the apparatus of idol and fetish and tom-tom" (173). To set human being back on evolutionary track, Germany must be beaten; there must be no overconcern with the severity of the outcome, the peaces into which the enemy will be torn. "Germany has shown unmistakably the way to her heart; it is for Europe to take it" (201). When Trotter concludes by pointing to World War I Germany as "the strongest example of the predacious led society that history records" (251), he has no idea how much more recording history there is yet to come. Somewhere here there's a heart to eat out.

The conflict between socialized gregariousness (England) and aggressive gregariousness (Germany)—"a divergence which almost amounts to a specific difference in the biological scale"—has the evolutionary significance of every all-out struggle for the survival of the species.

> It is a war not so much of contending nations as of contending species. We are not taking part in a mere war, but in one of Nature's august experiments. It is as if she had set herself to try out in her workshop the strength of the socialized and the aggressive types. To the socialized peoples she has entrusted the task of proving that her old faith in cruelty and blood is at last an anachronism. To try them, she has given substance to the creation of a nightmare, and they must destroy this werewolf or die. (174–75)

> Germany has left the path of natural evolution, or rather, perhaps, has never found it. Unless, therefore, her civilization undergoes a radical change, and comes to be founded on a different series of instructive impulses, it will disappear from the earth. (193)

The evolutionary progress Trotter charts as coming soon postwar (and for the first time: up until right now social evolution has been limited to "movements of oscillation rather than of true progress" [255]) begins with the amoeba and culminates in the socialized and consciously directed herd:

> In essence the significance of the passage from the solitary to the gregarious seems to be closely similar to that of the passage from the unicellular to the multicellular organism—an enlargement of the unit exposed to natural selection, a shielding of the individual cell from that pressure, an endowment of it with freedom to vary and specialize in safety. (103)

> The needs and capacities that were at work in the primeval amoeba are at work in him. In his very flesh and bones is the impulse towards closer and closer union in larger and larger fellowships. To-day he is fighting his way towards that goal, fighting for the perfect unit which Nature has so long foreshadowed.... That perfect unit will be a new creature, recognizable as a single entity; to its million-minded power and knowledge no barrier will be insurmountable. (213)

The step from multicellularism to the perfect unit is achieved by the society of the hive, which out of many members creates one animal: "This new animal differs from the other animals of the metazoa which it has outdistanced in the race of evolution, not merely in its immense power, energy, and flexibility, but also in the almost startling fact that it has recovered the gift of immortality which seemed to have been lost with its protozoal ancestors" (106). Each bee, while "possessed by an enthusiasm for the hive more intense than a mother's devotion to her son," "works herself to death" (106). When Freud briefly commented on Trotter's elevation of gregariousness to an instinct, he pointed to the drive's ingredients, which he shook out of the family pack: the young child forms group identifications with siblings because there is no more conclusive way available to him for resolving the total conflict over sole access to the mother. How German is that? Instead Trotter puts a bee under the bonnet of the motor or motive force of English social identity and identification. "England has taken as her model the bee" (201) or, perhaps, the WASP, which gives hives to workers protected and projected by the mother of an identification.

Mourning Ant Melancholia

> The thought alone that the 3,000,000 Bolshevists presently in
> German hands could be sterilized, making them available as
> workers while excluding them from procreation, opens vast
> perspectives.
>
> —ADOLF POKORNY TO HEINRICH HIMMLER, IN ALEXANDER MITSCHERLICH
>   AND FRED MIELKE, *DOCTORS OF INFAMY: THE STORY OF THE NAZI
>   MEDICAL CRIMES*

> Man and every other living creature has the striving to keep
> itself and its kind alive and to reproduce it—all the habits of
> life spring from this striving.
>
> —HANNS HEINZ EWERS, *AMEISEN*

In 1925, along the sidelines of his at once occultist and psy-war series of
novels, Ewers recorded his lifelong obsessional study of ants and then in
1943 reissued it, really paying for his authorship of books like *Vampir* when
he recants in the new edition's preface the "shading and glitter of that period of decadence," which he couldn't separate from the book as it stands
(to our suddenly increased span of attention), short, of course, of writing a
completely new one. It's the short stop of denial that gets his study of ants,
which virtually newsreels with Nazi compatibles and possibilities, into
his past to pick the undead corpus clean. Although he doesn't credit bees
or wasps (though maybe termites) with the same advanced state held by
the ants, he follows Trotter all the way into the science fictive preoccupation with the insect, the most primeval, but, with a little evolution-styled
imagination, easily futural species. The science friction sparks static from
the lost war. Ewers ridicules Forel's treatise on ants, in which the author
extended the whole labor, which for him was based on the experience of
World War I, into a recommendation for the future of pacifist armies and
Esperanto (*Ameisen*, 353). But Ewers dates his own first encounter with
ants to his sojourn in prisoner-of-war camp in Oglethorpe, Georgia (370).
He closes the book with a reference to the wartime fad in New York of belief in transmigration of souls—to which Ewers adds (it's his parting shot)
that Bismarck was interested in returning as an ant, a creature he identified
as so disciplined, so happy to work for the common good of the *Volk* (382).
At the same time, the Jewish introject is still neutral to good. Mosaic law is
cited in the regard it holds for the harvest leftovers that the ants produce

and which it reserves, by law, for the poor. At one of the more difficult turns in his empathizing with ant psychology, Ewers almost refers to Freud's science, certainly not by name, but nearly in the claim he makes for "sexual psychology" as the only one among the human sciences able to consider the prospect not only of a master instinct but of a slave one too (301).

Ants, Ewers proclaims, are top of the line of their animal type, just as man is top man of his line. The similarities between the two equals, lonely at the top, are remarkable. Ants keep, herd, and "milk" "cattle." But whereas we copied nature when we took to milking cows or goats, ants copied nothing at all when they started "milking" the sweet excrement of their farmyard bugs (189). Certain tropical ants even cultivate their own hanging gardens. Like us at our wheel or the spider out of its own body, the ant spins too, but the ant takes the thread not from its own body but from the larva, which has the natural capacity for spinning cocoons. When they thus use the larva for their colony construction, the ants go *"against nature, beyond what she wanted and determined"* (151). Ants build community dwellings linked to sister cities by highways (98). They communicate at some distance in a "language...reminiscent of telegraphy on the Morse machine: short, long, long, short − − . . . − . − − . . − ." (368). The queen ant, unlike queen bee, is not just an "egg laying machine" but truly mothers and raises her children, her people (57–58).

Although the ants get top prize, both of us are into hygiene. That ants bury their dead gets buried by the scientific literature as another example of hygiene. But, says Ewers, they grieve too. Plus, even for us burial is at the same time an act of hygiene. We'd surely keep our dead around if we could get away with it. The sick too are cared for and healed by nurse ants. The fatally wounded, however, are removed from the colony for speedy disposal (72–75). Whenever the ants diverge from humans within this area of overlap by the degree of their radicalization of the same concept (hygiene and euthanasia), the compatibility between ants and the Nazis rises to top selection. "But for my sensibility it seems more humane to transfer those afflicted by fatal illness or incurably insane to a quick death, rather than extend the torment of their living on for as long a time as possible, the way we humans are given to do; it demonstrates in addition a healthier sense of the general good of the *Volk*" (75). The biggest *Dasein*-rhyme between us and them is warfare. Ants fight among themselves, *Volk* against *Volk*. In their wars the victorious ants rob supplies and cattle or take possession of the conquered colony. Sometimes alliances are formed with former enemies, and these alliances can even lead on occasion, "in the case of weak peoples," to a merger (81). When a colony is taken over, it is reorganized—

to the point of one generation's extinction and the next one's enslavement—around total control of reproduction.

Ewers, who dedicates his book to the memory of his dear mother, stresses that ants have advanced to the top of their line through female domination. The preponderance of one gender hinders incest. The "natural thought" of the ants is for the queen-to-be to go out and marry the citizens of another *Volk*, but never across the lines of race or species: "To put it in human terms: the Swedish woman might take a Norwegian, Englishman, German, Dutchman for husband, but never a Negro or a Papuan; the Chinese woman might choose a Japanese or a Korean, but not an Arab" (49). But exogamy is also tough: most females die along the way, and "only a very few... get to the point of creating a *Volk* of her own out of her own body" (52). All down the line, selection in ant survival is "superhuman" (54).

The males don't live long and tend to disappear after conjugal duties are over (and out). Because once is enough. After one fertilization with the seed she at the same time stores indefinitely, the queen can keep on laying eggs without any time out for regular insemination (35). The female doesn't even require male insemination the first time around: it works, but she doesn't depend on it for her futurity (64). "The strongest in antkind are the infertile females, who moreover put the fully developed males of humankind to shame" (79). One of the queen's prerogatives is to lay eggs and give birth just like a virgin. Parthenogenesis is how the male, every one another Christ, comes about, out of the unfertilized eggs. But at some point, male and female reproduction must occur, though perhaps not during my generation. "Otherwise after a series of generations, the species would die out, since in the entire animal kingdom, starting with the amoeba, we know no case in which an unlimited parthenogenesis—or even only an unlimited splitting—were possible: the natural coupling of the sexes always has to intervene again every so often. Forever, therefore, the authentic female cannot be missing; with some generation or other genuine females must appear next to the males, and join in a regular wedding" (65–66).

"The concept of the ant *Volk* did without the co-work of the male; it wanted an Amazon state, a purely female state. The female rid of the reproductive function has the more developed brain: you don't need brains for the reproductive act" (44). The individual ant counts for nothing. The totality or community of ants is the only meaningful unit. *Volk* rules all specializations and diversifications of ant functions (44). For example: "No other species, not even mankind, cares so thoroughly for their young as the ants do—but at the same time the individual egg, the individual larva is without any value: they are calmly eaten up or passed around to others for nourishment if it seems expedient" (42). In war the ants will seize the enemy kids for nourishment or to raise as slaves. But Ewers supposes, if we are to believe Greek mythology, we too have been known to devour our tight young morsels.

Ants encounter certain social genres of difficulty reminiscent of human problems. For example, it is possible for two ant peoples to cohabit a colony, although there are tensions inherent in this situation, just as with the Negro in America, the Japanese in California, the Irish in England, the Jew in Eastern Europe (244). And ants can allow their collective life's work to be and go wasted when it comes to the beetles. It only takes a few for an invasion, because each one already enraptures the ant populations with their long hair and drugs them with the odor and juice coming out of their pores. These beetles Ewers also calls "vampires" (226). Another kind of beetle doesn't invade but waits around outside the colony for ants to come by and go for the hair, the juice, the ecstasy. But once the ants lie about drugged, this freelance "vampire witch" crawls down from its pillar and "pursues her hideous vampiric trade" and "sucks them dry" (228–29). The only way the beetles overstay their invasion is if they start running low in juice while the worker ants keep on licking until one hot day a golden-haired beetle is wounded. Once that happens, the beetle is eaten up right away. It's that kind of love, the kind "cannibalistic sex murder" also represents (231–32). The survivor beetles must emigrate. But even then their brood of little beetles, still under ant care, devours great amounts of ant eggs and larvae. After a season of exile spent with weaker ants who don't lick so hard so that in time their supplies can replenish, the banished beetles return to resounding welcome; sometimes the host ants will even go and pick them up and bring them back home in triumph (232).

But certain kinds of ants propagate themselves by taking over another kind's colony. The "bloodred queen" specializes in flying out to take over the "grey skirts." She kills all her grey peers and steals all the eggs and larvae and keeps them in the chamber she has occupied; they serve her now as food, now as the future servants who will be for her, not against her. In the meantime, with the young queen getting all the attention now, the old queen dies of neglect. That's the most direct approach. The young queen-to-be may be able to make an arrangement whereby she and the black-grey queen together raise their separate broods until one fine day the red ones see the light and drive off the black-grey ones.

The *Lumpen* ants are treated to a variation on the takeover theme. The pretender queen enters the *Lumpen* colony and acts like the reigning queen's

Abb. 76. Versuch der Einnebelung eines Tanks mit eigenen Mitteln (nach F. Heigl).

Attempted fog cover-up of a tank by its own means. Bottom of exhibit 30, *Der Chemische Krieg.* Reprinted by permission of Koehler-Mittler.

soul sister. Even though she's plainly an alien, someone so dear to our queen must be good, the host ants conclude. But under the cover of this show of intimacy, her embrace tightens until the old queen's off with her head. The new queen takes over with her own brood; in the near future the step-ants die out as a *Volk* (272–74).

The queen "embodies all that for which the ants live and die: the prototype of the rigorously national work state" [Urbild des streng nationalen Arbeitstaates]. "In some unexplained, mysterious manner ungraspable by us humans, the life of the original founder of the state appears to stand in connection with that of her *Volk:* when the queen dies, all the citizens contract a remarkable dysphoria. Mourning, which goes to the point of dissatisfaction with life, is how we humans might put it" (56–57). But the other extremity where we and the ants are pretty much alone in animal history is the crime of matricide. The bloodred queen sometimes succeeds in seducing the worker ants into killing their queen mother. Sometimes the worker ants will already be rallying to her claim to the throne because the current queen suddenly seems so old by comparison. When the new queen thus claims the interest of the ants, the ex dies from lack of nourishment and care. There's a rapport between us and the ants on this crime score. "With the difference however that the aberration only afflicts individuals, seldom entire groups, whereas with the ants, which are able to feel in common so thoroughly, so very much more socially and nationally, the whole *Volk* is afflicted. In antkind we observe the reversal of the original instinct" (271).

Ewers's insistence throughout is that the ant state form is adopted not by "instinct" but by virtue of the intelligent life. At the close of the book, he refers us to the vast archive of literature written in the recent past pro and contra equal soul rights for women. But even today we can't extend the soul or psyche to animals, even the most highly developed ones (381–82). The dedication to the mother's memory comes back here: a whole species, capable of mourning, can conceive themselves a *Volk* that for the good of the state will even murder the (dead) mother and put her to rest within their renewed collective, their new national formation and consciousness. But one of Mother's ghosts writes Ewers's last word on behalf of the irrational vampiric bond. The golden-haired beetles can even wipe out the proud bloodred race with the hold their fire water has over them, too (301).

Mickey Marx

It is difficult to see why these true socialists mention society at
all if they believe with the philosophers that all real cleavages
are evoked by the cleavage of concepts. Like all German ideolo-
gists, the true socialists continually mix up literary history and
real history as equally effective. This habit is, of course, very
understandable among the Germans, who conceal the abject
part they have played and continue to play in real history by
equating the illusions, in which they are so rich, with reality.

—KARL MARX AND FRIEDRICH ENGELS, *THE GERMAN IDEOLOGY*

Only since 1932 has the complete *German Ideology* been available near you,
everywhere, and now. With the release, "the gnawing criticism of the mice"
(Pascal, xv) that Marx had detected scurrying through his underworld tract
could at last be admitted—into the Marxian system. They say *The German
Ideology* is "the first full statement of Marxism" (Pascal, ix). But it promotes
itself as another "how to" book on ghost busting.

> The phantoms of their brains have gained the mastery over them.
> (Marx and Engels, 1)

> The phantoms formed in the human brain are also, necessarily,
> sublimates of their material life-process, which is empirically ver-
> ifiable and bound to material premises. (14)

Marxism shows us the way to a ghost-free future: and the prescribed
bringing to consciousness of the underlying material and social conditions
would indeed perform the bust—if, however, the phantoms had not at the
same time already entered a new advertising medium, the happy medium
created through a split-level distribution of social theory between its esoteric
science and the popular literature that keeps its libido pool stocked with a
following or understanding: "The very fact that it is concerned with social
exoteric circumstances means that it must carry on some form of propaganda." (81)

So that German social theory can carry on, not as politics but via metaphysics, anthropology, or, in short, psychology (83), propaganda splits social science. You saw it first with Marx and Engels: they traced German ideology's call for primal submissions to the haunted split-level of theory.
Inside the gap between social science and propaganda, it's the same difference between the reality of war and its anticipation or make-believe.

> And so the prophet bids his sacred host be calm, even at the
> prospect of a conflict with real weapons; you do not really risk
> your life; you merely pretend to risk it. (193)

Thus propaganda or war readiness turns on a pretending or testing rapport with risk. Marx and Engels already covered this rapport on the social-scientific side:

> Whenever, through the development of industry and commerce,
> new forms of intercourse have been evolved, (e.g. insurance companies etc.) the law has always been compelled to admit them
> among the modes of acquiring property. (61–62)

But the preemptive—pretending and testing—mode of risk and (same difference) grief management that insurance sells cannot be bought back as the time share of socioeconomic causes. Already on the side of propaganda, insurance cannot switch back from social science's other side. The newly founded rapport with risk, with a self-other bond always at risk (and that's the bond), grows up a psychology of group protection or projection that's no longer enrollable in Marx's classes. By 1932 (at the latest) the testing rapport with risk had assumed a propagandistic or psychological agenda nonreducible to its scientific status or social origin.

It proves possible, maybe necessary (if you go with the mice), to read the ingredients of the debate between Adorno and Benjamin (same time, same station) off the back of the 1932 release of *The German Ideology*. In the three corners of their match or mismatch: Marx, Freud, and Mickey Mouse. Benjamin's double take on Marxism and Freudian group psychology followed his upbeat reception of Mickey Mouse as the group mascot. It's the antidotal shock inoculation that mass culture, with Mickey Mouse at the front of the line, administers. The shots of catastrophe preparedness control-release the psychotic breakdown our ongoing technologization or massification otherwise telecommands. But, Adorno complains, with "Mickey Mouse things are far more complicated, and the serious question arises as to whether the reproduction of every person really constitutes that a priori of the film which you claim it to be, or whether instead this reproduction belongs precisely to that 'naive realism' whose bourgeois nature we so thoroughly agreed upon" (Taylor, 124). Which is to say, the theory of mass ego or mass identification that reproduces the inoculating shock or shot of catastrophe packs its own case of repression. Adorno argues that catastrophes (which appear to go down as prehistory) represent and repress only the recent past, a past primalized, moreover, through the repression of the

scientific or objective inside view brought to us by Freudian psychoanalysis and Marxian social theory. Benjamin's mass ego or collective consciousness, like Jung's less-conscious conception, is "open to criticism," Adorno
writes, "on both sides; from the vantage point of the social process, in that
it hypostasizes archaic images where dialectical images are in fact generated by the commodity character, not in an archaic collective ego, but in
alienated bourgeois individuals; and from the vantage point of psychology
in that a mass ego exists only in earthquakes and catastrophes, while otherwise objective surplus value prevails precisely through individual subjects and against them. The notion of collective consciousness" serves thus
only, Adorno concludes, "to divert attention from true objectivity and its
correlate, alienated subjectivity" (Taylor, 113). That's why Adorno wants to
get Benjamin back to the social science test: Benjamin's notion of testing as
the ready-made mass rapport with technologization not only exchanges an
old taboo for a new improved one but also misdirects Benjamin's own
larger-scale rapport with Marxism away from mediation through the total
social process toward the metaphorical, the concrete, the mere as-if. But as
Adorno would go on to prove in his own Mickey Mouse essays on jazz and
the fetish character of mass music, the metaphorical-concrete-as-if doesn't
go away with social conditioning. Indeed, as Benjamin saw it, the trigger-
happiness of gadgets, the push-button origin of the test, injects into whatever gets techno-reproduced right down to the moment a "posthumous
shock" ("Über einige Motive," 630). "The phantoms of their brains" had
encrypted themselves deep down and for keeps inside the test, risk and
grief management, the propagandistic bond with warfare and catastrophe,
and the psychologization, the merger, of Marxian and Freudian sciences.

At the three corners of the debate that, both Adorno and Benjamin
agreed, gave the complete picture, the good news and the bad news of
their otherwise allied reception of mass culture, the discursivity markers
and mascots were, out there in simulcast, following the bouncing ball of
polymorphous assimilation and unification. The merger of Marxism and
psychoanalysis inside social theory was brought to consciousness by the
Frankfurt school. Otherwise and out there it was a metapsychological fact.
That's the way sociologist Hendrik de Man went—from committed Marxist
to, thanks to World War I, an incomplete one. Freud's "theory of the drives,"
de Man writes, "has a significance for the personal behavior of mankind
similar to the one which the Marxist theory of interests has for its collective
behavior" (Cremerius, 105).

Analyzing the collapses of world war and world worker movement as
the feedback of extraeconomic or psychic factors, he turned to the study of

psychology, psychotherapy, and psychoanalysis. He too copped the consequences of society-wide psychic trauma when he reunified psychological
treatments and theories from Wilhelm Wundt to Carl Jung. And he gave
Freud the credit for a reunion that Freud, however, had, beginning in 1914,
regularly warned against. But the significance of Freud's science thus goes
without saying—without resisting or integration: the Freudian psychoanalysis de Man tried to incorporate into his otherwise Marxism-based social
theory intact and undisclosed he at the same time used interchangeably
with those Jungian and Adlerian notions that were advertised as Freud
resistant.

Bouncing across the range of symptoms produced by the discursivity
mergers, Mickey Mouse scored big time in a veritable Rorschach Blitz. Nazi
film journals reported in 1936 on Mickey Mouse's premiere in the Soviet
Union: Moscow critics recognized Disney as a genius and his achievement
as consummate social criticism (Im Reiche, 90). With Disney the public opinion that went around, came around (even in Nazi Germany): as late as 1940,
Nazi socialist ideologues celebrated Disney as injecting the socius with
magical antidotes to sociology (103). Early local criticisms of Mickey Mouse
in Nazi Germany (for example, as the manic measure or rat race of Western
degeneracy) were premature articulations still in line with certain pre-
Nazi diagnoses based on the forensic psychiatry of, say, Kraepelin and Wey-
gandt. The 1931 issue of Der Querschnitt, for example, records the psychiatric consensus:

> The chronic film image of Mickey Mouse exhibits unmistakable
> symptoms of his creator's paranoid mental state. But even in the
> vast majority of the audience we can observe an abnormal state
> similar to that of Mickey Mouse. (Im Reiche, 62)

But the spontaneous syndication of psychiatric assessment by the Nazi locals was not followed by the leader. Goebbels records in his diary on 20
December 1937:

> I'm giving the Führer for Christmas 30 class films of the last 4
> years and 18 Mickey Mouse films. He's already quite excited and
> very happy. This treasure will hopefully grant him much plea-
> sure and relaxation. (Im Reiche), 11)

Here we watch sitcom-style the upwardly mobile move that psychotherapy was able to make (in or even in Nazi Germany) toward establishing itself alongside—and that means also against—the interests of psychiatry.
The contest prize was equal but separate insurance coverage.

„Ach, Herr Doktor, ich habe so fürchterliche Kopffchmerzen."

„So, bitte, dann legen Sie sich mal auf den Diwan und sprechen jeden Gedanken aus, der Ihnen gerade einfällt."

These four images comprise a vertical comic strip decorating the page of a magazine article, "The Psychoanalysis of the Jew Sigmund Freud," one in a series of articles titled "The Role of the Jew in Medicine." The captions translate as follows:

1. "Oh, Doctor, I have such terrible headaches."
2. "Well, lie down on the couch and tell me every thought that comes into your head."
3. "Roast—mineral spring—blotting paper—handkerchief—dagger—"

„Braten — Heilquelle — Löschblatt — Taschentuch — Dolch — —"

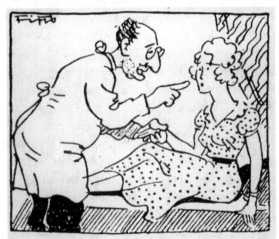

„Halt! Dolch! Jetzt haben wirs. Der Gedanke Dolch zeigt Ihre sexuellen Wünsche. Ihre Kopfschmerzen kommen also daher, daß Sie in Ihrer Ehe keine Befriedigung finden. Daraus ergibt sich von selbst, wie Sie geheilt werden können — — —"

4. "Stop! Dagger! Now we've got it. The thought 'dagger' shows your sexual wishes. Your headaches stem from the fact that you aren't finding satisfaction in your marriage. It follows from this just how you can be healed..."

Reproduced from a photocopy of the original article in *Deutsche Volksgesundheit aus Blut und Boden* (August–September 1933): 15–16.

Nazi adoration of Disney (who was rumored to be in fact Walter Dist-ler, native German through and through) supported the years of tortured indecision, renegotiation, and ambivalence occasioned by the German re-lease (coming soon even at that late date) of *Snow White*. The movie would in fact never be shown in Nazi German theaters. Hitler, who requested a copy on 5 February 1938 for his private cinema, simply loved it. But it was not enough that Disney was the one (and only) director to receive Leni Riefenstahl on her 1938 visit to Hollywood. That alone could not offset the hurt caused by the anti-Nazi activities (from petition signing to the pro-duction of anti-Nazi films) supported by the rest of the industry. Even in-side his own studio, Disney told Riefenstahl as he was receiving her, he could not screen the copy of *Olympia* she had brought along, since every-one else in his organization right down to the projectionist was dead set against the Nazi cause.

But back in Nazi Germany, it did remain possible to apply to the Reichs Film Archive for private screenings of *Snow White* and, after 1941, of Mickey Mouse films. In 1944 one reason recorded for a Nazi minister needing to view *Snow White* was "to obtain information on animation technique in connection with the planned production by the Reichs-Ministry for Arma-ment and War Production of technical-instructional films" (*Im Reiche*, 137).

The goals of the discursivity merger between Marxism and psychoanaly-sis that could never be attained as such (a waste!)—not without group-psy-chological compatibility between the two—nevertheless produced among its side effects a Nazi unified psychotherapy that competed for insurance coverage and, on both sides, a psychologization of the goals and contexts of social theory that belonged, in effect, to two phases of total war or, in other words, of media war. In the 1920s, American sociology and the Ger-man military were busy assessing the propaganda methods and effects aired during World War I. The sociologists were enlisted to prevent the coming American loss of the peace: conceiving the Great War as the war to end all wars, American military PR went all out to demonize the Axis powers. This left all sides of the conflict hanging over a peace for which the psy-chological reserves of preparedness and readiness had been completely ex-hausted. The German military conceded along with their defeat that the Allied propaganda efforts could only go out of control, since they remained one-sided: the German command failed to mount a counteroffensive, nei-ther mobilizing the mass media nor, on the same front, exploiting "all of their weapons with the maximum impact upon the enemy's will as the chief criterion" (Lasswell, "Political and Psychological Warfare," 23). But on the inside of their out-of-control projections of the German demon, American propaganda systematically applied the quantitative methods of modern social science to the presentation of the enemy's atrocities: commissions of experts were convened to collect the evidence, treat the data statistically, and deliver the findings. But this is where the Germans stopped taking notes: the German military took the World War I defeat as a lesson in the psychologization of warfare. While psychological factors were being control-released within the postwar American sociological reflection on, and extension of, Allied propaganda, the German military sent psychology to the front of the line of its remobilization efforts and replaced "propaganda" with what the German military took to calling "psychological warfare." American sociologist Lasswell gives the background story:

> The psychologists wanted "a place in the sun"; that is, they were eager to demonstrate that their skills could be used for the national defense in time of war. Early in the Second World War a group of Americans translated some of the important German literature into English for the purpose of opening the eyes of the military to the usefulness of psychology, not only in testing for specific aptitudes, or in propaganda, but in considering every phase of the conduct of war under modern conditions. ("Political and Psychological Warfare," 23)

The 1941 translation and compilation of an owner's manual to this second coming of world war, *German Psychological Warfare,* reached the conclusion, in concert with the Frankfurt school theorists, that "National Socialism is psychoanalysis in reverse." All propaganda packs a reversal, a double psychologization, that is, a psychologization and a sociologization. The Nazi socialist reading of the enemy's socioeconomic interests (like the Entente propaganda strikes directed against the Central Powers in World War I) is Marxism in reverse. It's brought to us not via politics but via metaphysics, anthropology—in a word, psychology. It wasn't enough for Marx and Engels to issue the disowner's guide to propaganda. But both sides of world war had all along been packing into their propaganda Marxistoid analyses of the inequities of the enemy's social organization: the first time around, Germany was called a feudal order of warlords; Germany called America's national interests on their really giving shelter or cover-up to the interests of Anglo-American capitalists. Indeed, Germany made one propaganda move during the Great War that is truly hard to evaluate, if only because it gave itself as much time as a vampire takes when he goes underground to await the passing of centuries for his resurrection and new start in life, in the lives of others. Injecting the Russian Empire, with Marxist-

Leninism, literally sending Lenin back from his exile in a sealed train, like a carefully administered toxin, did achieve the short-term goal of all quiet on the Eastern front. But thrown into the evolutionary wash of upheaval, the Soviet system was, in longer term, given a half-life to hold an empire of projections together that would then topple by that same better half-life. By the close of the twentieth century, one might say, less in fact than as fantasy, that Germany finally won the First World War.

The materialist look that Lasswell's theory of psychological warfare assumed for the cold war is another case of doubling on contact, on cover-up: "Propaganda—like diplomacy, armed forces and economic arrangements—is an instrument of total policy. In the long run its aim is to economize the material cost of power" ("The Strategy of Soviet Propaganda," 57–58). That Nazi research-happiness did not, after all, expend itself on Marxist theory within its uninhibited agenda—one limited only by service to the war effort, which historically is not a limit at all—does not necessarily confirm Marxism's projected correctness. One could also almost say that even Nazi research was not interested in Marxism. Checklist prospects open wide: the usefulness of Jung's theory or therapy beyond its name value fails a similar test.

The post–World War II American assessment of Allied shortsightedness with regard to the Nazi takeover of world war propaganda was that the West could not afford to notice what it felt it couldn't deny—that Nazi socialists had been so uninhibited that they could go ahead (no problem) and borrow from communist propaganda techniques. The projective segregation was hard to shake. For example:

> Although public opinion as we understand it cannot exist in totalitarian states, its place is taken by an official image of the world expressed through the media of mass communications. ("Political and Psychological Warfare," 48)

But when the American military discovered (in 1941) that it was in the first place psychology, psychoanalysis, and the psychotherapies that Nazi research had admitted into its war effort, the challenge of psychological warfare could begin to be met. But even after the Nazi war effort began running on empty, on the emptiness or lack that had all along been anticipated or denied—that is, psychologized (for example, in Heidegger's thinking of standing reserve or *Bestand* as one of the basics of technology's metaphysical emplacement or in Nazi military psychiatry's diagnosis of war psychosis in terms of depletion of psychic reserve fuel)—its military psychological complex remained, in theory, unbeatable.

But not to worry, the American psychological war effort did not openly appropriate the Nazi administration of the discursivity merger, of the emergence of Greater Psychoanalysis, before first making some streamlining adjustments. American psy warriors (as they were called) learned from the big mistake in Nazi Socialist mobilizations of psychic apparatuses and media technologies: the Nazis just didn't know when to stop winning. According to Gregory Bateson, the Germans could not see the long haul or recurrence *(Wiederholung)* of once and future losses for all the short-term goals of victory: "The Germans have a cry *Sieg zum Todt*, conquer unto death, which ironically describes the time structure of their wars, winning all the preliminary battles and losing the war" (*A Sacred Unity*, 212). H.D. Lasswell, the first American sociologist between the wars not only to take note of the psychological effects of military propaganda but even the first (he was on a roll) to mount an openly psychoanalytic social theory, defined American psychological warfare in terms of the limit:

> The best success in war is achieved by the destruction of the enemy's will to resist, and with a minimum annihilation of fighting capacity. The political aim is limited destruction. We are looking at the conduct of war in the perspective of psychology when we are seeking to widen the gap between the physical destruction of capabilities on both sides and the magnitude of the impact upon the enemy's intention to resist. ("Political and Psychological Warfare," 22)

The discovery of the limit alongside a savings in expenditure of destructiveness in the course of war sets a limit to victory and thus to warfare. It creates the conditions for a media war as total or totaled war's last stand or auto-overcoming.

According to Adorno, Freud's declaration that sociology was but applied psychology copped a high of omnipotence of thoughts that characterizes his analysis of group phenomena. And yet what's so great about Freud's group psychology, Adorno has to admit, is that it brings it all back into the home and sets the group on the relationship to the primal father. This relationship is at the same time fundamentally a social and, indeed, a sociological one ("Postscriptum," 88). In 1955 and then ten years later in a postscript, Adorno folded out these internal relations between sociology and psychology as an unresolved contradiction heading off neo-Freudian approaches at the impasse. A totally socialized or sociologized world like our own, Adorno argues, no longer knows from psychology. That's why a social-reality and adjustment oriented neopsychoanalysis, one that had admitted sociology into its remake of Freud's science, loses the lead in critique of the mass-media consumerist society that Freudian psychoanalysis, in its seeming disconnection point by point from social issues, had comprehended right down to the component parts (of identification, projection, and destrudo).

The internal contradiction between psychology and sociology is the one neopsychoanalysis symptomatizes in the no-win division it introduces between two options in the therapy and theory of the ego: type A, weaken the ego (the way to go with neurotics), or type B, strengthen the ego and its defense mechanisms (the plan preferred for psychotics). That neurotics alone should bring material to consciousness while psychotics must be rendered functional is a private-public division that Freud kept unresolved; for him psychopathology was a continuum on a scale from neurosis to psychosis. By resolving (or revolving) along the divide of a therapeutic separation the ambiguity or ambivalence of Freud's ego conception (which doubles as the internal contradiction Adorno brought up between sociology and psychology), neopsychoanalysis can make only wrong moves: weakening the ego makes the transference something less than transitory; strengthening the ego collaborates with the defense work of pushing the unconscious back into itself (from where, however, its "destructive being" achieves the widest range of enactment).

The neo-Freudians replace drives with character traits. But the character they push and hypostasize is not a continuous experience but the sum of effects of shock. The revisionists look away from the "shocklike structure of individual experience." In other words, the totality of this neo-Freudian character is a fictive one. In Adorno's words: "One could instead call it a system of scars, that are only integrated through suffering and even then never completely" ("Die revidierte Psychanalyse," 24). Thus personalized, the relationship between sociology and psychology goes like this: the most threatening moments of socialization go down as psychology, that is, as the subjective unconscious. But the personalizable moments have at the same time been transformed into generic brands, collective images—like the zeppelin moving across British airspace in peacetime, which Freud considers in one of his *New Introductory Lectures* (the one on Marxism) as having given the advance sign of World War I soon being on the air. Freud's image that hovers over the psychologization of warfare, the inside view of World War I, is tied down by Adorno now to Jung's dedynamization of the unconscious as a normative series of archaic images, now to Benjamin's notion of the dialectical image that was designed to theorize the series, bring it to a

Example of use of Mickey Mouse as mascot adornment or "fetish" on planes of the Third Reich Luftwaffe. Reprinted from *Im Reiche der Micky Maus: Walt Disney in Deutschland, 1927–1945,* 144.

kind of season finale, as a current myth mode that ultimately opens access to social relations. At the same time this brings Adorno back (from inside out) to his debate with Benjamin in the thirties on the links and limits of Marxism, psychoanalysis, and Mickey Mouse against the background of a kind of polymorphous perversity of mobilization that hits the center of totalization where no one can tell left and right wings apart.

A Nazi squadron of fighter planes (part of the Condor Legion) took wing under the official name of "Micky Maus." Each plane was decorated with a logo of Mickey Mouse waving a hatchet and riding a bomb. The miniaturizing replications of Mickey Mouse that were real popular in or even in Nazi Germany included, on toy-sized repros of the warplanes, the tiny Mickey Mouse logo. On their side the Allies named one type of radar device that had stereo earlike antennae "Mickey Mouse." On both sides Mickey Mouse rode the airwaves of total war. Total war *is* psychological warfare *is* mass psychology.

While Mickey Mouse was at war, treatment of the traumatized on the home front could also be based on symptoms available in toy stores everywhere. In the 1943 supplement to the annual journal of Nazi Psychotherapy (*Zentralblatt für Psychotherapie*), Gerdhild von Staabs unpacked the results of a psychotherapeutic intervention with children (called the "scenotest") that permitted reconstruction of primal scenes by patients playing (under the Berlin institute's supervision) with those extended families of

Another Mickey Mouse decorating a Nazi German warplane. The place names are souvenirs of various garrison stopovers. From *Im Reiche der Micky Maus*, 144.

dolls that come complete with your favorite barnyard animals. Among the illustrations of the doll scenes the children reconstructed and named, one picture stands out and forces a double take. It's true that the doll scenes pack a surplus of funerals, live burials, and graveyard visits. But there's only one scene that must be translated. It's the scene, game, or test that the child named "cow." It shows the animal's entrance stage right. In the picture, the doll family members are found lying about where they all fell down upon the cow's arrival. The therapist gives the translation: "bomb" (37–38).

The sceno-test was designed to promote short-term therapy as adjunct to psychoanalysis, as administered at the Institute for German Psychotherapy. The sceno-test that detonated the "bomb" was inserted at the institute in the course of the child's depth-psychological therapy (in other words, he was being psychoanalyzed). The test strengthens the ego and permits the child at play to graduate over the series of sessions from bomb sites to a kindergarten out in the country that appears bombproof. The neotherapeutic rebuilding of the ego's rapport with the unconscious via this change of

A Luftwaffe officer next to his Mickey Mouse–adorned war plane. Dates written by Mickey's feet, 22.7.1942 and 12.8.1942, commemorate two times he was shot down behind enemy lines and walked back to the German side of the front. From *Im Reiche der Micky Maus*, 144.

scenes is the rapid-fire alternative to transference interpretation. Another child constructs the scene of an air-raid shelter in the vicinity of a camp (the patient says it's for prisoners of war). That the shelter is without windows and doors (indeed, no one is permitted inside) is seen to share one complex with the "little soldier" attitude he adopts when he pulls himself together after sceno-testing and says to, or exchanges with, the therapist, "Heil Hitler." The therapist comments:

> That's why he builds an air raid shelter without an entrance and in which no one can seek refuge. There are thus safe places in life but no one is permitted access to them. Since all persons are experienced as enemies, everyone really should die. (27)

Even the most perfect interdepartmental research, Adorno argues in the fifties, presupposes a univocal continuity where in fact discontinuity is the rule. That's why the interdisciplinary mode readily fulfills ideological

German toy fighter plane (Tipp and Co.) with Mickey Mouse adornment, 1940. From *Im Reiche der Micky Maus*, 168.

functions ("Postscriptum," 88). But there is a continuity symptomatized as discontinuity between Freud's science and the new improved brands under Adorno's review in 1955 and again in 1965. It's Nazi psychoanalysis. It's where the sociologization of the psyche and the psychologization of the socius both worked double time. It's a continuity between our most protected and progressive sources of modernity and what we take to be our biggest symptom in the category of aberration and discontinuity. And it's a continuity that every master discursivity and antidiscursivity about faces each time it faces the division or, same difference, merger between sociology and psychology on a scale from Marxism to psychoanalysis.

Americanization is a charge that goes only so far, to the point where it can still be folded over what it covers up. The revisionary developments of the master discursivities—their sociologization in the course (ultimately) of psychologizing the socius at war—cannot skip the beat they follow of Nazi psychoanalysis. Adorno saw the Nazi ideology as a psychotic system that servd to protect those living under it from individual psychotic breakdown. But this can't be the most efficient way to guarantee the staying power ot neurosis's functional or therapizable mode. That's why the move to lock up in the other and disown the propaganda that emerges from the split between the esoteric science and the exoteric topics it must bring up

Carl Müller-Braunschweig, psychoanalyst working at the German Institute, reading Freud's *Civiliza-tion and Its Discontents*, probably in 1938. Reprinted from page 174 of *"Here Life Goes On in a Most Peculiar Way..."*

(the split between psychology and sociology) is not the way to go or stay. Because like the unconscious that the neo-Freudian alliance with the ego in the treatment of psychotics pushes back, the repressed continuity is back and overtakes even the most correct discursivity or antidiscursivity. That's right, it's about facing the continuity that was there: Nazi psychoanalysis, Nazi Marxism, Nazi deconstruction.

References

Abraham, Karl. "Psychoanalysis and the War Neuroses." In *Clinical Papers and Essays on Psychoanalysis*, vol. 2, ed. Hilda Abraham, trans. Hilda Abraham and D. R. Ellison., 1919; New York: Basic Books, 1955.

———. "Erstes Korreferat." In *Zur Psychoanalyse der Kriegsneurosen*, 31–41. Internationale Psychoanalytische Bibliothek no. 1. Leipzig/Wien: Internationaler Psychoanalytischer Verlag, 1919.

Adler, Alfred. *Cooperation between the Sexes: Writings on Women, Love and Marriage, Sexuality and Its Disorders*. Ed. and trans. H. L. Ansbacher and R. R. Ansbacher. Garden City: Anchor Books, 1978.

———. *The Neurotic Constitution*. Trans. Bernard Glueck and John Lind. New York: Moffat, Yard, 1917. [*Über den Nervösen Charakter: Grundzüge einer vergleichenden Individual-Psychologie und Psychotherapie*. Wiesbaden: Bergmann, 1912.]

Adorno, Theodor W. "Freudian Theory and the Pattern of Fascist Propaganda." *Gesammelte Schriften* 8 (1951): 408–33.

———. "Postscriptum." "Zum Verhältnis von Soziologie und Psychologie." *Gesammelte Schriften* 8 (1966): 42–92.

———. "Die revidierte Psychoanalyse." *Gesammelte Schriften* 8 (1951): 20–41.

———. "Zum Verhältnis von Soziologie und Psychologie." *Gesammelte Schriften* 8 (1955): 42–92.

Alexander, Franz, and Gerhard J. Piers. "Psychoanalysis." In *Progress in Neurology and Psychiatry*, vol. 2, ed. E. A. Spiegel, 500–517. New York: Grune and Stratton, 1947.

Ansbacher, H. L. "German Military Psychology." *Psychological Bulletin* 38, no. 6 (June 1941): 370–92.

Antonovsky, Anna. "Aryan Analysts in Nazi Germany: Questions of Adaptation, Desymbolization, and Betrayal." *Psychoanalysis and Contemporary Thought* 11, no. 2 (1988): 213–31.

Banse, Ewald. *Germany Prepares for War: A Nazi Theory of "National Defense."* New York: Harcourt, Brace, 1934.

Bateson, Gregory. *A Sacred Unity: Further Steps to an Ecology of Mind*. Ed. Rodney E. Donaldson. New York: Harper Collins, 1991.

Baudouin, Charles. "Esquisse d'une pathologie du risque." *Zentralblatt für Psychotherapie und ihre Grenzgebiete einschliesslich der medizinischen Psychologie und psychischen Hygiene: Organ der allgemeinen ärztlichen Gesellschaft für Psychotherapie* 8, no. 3 (1935): 108–13. Beginning in 1936 the journal's affiliation was retitled *Organ der internationalen allgemeinen ärztlichen Gesellschaft für Psychotherapie*.

Benjamin, Walter. "Über einige Motive bei Baudelaire" in *Gesammelte Schriften* 1, no. 2 (1980): 605–53.

Bernays, Edward L. *Crystallizing Public Opinion*. 1923; New York: Liveright, 1934.

Bettelheim, Bruno. "Individual and Mass Behavior in Extreme Situations." *Journal of Abnormal and Social Psychology* 38, no. 4 (October 1943): 417–52.

Binion, Rudolph. "Hitler's Concept of Lebensraum: The Psychological Basis." *History of Childhood Quarterly: The Journal of Psychohistory* 1 (fall 1973): 187–215.

———. "Reply by Rudolph Binion." *History of Childhood Quarterly: The Journal of Psychohistory* 2 (fall 1973): 249–58.

Boas, George. "Human Relations in Military Government." *Public Opinion Quarterly* (winter 1943): 542–54.

Bohleber, Werner. "The Presence of the Past—Xenophobia and Right-Wing Extremism in the Federal Republic of Germany: Psychoanalytic Reflections." *American Imago* 52, no. 3 (fall 1995): 329–44.

Bohleber, Werner, and J. Drews, eds. *"Gift, das du unbewußt eintrinkst..."* Der Nationalsozialismus und die deutsche Sprache. Bielefeld: Aisthesis Verlag, 1991.

Brady, Robert A. *The Spirit and Structure of German Fascism.* London: Victor Gollancz, 1937. Left Book Club edition—not for sale to the public.

Brainin, Elisabeth, and Isidor Kaminer. "Psychoanalyse und Nationalsozialismus." *Psyche* 36 (1982): 989–1012.

Bräutigam, Walter. "Rückblick auf das Jahr 1942: Betrachtungen eines psychoanalytischen Ausbildungskandidaten des Berliner Instituts der Kriegsjahre" [Review of the Year 1942: Observations of a Psychoanalytic Training Candidate at the Wartime Berlin Institute]. *Psyche* 38, no. 10 (1984): 905–914.

Brecht, Karen. "Adaptation and Resistance: Reparation and the Return of the Repressed." *Psychoanalysis and Contemporary Thought* 11 (1988): 233–48.

Bruntz, George G. *Allied Propaganda and the Collapse of the German Empire in 1918.* Stanford: Stanford University Press, 1938.

Bumke, Oswald. *Gedanken über die Seele.* Berlin: Springer Verlag, 1941.

Carotenuto, Aldo, ed. *Tagebuch einer heimlichen Symmetrie: Sabina Spielrein zwischen Jung und Freud.* Freiburg: Kore, Verlag Traute Hensch, 1986.

Chasseguet-Smirgel, Janine. "'Time's White Hair We Ruffle'—Reflections on the Hamburg Congress." Trans. Philip Slotkin. *International Review of Psychoanalysis* 14 (1987): 433–44.

Cocks, Geoffrey. *Psychotherapy in the Third Reich: The Göring Institute.* New York: Oxford University Press, 1985.

Cremerius, J., ed. *Die Rezeption der Psychoanalyse in der Soziologie, Psychologie und Theologie im deutschsprachigen Raum bis 1940.* Frankfurt a/M: Suhrkamp, 1981.

Derrida, Jacques. "Racism's Last Word." Trans. Peggy Kamuf. *Critical Inquiry* 12, no. 1 (autumn 1985): 290–99.

Deutsch, Helene. "Freud and His Pupils: A Footnote to the History of the Psychoanalytic Movement" [1940]. In *Freud As We Knew Him*, ed. Hendrik M. Ruitenbeck, 170–79. Detroit: Wayne State University Press, 1973.

Doyle, Arthur Conan. *The Case for Spirit Photography.* New York: George H. Doran, 1923.

———. *The History of Spiritualism.* 1924; New York: Arno, 1975.

Dräger, Käthe. "Bemerkungen zu den Zeitumständen und zum Schicksal der Psychoanalyse und der Psychotherapie in Deutschland zwischen 1933 und 1949." *Psyche* 25, no. 4 (April 1971): 255–68.

Durbin, E. F. M., and John Bowlby. *Personal Aggressiveness and War*. 1938; New York: Columbia University Press, 1950.

Eickhoff, F.-W. "On the 'Borrowed Unconscious Sense of Guilt' and the Palimpsestic Structure of a Symptom—Afterthoughts on the Hamburg Congress of the IPA." *International Review of Psychoanalysis* 16 (1989): 323–29.

Eifermann, Rivka R. "'Germany' and the 'Germans': Acting Out Fantasies, and Their Discovery in Self-Analysis." *International Review of Psychoanalysis* 14 (1986): 245–62.

Eissler, K. R. *Freud as an Expert Witness: The Discussion of War Neuroses between Freud and Wagner-Jauregg*. Madison, Conn.: International Universities Press, 1986.

Erikson, Erik Homburger. "Hitler's Imagery and German Youth." *Public Opinion Quarterly* (Winter 1943): 475–93.

Ewers, Hanns Heinz. *Alraune. Die Geschichte eines lebenden Wesens* [Alraune: The Story of a Living Creature]. 1919; Georg Müller Verlag, 1921.

———. *Ameisen* [Ants]. 1925; Munich: Zinnen-Verlag, 1943.

———. *Horst Wessel: Ein deutsches Schicksal*. Stuttgart and Berlin: J. G. Cotta'sche Buchhandlung Nachfolger, 1932.

———. *Vampir: Ein verwildeter Roman in Fetzen und Farben*. 1920; Munich: Georg Müller Verlag, 1922.

———. *Der Zauberlehrling oder die Teufelsjäger* [The Sorcerer's Apprentice or the Devil Hunters]. Munich and Berlin: Georg Müller, 1917.

Farago, Ladislas, ed. *The Axis Grand Strategy*. New York: Farrar and Rinehart, 1942.

———, ed. *German Psychological Warfare: Survey and Bibliography*. New York: Committee for National Morale, 1941.

Farrar, Clarence. "War and Neurosis: With Some Observations of the Canadian Expeditionary Force." *American Journal of Insanity* (April 1917): 693–719.

Federn, Ernst. *Witnessing Psychoanalysis: From Vienna back to Vienna via Buchenwald and the USA*. London: Karnac Books, 1990.

Fenichel, Otto. *The Psychoanalytic Theory of Neurosis*. New York: W. W. Norton, 1945.

Ferenczi, Sandor. "Beitrag zur Tic-Diskussion." In *Schriften zur Psychoanalyse*, 92–93. 1921; Frankfurt a/M: Fischer Taschenbuch Verlag II, 1982.

———. "Die Psychoanalyse der Kriegsneurosen." Internationale Psychoanalytische Bibliothek no. 1. Leipzig/Wien: Internationaler Psychoanalytischer Verlag, 1919.

———. "Two Types of War Neuroses." Trans. J. I. Suttie. In *Further Contributions to the Theory and Technique of Psycho-Analysis*, ed. John Rickman, 124–41. 1916; New York: Brunner/Mazel, 1980.

Freud, Sigmund. *The Standard Edition of the Complete Psychological Works*. Ed. James Strachey. London: Hogarth Press, 1953–1974. Cited in the text as *SE*.

Frankl, Viktor E. *Man's Search for Meaning: An Introduction to Logotherapy*. 1959; New York: Washington Square Press, 1964.

Fromm, Erich. "On the Problems of German Characterology." *Transactions, the New York Academy of Sciences, Section of Anthropology*, 25 January 1943, 79–83.

Gabler, Nea. "Edward L. Bernays and Henry C. Rogers: The Fathers of P.R." *New York Times Magazine*, 31 December 1995, 28–29.

Geuter, Ulfried. *Die Professionalisierung der deutschen Psychologie im Nationalsozialismus* [The Professionalization of German Psychology in National Socialism]. Frankfurt a/M: Suhrkamp Verlag, 1984.

Goebbels, Joseph. *Der Kampf um Berlin.* Munich: Eher, 1939.

Göring, Matthias H. "Die Bedeutung der Neurose in der Sozialversicherung" [The Significance of Neurosis in Social Insurance]. *Zentralblatt für Psychotherapie* 11 (1939): 36–56.

Gordon, Don E. *Electronic Warfare: Element of Strategy and Multiplier of Combat Power.* New York: Pergamon, 1981.

Grinker, Roy R., and John P. Spiegel. *War Neuroses in North Africa: The Tunisian Campaign (January–May 1943).* The Air Surgeon Army Air Forces. New York: Josiah Macy, 1943.

Grotjahn, Martin. *My Favorite Patient: The Memoirs of a Psychoanalyst.* Frankfurt a/M: Peter Lang, 1987.

Grunberger, Richard. *The 12-Year Reich: A Social History of Nazi Germany, 1933–1945.* New York: Holt, Rinehart and Winston, 1971.

Hall, Stanley. "Practical Relations between Psychology and the War." *Journal of Applied Psychology* 1 (1917).

Handbuch der ärztlichen Erfahrungen im Weltkriege, 1914–18 [Handbook of Medical Experiences during the World War, 1914–18]. Vol. 4, *Geistes und Nervenkrankheiten.* Ed. Karl Bonhoeffer. Leipzig: Barth, 1921.

Hartmann, George. "Toward a Reasonable Peace." *Journal of Abnormal and Social Psychology* 38, no. 2 (April 1943): 199–210.

Herman, Judith Lewis. *Trauma and Recovery.* New York: Basic Books, 1992.

Hirschfeld, Magnus. *Kriegspsychologisches* [Psychological Aspects of War]. Bonn: A. Marcus and E. Webers Verlag, 1916.

———. *The Sexual History of the World War—in Collaboration with World-Famous Physicians, Scientists, and Historians.* New York: Falstaff, 1937. "Has been edited and translated into English from the German work."

Im Reiche der Micky Maus. Potsdam: Henschei Verlag, 1991. Catalog to an exhibition at the Potsdam Film Museum.

Jones, Ernest. "Die Kriegsneurosen (war-shock) und die Freudsche Theorie." In *Zur Psychoanalyse der Kriegsneurosen,* Internationale Psychoanalytische Bibliothek no. 1, 61–82. Leipzig/Wien: Internationaler Psychoanalytischer Verlag, 1919.

———. "The Psychology of Quislingism." In *Essays in Applied Psychoanalysis,* vol. 1, 276–83. 1940; New York: International Universities Press, 1964.

———. "War and Individual Psychology." In *Essays in Applied Psychoanalysis,* 55–76. 1915; New York: International Universities Press, 1964.

———. "War and Sublimation." In *Essays in Applied Psychoanalysis,* 77–87. 1915.

Jung, C. G. "After the Catastrophe." In *Civilization in Transition,* trans. R. F. C. Hull, 194–217. 1945; New York: Pantheon, 1964.

———. "The Stages of Life." In *Modern Man in Search of a Soul,* trans. Cary F. Baynes, 95–114. 1931; New York: Harcourt Brace Jovanovich, 1933.

———. "The State of Psychotherapy Today." 1934. In *Civilization in Transition*, 157–73. ["Zur gegenwärtigen Lage der Psychotherapie." *Zentralblatt für Psychotherapie* 7 (1934): 1–16.]

———. "Wotan." 1936. In *Civilization in Transition*, 179–93.

Kafka, Franz. *Amtliche Schriften*. Berlin: Akademie-Verlag, 1984.

Kafka, John. "On Reestablishing Contact." *Psychoanalysis and Contemporary Thought* 11, no. 2 (1988): 299–308.

Kemper, Werner. *Die Störungen der Liebesfähigkeit beim Weibe*. Leipzig, 1942.

Künkel, Fritz. *Conquer Yourself: The Way to Self-Confidence*. New York: Ives Washburn, 1936.

———. *Ringen um Reife: Eine Untersuchung über Psychologie, Religion, und Selbsterziehung*. Constance: Friedrich Bahn Verlag, 1962.

Lacan, Jacques. "Desire and the Interpretation of Desire in *Hamlet*." Trans. James Hulbert. In *Literature and Psychoanalysis: The Question of Reading Otherwise*, ed. Shoshana Felman. 1959; Baltimore: Johns Hopkins University Press, 1982.

Lacoue-Labarthe, Philippe, and Jean-Luc Nancy. "The Nazi Myth." Trans. Brian Holmes. *Critical Inquiry* 16 (1990): 291–312.

Lasswell, Harold D. "Political and Psychological Warfare." In *A Psychological Warfare Casebook*, ed. William E. Daugherty and Morris Janowitz. Baltimore: Johns Hopkins University Press, 1958.

———. *Propaganda Technique in the World War*. 1927; New York: Peter Smith, 1938.

———. "The Psychology of Hitlerism." *Political Quarterly* 4 (1933): 373–84.

———. "The Strategy of Soviet Propaganda." *Headline Series* 86 (March–April 1951): 57–62.

———. *World Politics and Personal Insecurity*. New York: McGraw-Hill, 1935.

Le Bon, Gustave. *The Crowd: A Study of the Popular Mind*. 1895; English translation, London: T. Fisher Unwin, 1896.

———. *Enseignements Psychologiques de la guerre européenne*. Paris: Flammarion, 1916.

Lifton, Robert Jay. *The Nazi Doctors: Medical Killing and the Psychology of Genocide*. New York: Basic Books, 1986.

Linebarger, Paul M. A. *Psychological Warfare*. Washington, D.C.: Infantry Journal Press, 1948.

Lockot, Regine. *Erinnern und Durcharbeiten: Zur Geschichte der Psychoanalyse und Psychotherapie im Nationalsozialismus* [Remembering and Working Through: On the History of Psychoanalysis and Psychotherapy in National Socialism]. Frankfurt a/M: Fisher, 1985.

Maclean, G. A. *Insurance up through the Ages*. Louisville: Dunne, 1938.

Mahler, Margaret. "On Infantile Precursors of the 'Influencing Machine' (Tausk)." In *The Selected Papers of Margaret S. Mahler*, vol. 1, *Infantile Psychosis and Early Contributions*, 205–21. 1959; New York and London: Jason Aronson, 1979.

Marx, Karl, and Friedrich Engels. *The German Ideology*. Parts 1 and 3. Ed. R. Pascal. New York: International Publishers, 1947.

McDougall, William. *The Group Mind*. 1920; London: Cambridge University Press, 1927.

————. *An Introduction to Social Psychology*. 11th ed. Boston: Luce, 1916.

————. *Outline of Abnormal Psychology*. New York: Charles Scribner's Sons, 1926.

Meier, Norman C. *Military Psychology*. New York and London: Harper, 1943.

Metz, Paul. "Die Eignung zum Flugzeugführer als Anlagenproblem." *Zeitschrift für Psychologie* 143 (1938): 12–14.

————. "Funktionale und charakterologische Fragen der Fliegereignung." *Zeitschrift für angewandte Psychologie*, supplement, 72 (1936): 153–72.

————. "Die Orientierung beim Fliegen." In *Gefühl und Wille*, ed. Otto Klemm, 207–8. Jena: Verlag von Gustav Fischer, 1937.

————. "Die Prüfung der Fl.-Orientierungsfähigkeit." *Soldatentum* (1935): 302–10.

Metzger, Hans-Joachim. "Kraft Durch Freud?" *Der Wunderblock* 7 (1978): 29–45.

Meyrink, Gustav. *Der Golem*. Leipzig and Zürich: Grethlein, 1915.

Mierke, Karl. "Psychologie des Kampfes und der Kriegsführung: Die soldatische Haltung zur Angst" [Psychology of Combat and Military Leadership: The Soldierly Attitude toward Anxiety]. *Zeitschrift für angewandte Psychologie* 72, supplement (1936): 1–25.

Mitscherlich, Alexander, and Fred Mielke. *Doctors of Infamy: The Story of the Nazi Medical Crimes*. New York: Schuman, 1949.

Mitscherlich, Alexander, and Margarete Mitscherlich. *Die Unfähigkeit zu trauern*. [The Inability to Mourn]. Munich: Piper Verlag, 1967.

Myers, Charles S. *Shell Shock in France, 1914–1918*. Cambridge: Cambridge University Press, 1940.

Numbers, Roland L. *Almost Persuaded: American Physicians and Compulsory Health Insurance, 1912–1920*. Baltimore: Johns Hopkins University Press, 1978.

Parsons, Talcott. "Racial and Religious Differences as Factors in Group Tensions." In *Talcott Parsons on National Socialism*, ed. Uta Gerhardt, 275–90. 1945; New York: Aldine de Gruyter, 1993.

Pascal, R. Introduction to *The German Ideology*, by Karl Marx and Friedrich Engels. parts 1 and 3. Ed. R. Pascal. New York: International Publishers, 1947.

Plänker, Tomas, and Ernst Federn. *Vertreibung und Rückkehr: Interviews zur Geschichte Ernst Federns und der Psychoanalyse*. Tübingen: Edition Diskord, 1994.

Poppelreuter, Walther. *Hitler der politische Psychologe* [Hitler, the Political Psychologist]. Langensalza: Beyer and Mann, 1934.

Prest, Thomas Preskett. *Varney the Vampire: or, The Feast of Blood*. 1847; New York: Arno Press with McGrath Publishing, 1971.

Rado, Sandor. "Pathodynamics and Treatment of Traumatic War Neurosis (Traumatophobia)." *Psychoanalysis of Behavior: Collected Papers*. 1942; New York: Grune and Stratton, 1956.

Reik, Theodor. "Der Schrecken." In *Der Schrecken und andere psychoanalytische Studien*, 7–44. Vienna: Internationaler Psychoanalytischer Verlag, 1929. 7–44.

Richards, R. L. "Mental and Nervous Diseases in the Russo-Japanese War." *Military Surgeon* 26, no. 2 (February 1910): 177–93.

Riedesser, Peter, and Axel Verderber. *Aufrüstung der Seelen: Militärpsychiatrie und Militärpsychologie in Deutschland und Amerika* [Mobilization of Souls: Military

Psychiatry and Military Psychology in Germany and America]. Freiburg i/B: Dreisam-Verlag, 1985.

Rivers, W. H. R. "The Repression of War Experience." *Royal Society of Medicine* (1917): 2–20.

Riviere, Joan. "An Intimate Impression." In *Freud As We Knew Him*, ed. Hendrik M. Ruitenbeck, 128–31. 1939; Detroit: Wayne State University Press, 1973.

Roth, Karl Heinz. "Die Modernisierung der Folter in den beiden Weltkriegen: Der Konflikt der Psychotherapeuten und Schulpsychiater um die deutschen 'Kriegsneurotiker,' 1915–1945." *Hamburger Stiftung für Sozialgeschichte des zwanzigsten Jahrhunderts* 3 (1987): 8–73.

Roussy, G., and J. Lhermitte. *The Psychoneuroses of War*. Trans. Wilfred B. Christopherson. Ed. William A. Turner. London: University of London Press, 1918.

Royce, Josiah. *War and Insurance*. New York: Macmillan, 1914.

Sachs, Hanns. "The Delay of the Machine Age." Trans. Margaret J. Powers. *Psychoanalytic Quarterly* 11, nos. 3–4 (1933): 404–24.

Salmon, Thomas W. "Recommendations for the Treatment of Mental and Nervous Diseases in the United States Army." *Psychiatric Bulletin of the New York State Hospitals* (1917): 355–76.

Scherke, Felix, and Ursula Gräfin Vitzthum, eds. *Bibliographie der gestigen Kriegsführung*. Berlin: Verlag Bernard & Graefe, 1938.

Schiche, E. "Über Todesahnungen im Felde und ihre Wirkung." *Beiheft zur Zeitschrift für angewandte Psychologie* 21 (1920): 173–78.

Schult-Hencke, Harald. *Einführung in die Psychoanalyse* [Introduction to Psychoanalysis]. Jena: Fischer, 1927.

Seif, Leonhard, ed. *Wege der Erziehungshilfe: Ergebnisse und praktische Hinweise aus der Tätigkeit es Münchener Arbeitskreises für Erziehung*. Munich: J. F. Lehmanns, 1940.

Simmel, Ernst. "Anti-Semitism and Mass Psychopathology." In *Anti-Semitism: A Social Disease*, ed. Ernst Simmel, 33–78. New York: International Universities Press, 1946.

———. *Kriegsneurosen und "Psychisches Trauma."* Leipzig and Munich: Verlag von Otto Nemnich, 1918.

———. "Psychoanalyse der Massen." In *Psychoanalyse und ihre Anwendungen: Ausgewählte Schriften*, ed. Ludger Hermanns and Ulrich Schultz-Venrath, 36–42. 1919; Frankfurt a/M: Fischer Taschenbuch Verlag, 1993.

———. "War Neuroses." In *Psychoanalysis Today*, ed. Sandor Lorand, 227–48. New York: International Universities Press, 1945.

———. "Zweites Korreferat." *Zur Psychoanalyse der Kriegsneurosen* (1919): 42–60.

Simoneit, Max. "Die allgemeine Wehrpflicht als psychologisches Problem." *Soldatentum* (1936): 58–62.

———."Ehre und Ehrhaftigkeit in der soldatischen Lebensform." *Soldatentum* (1934): 118–122.

———. "Soldatentum als Lebensform." *Soldatentum* (1934): 65–69.

———. *Wehrpsychologie: Ein Abriß ihrer Probleme und praktischen Folgerungen*. Berlin: Verlag Bernard and Graefe, 1933.

Spiegel, Rose, Gerard Chrzanowski, and Arthur H. Feiner. "On Psychoanalysis in the Third Reich." *Contemporary Psychoanalysis* 11, no. 4 (1975): 477–505.

Spielrein, Sabina. *Die Destruktion als Ursache des Werdens.* 1912; Tübingen: Edition Diskord, 1986.

Staabs, Gerdhild von. "Der Sceno-Test: Beitrag Zur Erfassung unbewusster Problematik bei Kindern und Jugendlichen." *Zentralblatt für Psychotherapie* 1943, supplement 6.

Stoker, Bram. *Dracula.* Westminster: Constable, 1897.

———. *The Lady of the Shroud.* 1909; London: Jarrolds, 1966.

Störring, Gustav. "Die Verschiedenheiten der psychopathologischen Erfahrungen im Weltkriege und im jetzigen Krieg und ihre Ursachen" [The Differences between the Psychopathological Experiences in the World War and in the Current War and Its Causes]. *Münchener Medizinische Wochenschrift* 89, no. 2 (January 1942): 25–30.

Tausk, Victor. "Diagnostische Erörterungen auf Grund der Zustandsbilder der sogenannten Kriegspsychosen." In *Gesammelte psychoanalytische und literarische Schriften,* ed. Hans-Joachim Metzger, 219–44. 1916; Vienna and Berlin: Medusa Verlag, 1983.

———. "Zur Psychologie des Deserteurs." In *Gesammelte psychoanalytische und literarische Schriften,* 169–98. 1916.

Taylor, Ronald, ed. *Aesthetics and Politics.* London: NLB, 1977.

Theweleit, Klaus. *Male Fantasies.* Vol. 1. Trans. Stephen Conway. Minneapolis: University of Minnesota Press, 1987.

Trotter, W. *Instincts of the Herd in Peace and War.* 2d ed. London: T. Fischer Unwin, 1919.

Vambery, Arminus. *His Life and Adventures Written by Himself.* New York: Cassell, 1914.

Viereck, George Sylvester. *Spreading Germs of Hate.* New York: H. Liveright, 1930.

Virilio, Paul. *War and Cinema: The Logistics of Perception.* Trans. Patrick Camiller. New York: Verso, 1989.

Wallerstein, Robert. "The Future of Psychiatry." *Psychoanalytic Quarterly* 58, no. 3 (July 1989): 342–73.

White, Robert. *The Abnormal Personality: A Textbook.* New York: Ronald Press, 1948.

Wiener, Norbert. *God and Golem, Inc.: A Comment on Certain Points Where Cybernetics Impinges on Religion.* Cambridge: MIT Press, 1964.

Wittkower, Eric, and J. P. Spillane. "Neuroses in War." *British Medical Journal,* 10 February 1940, 223–25.

———. "A Survey of the Literature of Neuroses in War." In *The Neuroses in War,* ed. Emanuel Miller. New York: Macmillan, 1940.

Würfler, Paul. "Zum Verständnis der Neurose, auch im Hinblick auf militärische Verhältnisse." *Der deutsche Militärarzt* 4, no. 3 (1939): 124–28.

Wuth, Otto. "Das Psychopathenproblem in der Wehrmacht nebst Besprechung einiger einschlägigen Fragen." Lecture held at the Militärärztlichen Akademie Berlin, 9–10 March 1939.

———. "Über den Selbstmord bei Soldaten." *Soldatentum* (1936): 84–90.

Zapp, Gudrun. *Psychoanalyse und Nationalsozialismus: Untersuchungen zum Verhältnis Medizin/Psychoanalyse während des Nationalsozialismus.* Inauguraldissertation zur Erlangung der Doktorwürde der medizinischen Fakultät der Christian-Albrechts-Universität zu Kiel, 1980.

Zentralblatt für Psychotherapie 6 (1933); 7 (1934); 8 (1935); 9 (1936); 10 (1938); 11 (1939); 12 (1941); 13 (1941); 14 (1942); 15 (1943); 16 (1944).

Ziemer, Gregor. *Education for Death: The Making of the Nazi.* New York: Oxford University Press, 1941.

Filmography

The Black Cat. Dir. Edgar Ulmer. Universal, 1934.

Die Büchse der Pandora [Pandora's Box]. Dir. G. W. Pabst. Ufa, 1929.

Das Cabinet des Dr. Caligari [The Cabinet of Dr. Caligari]. Dir. Robert Wiene. Decla-Bioscop AG, 1920.

Faust. Dir. F. W. Murnau. Ufa, 1926.

Die freudlose Gasse [Joyless Streets]. Dir. G. W. Pabst. Ufa, 1925.

Geheimnisse einer Seele [Secrets of a Soul]. Dir. G. W. Pabst. Neumann-Filmproduktion, 1926.

Der Golem: Wie er in die Welt kam [The Golem: How He Came into the World]. Dir. Paul Wegener and Carl Boese. Ufa, 1920. Remake of Wegener's 1915 *Der Golem*.

Invasion of the Body Snatchers. Dir. Don Siegel. Allied Artists, 1956.

Jud Süss. Dir. Veit Harlan. Ufa, 1940.

Lifeboat. Dir. Alfred Hitchcock. Twentieth Century Fox, 1944.

Mädchen in Uniform. Dir. Leontine Sagan. Deutsche Film Gemeinschaft, 1931.

Ministry of Fear. Dir. Fritz Lang. Paramount, 1944.

Nosferatu. Dir. F. W. Murnau. Prana, 1922.

Olympia. Dir. Leni Riefenstahl. Tobis Filmkunst GmbH./Olympia-Film GmbH, 1938.

Schloß Vogelöd [The Haunted Castle]. Dir. F. W. Murnau. Decla Bioscop, 1921.

Shoah. Dir. Claude Lanzmann. Les Films Aleph and Historia Films, 1985.

Snow White and the Seven Dwarfs. Dir. David Hand. Walt Disney Productions, 1937.

Der Student von Prag [The Student of Prague]. Dir. Henrik Galeen. Ufa, 1926. Remake of 1913 original directed by Stellan Rye.

Triumph des Willens [Triumph of the Will]. Dir. Leni Riefenstahl. NSDAP-Reichspropaganda Abteilung, 1935.

Index

Laurence A. Rickels is professor of German and comparative literature at the University of California–Santa Barbara, and adjunct professor in the art studio and film studies departments. He is the author of *The Vampire Lectures* (Minnesota, 1999), *The Case of California* (Minnesota, 2001), and *Aberrations of Mourning*, and the editor of *Acting Out in Groups* (Minnesota, 1999). He is a therapist as well as a theorist and has appeared on the Web in this double capacity as "Dr. Truth."

Benjamin Bennett is the Kenan Professor of German at the University of Virginia. He is the author of many books, including *Theater as Problem: Modern Drama and Its Place in Literature* and *Beyond Theory: Eighteenth-Century German Literature and the Poetics of Irony.*